Would it be all right with you
if life got easier?

Vildehiya Publications - Sacramento, California

YOU and MONEY

Would it be all right with you if life got easier?

Maria Nemeth PhD

Vildehiya Publications
1281 47th Avenue, Sacramento CA 95831

Copyright © 1997 by Maria Nemeth PhD

Cover Design by Mikell Yamada
Contents designed and produced by Sally Cooney
Illustrations by Bruce Marion
Cover Photo by Hope Harris

Printed in the United States of America

Library of Congress Cataloging in Publication Data
Nemeth, Maria, 1944-
    You & money: would it be all right with you if life got
    easier? / by Maria Nemeth.
    p.cm.
    Includes index.
    ISBN: 1-890507-50-4
    1.Finance, Personal. 2. Investments. I.Title. II. Title:
    You and money.
    HG179.N43 1997   332.024
                               QBI97-40425

SECOND
PRINTING
1997

Dedication

To Aunt Anna and Rita

Acknowledgments

This book is dedicated to *You and Money* graduates all over the world. First, because they asked for this book. Second, because they eagerly awaited it for these many years. But most importantly, because they have allowed me into their lives, to share in their personal discoveries, witness their courage, and participate in their breakdowns and breakthroughs. Thank you for your faith and patience.

First, I want to acknowledge my editor, Hal Zina Bennett. He was the editor that every writer dreams of: talented, supportive, encouraging, gentle but direct, willing to lend his best judgment, and appreciative of the author's quirks and vulnerability. Also, thanks to Susan Sparrow for her excitement and confidence in the several versions of this work.

There would be no book without the contribution of these people: Rita Saenz, who, with a loving hand, has always helped me to separate the wheat from the chaff in life. Sally Cooney, patient friend and book designer, who made this book a reality. Dr. Patricia Elliot, a great coach, jumped in mid-stream at one point and called me daily with support and encouragement. A special thanks to Ellie Owen, PhB (Ph Balance), my friend and my river guide, for her gentle wit and constant support. Nan Goodart and Dr. Glenda Lippman are brave friends, always willing to tell the truth. They encouraged me to re-start this version of the book from scratch. Millie Loeb has encouraged me and given me feedback and support for many years. Charlotte Higgins, a busy author, who called daily to help me with Monkey Mind during the critical last stage of completion. Wendy Jordan, benefactor extraordinaire, for her faith and generosity. Kit Snyder, who worked with me several years ago to start this project when I was absolutely not a writer. Zana Blazer, who co-initiated the first version of the *You and Money* course for women.

I have found that there is always a reliable support group, eager to lend a hand, compassionate and empowering. These people, have appeared in my life to help me or stick by me through breakdowns and breakthroughs. Thank you for love: Aunt Gloria and Uncle Arnold, Lisa, Chuck and Rachael Simon, Rev. Beth Ann Suggs, Nancy DeCandia, Julie Bowden, Cath Christianson, Mic Harper, Charlotte Kelly, Dave Golz, Clysta Kinstler, Suze Miller, *You and Money* Associates in Austin, Bill Bennett, San Francisco Bay Area coaches: Susan Zerner, Ann Grassel, Chris Dunlap, Sheila Cotton, Irene Goleski, and Linda Alfano, who gathered when I needed them to brainstorm and Treasure Map, David Cawthorn of Tzedakah Publications, Theron Turner, Constance Pedron, Holt Reeves, Bruce and Judy Parks, Susie and Andrea Saenz, and Margi Mainquist.

Contents

INTRODUCTION:
Your Journey Begins

Your Journey Begins

"Our goals begin with our dreams."

Audre Lorde

This book is about you and your relationship with money. It is about scarcity and abundance. It is about how you use your energy when receiving, spending, earning and thinking about money. It is about creating the best possible relationship you can have with money. And it is about having what you truly want in life while gaining clarity and ease on the path you will pursue to fulfill your fondest goals.

What is money? Joseph Campbell, noted mythologist and thinker, called it "congealed energy." It is human energy, your energy, symbolically held in a tangible form. Depending on the relationship you have with it, it can be the source of great joy and creativity ... or it can be pure torment.

Money is only one form of human energy, of course. Other forms include physical energy, love, time, creativity and spiritual power. Presumably, we are here to learn about all these forms of energy, for it is certainly true that every day brings new lessons and challenges for all of us in these areas. If you are like most people, the majority of these challenges have something to do with money!

Bringing forth and directing the way energy is used may be the greatest of the lessons we are born to learn. Like a hologram the lessons you learn in one area affect all the others. I picked money because, in this culture, it is the most tangible of the energies. You can count it, measure it, hold it in your hand, and use it to make things happen. In so many ways, this makes it easier to talk about and work with. Given life's holographic nature, the discoveries and the changes you make in this area will affect your whole life.

Unconsciously, we know early on that our relationship with money is a mirror for our relationships with all other forms of energy. Apropos of this, there is an old Spanish toast: *Salud, amor y pesetas y tiempo para gastarlos!* Health, love, money, and the time to enjoy them! These are four forms of energy that empower our lives. Without any one of them, life becomes difficult. They are all interdependent. If you have a powerful and rewarding relationship with money, you will increase your ability to deal with health, love and time as well.

This book is not about living an austere life. On the contrary! It is about discovering what *living the good life* truly means to you. How do you want to spend the rest of your life, or at least the next phase? What really brings you joy? If what you want to attain requires more money, then you will find practices here that will get you in shape to have it and direct it wisely, with *gusto*!

My Own Story

Fourteen years ago, if you had asked me to talk about my relationship with money, I would have been mortified. That year I gambled and lost. I invested thirty-five thousand dollars on an unsecured promissory note to a man I had known for six months. It was not even my own money. I had borrowed it from a family member.

The man to whom I loaned this money promised I would get a 30 percent return on my investment. The money was supposed to be used to make short term loans to buyers who needed to close real estate escrows. It was a fraud. There were no escrows. Within a few months, all the investors lost everything.

Like many of you who will be reading this book, I had read money investment books and attended money seminars. I had a financially sound private practice as a clinical psychologist. Based on the action I had taken, there was obviously a great disparity between what I knew on a thinking level about money and the actions I took.

When I lost the money, I felt terrible and stupid. I hoped no one would find out what had happened. However, Fate had other plans for me. Two weeks after I discovered my money was gone, I got an unexpected phone call from a local newswoman:

"Dr. Nemeth, the university gave us your name as associate clinical professor there, and because you are a psychotherapist. You may not be aware of this, but Sacramento has been having a run of investment frauds. I'm doing an article on it. We need to know from a professional if there is any type of personality or character flaw that allows people to get taken by these schemes. Is there something wrong with their thinking process?"

Oh, my God! I was caught! At first, I wanted to say I was way too busy to talk. I wanted to hang up the phone before she asked another question. I saw my whole reputation going down the drain. What if I told this reporter the truth?

"I lost money in one of those scams." I heard the words

slipping out of my mouth and I was horrified. I stared into the receiver, feeling my heart going right down through those little black holes. What could I possibly be thinking!

After a long pause, the reporter finally asked: "Are you sure you want to tell me this? Do you really want me to print this?"

I considered. She might as well, I thought. Maybe others will learn from my mistakes. Surely others have blind spots when it comes to money.

At one point, the reporter tried to find excuses for my actions.

"Obviously you were taken in. He played upon your trust and relationship with your friends who were also investing."

"Well, maybe. But, do you want to know the real reason I invested with him without reading the fine print?" By now, the relief from telling the truth was making me feel a little heady.

"Yes. Tell me."

"It was greed."

"Rich or poor, it's nice to have money."

Dorothy Parker

The instant the words were out of my mouth, I knew it was true. Greed. Wanting to beat the system, make a quick profit. I had not listened to financial advisors and friends who warned me about how risky the investment was. I had been blinded by the possibility of a fabulous outcome. I had not wanted to bother with the finer details, such as knowing the long-term track record of the company. I did not even ask to see the actual escrow papers of the deals I was supposed to be financing!

The reporter's interview was lengthy. The article the reporter wrote detailed how people from all walks of life can experience moments of money madness. Greed was the form the madness took with me.

Soon after the publication of my interview, friends and neighbors called, revealing their own financial nightmares. They had stories of scams, bankruptcies and unexpected losses. People told me about their spending binges, or how they hid money from their spouse. I heard stories of families being torn apart because some were left more money than others when their parent or loved one died.

People told me about goals they had abandoned. They spoke of dreams delayed or unachieved because of the fear of taking even the slightest chance with their money. A bank vice president told me about a couple who kept more than $250,000 in a low interest, simple savings account because they were too afraid to invest in money market certificates.

Soon, I had a big file of personal stories illustrating how

upset we can get in our relationship with money. Among those who told the truth about their disastrous money experiences were bankers, real estate brokers, certified financial planners, and stockbrokers. These were individuals one would expect to know better. The truth was, they *did* know better. Their knowledge was simply not getting translated into personal action.

A well-known financial consultant confided, "When it comes to other people's money, I know just what to do. But I can't follow my own financial advice. I'm like the child of the cobbler going without shoes."

Certain people with whom I spoke did not have disastrous relationships with money. Instead, they talked of the tedious predictability of their money lives. They made enough to pay the bills and make necessary major purchases. Their credit card debt was too high, but they felt they would get around to paying it off ... someday. Many of their goals and dreams had been delayed until that proverbial *one day*, a day that would never come unless they made a real shift in their lives.

> "I have enough money to last me the rest of my life, unless I buy something."
>
> Anonymous
> Quoted by Hanna Holborn Gray
> Christian Science Monitor

Your Money and Your Life

I am convinced that one of life's purposes is for us to learn how to use energy wisely to bring our dreams into reality. When we direct energy consciously, our experience will be one of satisfaction and creativity. When we misuse energy, our experience will be one of frustration, disappointment and thwarted dreams.

For most of us, money is central to our lives. Whether rich or poor we have a relationship with money as soon as we are old enough to count. Money provides us with security, stability, a way to take care of our families, make a contribution, and have fun. These are some of the same reasons we seek relationships with other people. As in our relationships with loved ones, we often get mired down by our anxieties. When this happens, there is no joy, peace of mind or freedom, whether with people *or* money.

I remember when I first asked people about their relationship with money. Often they had a horror story to tell, or they clammed up immediately. One woman laughed and said;

"My relationship with money is like a one-night stand, here today, gone tomorrow, and doesn't even know my name."

"Lack of money" was a common thread running through

most of the discussions. Money was frequently named as the number-one cause of stress. It did not matter whether the concern was real (as with someone on welfare) or imagined (as with a millionaire). Almost everyone's solution to the money problems they were having was simple: "Just give me more money. Then things will get better for me."

I even encountered people who questioned whether they had the right to continue living if they could not afford to meet their basic needs. Others believed that winning the lottery could solve all their problems. Some worried that their desire for money conflicted with their spiritual beliefs. Many felt victimized or helpless, as though money was an outside force controlling their lives. They felt they would never be free of its tyranny.

In 1996, the Louis Harris and Associates survey for the Lutheran Brotherhood found that one third of the adults who responded said they have trouble sleeping or relaxing because of financial anxieties. Decisions they had delayed because of financial obligations included: buying a house, changing careers, having children, and getting married.

The You and Money Course Begins

Prompted by my exploratory research I decided to sponsor an informal workshop on money, scarcity and abundance. Friends joined me. We set aside time when we could get together and focus on our relationship with money. This early effort to bring clarity into our own lives was the first in a series of seminars that would evolve into the current *You and Money* course.

The first question we chose was how to confront our unconscious beliefs and feelings about money. That's a paradox, of course. If it is unconscious, how do you know what to confront? Well, we plunged right in and began by asking: "What *don't* I want to look at regarding me and money?"

Old fears, unfulfilled dreams and financial mistakes arose in our minds. Repeatedly, we faced the hard choice of *telling the truth* or *trying to look good*. A responsible administrator of a multi million dollar program confided: "It would be easier for me to fly to the moon than balance my personal checkbook to the penny." For another, balancing the checkbook was a piece of cake, but the thought of ever having fun with money while reaching satisfying financial goals seemed like a bad joke.

As each of us looked at our own particular brands of money madness, telling the truth to ourselves and each other, an unusual phenomenon occurred. We experienced breathing room in our lives. Suddenly, we could see what we genuinely wanted in life. We gained the fortitude to pursue goals that had seemed impossible. This happened no matter how old or young the participant, or what shape our finances were in before the seminar.

In a later *You and Money* course, one participant's story was particularly poignant and inspiring. She was in her 70's, a retired librarian, who because of her financial worries had given up her cherished dream to join the Peace Corps and teach English in a faraway place. A long, conscious look at her relationship with money freed her to realize that dream. Not long after the last meeting of their group I received a postcard she sent me from Sri Lanka. She was organizing libraries and teaching English as a Second Language classes as a Peace Corps volunteer. She had realized her dream!

Hers is not the only story. Graduates of the *You and Money* course have freed themselves from crippling debt, built successful businesses, purchased their dream homes, and so much more. They have discovered new, more effective ways to use the energy we call money. It is to those brave souls, and the thousands of other people who have allowed me to support them to make their dreams a reality, that this book is dedicated.

Purpose of the Book

That first gathering of friends who were willing to share their experiences with money was a turning point in my life. On the one hand it helped me to clarify some of my own beliefs about money and allowed me to get in touch with my often-hidden feelings about it. But there was something more than this involved. When I saw how my own life was changed for the better, and how other people's lives were affected in such positive ways, I felt that I had been given a life's mission. I do not mean this in a boastful or arrogant way. To me it was like being handed one of the most valuable gifts of my life. Here was another way I could give my own life meaning and purpose. I could create the setting and provide the tools for others to gain clarity and empowerment with money.

I offered the workshop to others and it caught on. Within a short period of time I found there was a great demand for this work. Soon I was getting requests from other parts of the country, and within a few short years I found myself traveling to other states. Today, the success of the *You and Money* course has grown far beyond my wildest dreams.

Along with a growing demand for the workshops, I was inundated with requests for a book. Fifteen years after the inception of the course I've finally completed that book, which you now hold in your hands.

With this book as a guide, you can see how you hold barriers in place, see what you can do to dissolve those barriers, and get exactly what you want from life. In very practical terms, you will learn:

* A practical framework to help you discover and attain authentic goals in life, rather than what you *should* or *ought to* have.

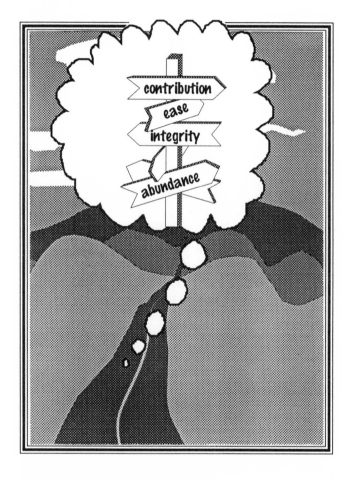

* A four step problem-solving process that works in virtually every area of life but which is particularly effective in money matters.

* Ways to free yourself from major limiting decisions about being successful that you may have made in the past and how to go beyond those limits to have what you truly value.

* A method to discover the specific nature of your personal Standards of Integrity, and how to use these standards to shape your goals and dreams.

* Processes that can be applied to areas other than money, such as transforming obstacles, including grievances with other people, so that even very painful experiences can become empowering.

* A method to discover your life's intentions and how those intentions apply to your relationship with money.

This limited list only hints at what you will find in the pages ahead. If you are prepared to do the work, you can and will realize extraordinary results. That is what I have learned during 25 years of conducting seminars. Those who relied on being entertained, instructed, or spoon-fed material got short-term results. They sometimes achieved insight, but little action came from it. In *You and Money* we call this the "Booby Prize."

To get the most from these pages, think of the author as your guide, a personal coach, your mentor--someone to support you to go beyond your self-created constraints. Like the hero on the path, or the athlete on the field, dare to allow yourself to be your best.

Before you read much further, make sure you have a notebook or journal. Keep a record of the journey you are about to take. The notes you jot down in your journal may become your own private workshop. If you do this, you can follow in the footsteps of so many *You and Money* graduates who have turned their dreams into realities.

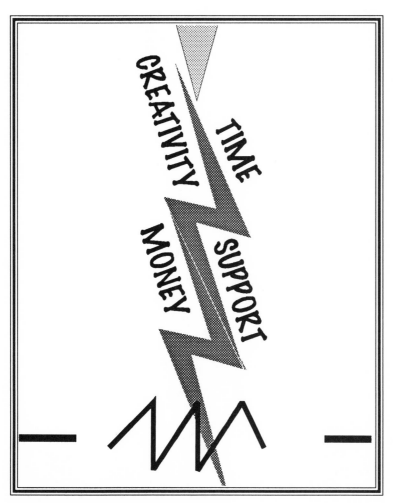

CHAPTER ONE:
Money, Energy and the Hero's Journey

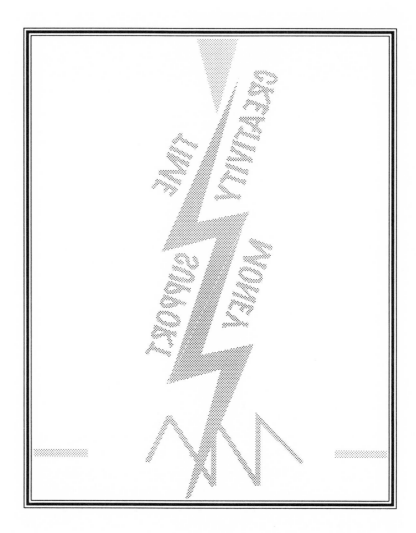

Money, Energy and the Hero's Journey

"Money is congealed energy and releasing it releases life possibilities."

Joseph Campbell

Your life can be simple and satisfying. It can be a natural and direct expression of the person you truly are. Using the talents you already have, you can attain your goals. Does it sound like a miracle? Maybe it is, but it is a miracle that is within everybody's reach. It can be your miracle.

Look at people who get what they want. For fifteen years I have traveled around the country, leading the *You and Money* course and talking with people who are successful. Do they possess attributes that set them apart from people who do not see their dreams come true? No. This is what I found: the only difference between people who are successful and people who aren't is that people who are successful are successful, and people who aren't, aren't! People who are successful have no more talent, intelligence, physical energy, or creativity than others. They often have the same fears, doubts, aspirations and worries.

If there is no basic difference between people who are successful and people who are not, what separates the two? People who are successful have learned to use energy. They focus their money, time, creativity, vigor and intelligence to bring their desires into reality.

So how do you learn to focus energy in these ways, so that you, too, can bring your dreams into reality? Money is a potent form of energy and can be the perfect focal point for working out life's important lessons. Your relationship with it is symbolic of all your other relationships with energy. Look at the parallels: do you ever have enough money? Time? Physical energy? Must you hoard money to feel secure? Must you reserve your love of others in order to feel safe? Do you waste money? Time? Do you know exactly how much money is in your checking account right now? Do you have an accurate picture of your current physical health?

Money is an emotionally charged subject. Many of us would rather talk about our sex lives than discuss the paycheck we bring home each month. I remember an incident that happened when I was seven years old. We had cousins over for dinner. At the table I wanted to sound adult, so I asked my grown cousin Irwin: "How much money do you make?" Everyone stopped talking. It was alarming, given the usual noise at dinner. Mother, clearly embarrassed, looked at me. "Maria, that's something you should never ask people." All the adults laughed. Me? I had just learned something important about money: it is too personal to talk about.

It is certainly no secret; the subject of money makes many of us ill at ease. That is because it is a subject that reaches into virtually every area of our lives. With just a little probing we might, for example, discover how we use it to fuel or frustrate our dreams, or to define our view of the world around us.

What is my relationship with money? That question may be one of the most important questions you will ever ask. When you know the answer, your path to a fulfilled life will be clear. It will be as if a guide had forged ahead into the wilderness, clearing the path for you.

A Bird's Eye View of Reality

You and I are designed to bring elements from *metaphysical* reality into *physical* reality. After many years of watching participants from the *You and Money* course grow and thrive, I have found that people who are successful are those who have learned and then effectively demonstrated this principle. They have learned how to carry their dreams, from the metaphysical realm, into reality, the physical realm.

To better understand this principle, study the following visual model of how it works. It will help you gain some perspective on what it takes to lead a fulfilled life, as well as chart out the work we will be doing in this book.

Let us suppose that there is an imaginary line that divides two aspects of reality as we have come to know it:

Metaphysical and Physical Reality

One aspect (the top portion of the diagram) is called physical reality. For our purposes, we will say that objects in this realm have high density. You can see, taste, feel or smell them. They can be measured and are subject to the constraints of space and time. One law of this domain is called impermanence: things grow, die and are replaced.

Another aspect of reality (the bottom portion) is called metaphysical reality. Whatever exists here is intangible and cannot be measured by the usual physical means. This is the home of imagination, vision and intention. These elements exist over time and are not necessarily subject to imperma-

Physical Reality

The Border

To be financially successful

To be a loving mate

To be an adventurer   To be physically fit

To be a compassionate person

Metaphysical Reality

nence. For example, you may have an intention to be physically fit that lasts you all of your life and is not dimmed by age. Whole cultures can have a collective vision that exists long after any individual dies. Though they are not material, they nevertheless play a profound role in shaping what goes on in the physical reality.

As human beings, we thrive when engaged in the process of bringing elements from the metaphysical into the physical realm. I think what we are looking at here is a result of our genetic programming. The urge to manifest our visions and intentions may have started millions of years ago, probably as a survival mechanism. After all, we were not born with fur, fangs or the ability to run as fast or fight as forcefully as our predators. But we do have the ability to think about the *possibility* of something existing that would help us make up for our physical vulnerability.

Let us imagine for a moment a caveman being chased by a tiger. He scampers up a tree just in time to avoid this raging animal. In the tree with him is a monkey, screaming in alarm. Both man and beast scream for a while as they watch the tiger try unsuccessfully to climb the tree. Then the caveman stops. He notices a stick and stone lying on the ground. The process of discovering and using intention begins. The caveman begins to think something like: "What if I took that stick and attached it to that stone with the vine from this tree? Next time, maybe I could hit that tiger before he gets me." He is forming a goal motivated by an intention, to be physically safe, that can later be translated into physical reality.

This is how it works to bring dreams and intentions into physical reality on a more personal level. You have an intention. This intention takes form in statements such as the following:
* To be physically fit
* To be an adventurer
* To be a loving mate

Each of us has a number of major intentions that are meaningful for us. For the man confronted by the tiger, the intention, to be physically safe, has obvious value in terms of his survival. This same intention is present when you check your parachute, buckle your seat-belt, or fasten the bindings on your skis.

But now let us look at something closer to home, for example, your intention for reading this book. Let us say that your intention has to do with money, that is, to be financially successful. (See the diagram on page 15.) While we will be exploring the meaning of intentions in more depth throughout this book, for now, consider that personal intentions are the inner drives that motivate and excite you. They may persist over the entire course of your life. They do not reflect what you *should* want in life, but what you *do* want. They come from a deep inner core of your being. They are worthwhile. Intentions start with *to be* rather than *to do*. Doing happens in physical reality.

You are invigorated when you know your life's intentions. At times you can get "high" on them, because they are so grand. But a life of unrealized intentions can be just as stale and frustrating as a life of no intentions at all. Something must be done to manifest them, and herein lies the drama of it all. Indeed, unrealized intentions can haunt us, constantly reminding us that we have not lived up to our life's potential. Thus, they can be the source of frustration or the impetus to move us forward on our path to success.

> "Nothing contributes so much to tranquilizing the mind as a steady purpose - - a point on which the soul may fix its intellectual eye."
>
> *Mary Wollstonecraft Shelley*

In order to manifest an intention, you have to *do* something. You must take action. What is more, this cannot be just any action: it must be action that focuses your life's energy. So, where do you begin? First, you send up a trial balloon, called a *goal*. (Look again at the diagram.) A goal is the projection of your intention into physical reality. The attainment of a real goal can be measured. For example, if you have a goal to increase your income by 20 percent by the end of the year you will know whether or not you have attained that goal by December 31. That goal is measured through simple mathematics.

A goal is a promise that you make to yourself. In the *You and Money* course, we use this definition of a goal: "an area or object toward which play is directed in order to score." Remember play? Play is action that you engage in with a certain spirit of exploration and excitement. A goal is something you want, not something you should or ought to have.

Take the example of manifesting the intention to be financially successful. First of all, does that seem like a daunting enterprise? It does to many people. We get to the heart of the matter by looking at a simple, straightforward definition of *success*, a word we will use often in this book. Success is doing what you said you would do. **Period.** You are being successful when you consistently keep your word. So, if you promise yourself to save two hundred dollars a month toward investing in a financial portfolio, and you keep your promise, you are demonstrating the intention of being financially successful. Forget about the size of the promise for a moment. Thinking the promise has to be enormous deters most people from ever starting on the path to financial success. If you really get this principle, the size of your promises will expand over time.

In order to make the intention of being financially successful real, you may want to create the goal of buying a house (the balloon in the diagram). Does the house exist as a physical reality in your life right now? No. Creating the goal focuses your energy toward getting one. In that way, a goal is a bridge between the metaphysical and the physical realms.

What we are talking about may seem obvious. Let me caution you about this interpretation. The people I have met who actually get what they want have made their dreams into measurable goals. Napoleon Hill knew the powerful principle of having goals and wrote about it extensively in his famous book *Think and Grow Rich*. He wrote, "The mind is our greatest asset. From it have emanated goals that have made the most impossible dreams into everyday realities."

How do you bring the house of your dreams, the house that you visualize in the metaphysical realm, into physical reality? You energize your goal. (See the diagram on page 19.) There are many forms of energy you can invest toward your goal. You may invest time looking for a house or consulting with a real estate agent. You may call upon friends or relatives to lend their emotional or financial support to your project, counting upon their energy to keep your energy going. You may invest creative energy looking for the best buy or financing package. You may even change jobs or professions or move to a new city, where your idea of a nice house is less costly. You may decide to stop spending money on a new car or vacation and save it for the house. Your intention, to be financially successful, provides the vessel that directs this energy and carries you toward your goal.

Trouble at the Border

All this is well and good. But, you may say, I seem to run into trouble at the border between metaphysical and physical realities. It is true that there is a shift in energy at this boundary. For example, it is much easier to *dream* about the house than to pick up the phone, call a real estate agent, fill out papers to qualify for a mortgage, or check a prospective house for termites. To move anything in the physical realm requires a lot more energy. Just think about moving an imagi-

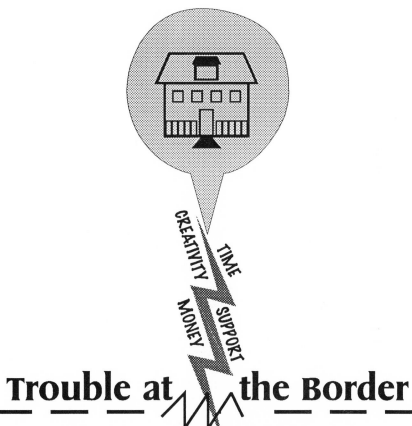

nary piano in the metaphysical realm. Compare that output of energy to the output required to move an actual piano in the physical realm. It is easy to get tired in the latter case. To top it off, as difficulties mount in the physical realm, there is a little voice that starts chattering away in your head:

* It wasn't supposed to be this hard.
* Maybe now is not the right time.
* If I were meant to have a house, it would be much easier to get one.

About the same time that these thoughts are running through your head, you discover your credit report is inaccurate (obviously not in your favor). You are tempted to lie about recent debts that you have not paid, or to ask your brother to deposit $10,000 temporarily into your savings account so you will appear to have more money than you do. You also find you must change your spending priorities to afford the house. Working through these problems is not necessarily a lot of fun. But it is part of the process of being financially successful.

Everyone encounters trouble at the border. We often forget this. I know I did. About twenty years ago I began writing a book on crisis intervention. I had traveled around the nation giving seminars on working with people in crisis. I had all my charts and graphs, and enough seminar notes to wallpaper the inside of the Taj Mahal. I was excited. My friends were excited. I was going to be an author. I remember sitting down to the typewriter the first time. I had a cup of Earl Grey tea by my side. Mozart was playing in the background. I paused, my hands above the keys, ready to start. Suddenly, my chest got tight. My arms got heavy. This was not in the travel brochure! It was supposed to be fun. I tried to write an opening paragraph. Twelve rewrites later, I was sure I didn't know enough about the subject. It was too hard. The paragraph I had written sounded stilted and boring. I stopped, thinking that next week I would feel better. But the same thing happened the next week, and the next. I finally stopped trying to write. I said to myself, "Obviously I don't know enough about the subject, or else it would be easier." I put off writing the book for the arrival of that mythical *One Day When I Would Know Enough.*

Eighteen months later, walking down Westwood Boulevard near UCLA, I noticed a display in a bookstore window. Turning, I saw a large stack of bright red books with big white lettering, *Crisis Intervention.*

I walked in, heart in my throat. Picking up the book, I saw that the author had written almost exactly what I would have! Turning to the author's profile, I saw he had no greater or lesser experience than I had with the subject. Why was he the one with a published book? Why wasn't it I? What did he know that I didn't know? I felt terrible, resentful. Life was so unfair! And then I stopped, suddenly realizing that the answer to all my questions was really a very simple one: *He had written the book* and *I had not.* As obvious as that might sound, it was a revelation for me. I immediately grabbed one of the books, took it to the counter and paid for it. I have kept that book with me all these years, putting it on a shelf where it will always be in clear sight. It is a constant reminder to me of what it takes to cross the border between the metaphysical and physical realms. That red book has become a kind of talisman, reminding me of what I must do every time I am tempted to listen to my doubts about writing.

The purpose of this book is to assist you to make your own journey from the metaphysical to the physical more exciting and productive. When you know how the border crossing looks and feels, you can predict and plan for challenges that arise. You can get support from family or friends (see chapter 15). You do not have to try to muscle it through on your own. When the going gets rough, you do not need to lose courage and invalidate your goal or the intention behind it. In fact, you may come to see that any distress you may experience in the face of difficulty is a measure of your willingness to move outside your comfort zone, to stretch beyond your present capacities or place in life and expand both your skills and your strengths.

Never give up on having goals that excite you. Without them you too easily fill your life with aimless activities that waste your energy: it is called "driven behavior." And without working toward goals that excite you, you sit at the sidelines, waiting for the "signal" that indicates now is the right time to enter the game, to continue living fully. When you engage in driven behavior or sit waiting on the sidelines, you are missing out on life. You are like the migrant to the promised land, staring at the border but doing nothing to cross.

I am convinced we are here on earth to put our intentions and dreams into action. To do that, we must learn about border crossings because it is here that most of us stop. The point to remember is that the only guards patrolling those borders are of our own making. There is always some trouble at the border, but its impassability is our creation, and we can make it vanish!

Doing Life the Easy Way

Would it be all right with you if your life got easier? This is a simple question. Buddhists ask their students such questions when they want them to learn an important lesson. It is a question I have asked myself for many years, and I am still asking.

You might think that the question should elicit an automatic "Yes!" Guess again! When I ask it in workshops and private consultations, there is sometimes a moment of hesitation as the question sinks in. Perhaps we get used to doing things the hard way. Remember "no pain, no gain?" Or, we think that if we relax our guard, things will worsen.

"The less effort, the faster and more powerful you will be."

Bruce Lee

Much of the time, too, we reap hidden benefits from doing things the hard way. For example, don't you really believe, in your heart of hearts, that the best way to succeed is to do it on your own, without depending on the support of others? The hidden gain might be a false and fleeting feeling of pride that you don't really need anybody "interfering" in your life. Haven't you sometimes thought that asking for help is a sign of weakness? The hidden gain when you do succeed seems to be proof of your "strength." If you have ever felt or acted in these ways, join the crowd! Most of us have approached our goals as if we were lone rangers, rugged individualists, proud of our ability to tough it out all alone. Doing it alone is definitely doing it the hard way. One young man in the *You and Money* course called it the "I'll-Do-It-Myself-Mother" syndrome. Anybody who was ever six years old will remember that one.

There are many other ways we make life difficult for ourselves. For example, are you afraid to fail? Are you afraid to succeed? Do you pull back in revealing your personal strength or true capability because you are "protecting" someone else from that truth? Whether it is succeeding or failing, fear haunts us when it comes to some of the most important decisions of our lives. Your psychological reasons for fear may not turn out to be important when you discover how universally prevalent fear is, particularly around issues of money. Given that such fears are more common than not, you can either run from them or allow them to teach you.

Most of us act like failure means the end of the world. We look at slogans such as: "If you are not failing, you are not aiming high enough," and we say to ourselves: "Yeah, sure! Whoever said that has never been in my position." So we go throughout life trying to avoid failure, or taking it personally every time we do fail at something. Fearing failure we go through life never really testing our wings, never discovering our strengths and natural skills and talents.

I do not suggest that you deliberately seek out failure or have a cavalier attitude toward it. Most of us try to avoid failure or mistakes. We tend not to look upon failure as positive feedback or constructive. It is doing life the hard way. There is not enough room for creativity, spontaneity or learning. We become old before our time because we trade our dreams for illusions of security. Helen Keller, blind and deaf from the time she was 19 months old, said something that I have carried with me for the days when all I want to do is retreat into the simple security of no mistakes:

"Security is mostly a superstition. It does not exist in nature, nor do the children of men as a whole experience it. Avoiding danger is no safer in the long run than outright exposure. Life is either a daring adventure or nothing."

Life is hard when you do not do what you truly value because you are afraid. When you always try to live within your comfort zone, life becomes stifling and therefore truly uncomfortable. In his classic novel *The Web and the Rock*, Thomas Wolfe said something that could inspire us all to move beyond our fears and thus to stretch beyond our comfort zones:

"If a man has a talent and cannot use it, he has failed. If he has a talent and uses only half of it, he has partly failed. If he has a talent and learns somehow to use the whole of it, he has gloriously succeeded, and won a satisfaction and a triumph few men ever know."

In a paradoxical way, the easy life includes the experience of discomfort and pain. It is when we try to *avoid* naturally occurring pain or discomfort that life becomes difficult.

The Real No Pain/No Gain

Discomfort and pain are worthy companions when you examine your relationship with money. In the *You and Money* course, one woman, the director of a large county agency, told me that she would sooner walk over hot coals than attempt to balance her checkbook to the penny. Does this sound silly to you? I guarantee that there is some aspect of your relationship with money that you have not looked at or mastered because it is uncomfortable for you. Avoidance is a natural response.

The secret to an easy life is to learn to use pain and discomfort as teachers. Pain may be a sign for you to explore another path. Discomfort may indicate that you are "at the border," and with one more push you will move beyond it. One woman in my course reported these feelings the day she promised to add up her credit card debt as a first step toward changing her relationship with money.

At the border, you have a decision to make. You can view discomfort as a marker for a boundary or limitation, or you can use it to prepare to reach beyond. Through that "boundary" may lie the land of infinite possibility, within which are the promise and the power of your dreams and intentions.

Let me give you another example. Roger had a dream of opening a bagel bakery. He worked for a state agency and was comfortable in his job. But he had a vision of owning a bakery that made the best bagels around. He visited Chicago and New York, checking out the best bagel flour -- just the right amount of gluten. Then he came back home and looked seriously at opening his store.

Panic set in. Should he leave a comfortable job with seniority, benefits and security and go out on a limb? Should he put off his dream until after retirement -- seven years down the line? He decided to cross that border with caution by going into partnership with a friend, working at the store part time. He made sure he had the support of his wife and friends. The partnership went okay but it was not exactly what he wanted. Two years later he left his regular job to open his own bagel outlet. Now he is doing extraordinarily well.

His decision may not have worked for you. Only you can see the lessons that are at your border. Crossing the border is a personal process that requires you to be clear about your choices and to be willing pass *through* discomfort.

Doing Life the Hard Way

The following are examples of doing life the hard way with money. They are taken from the lives of people who have attended the *You and Money* course over the years. These people were not comfortable. You may notice their candor and willingness to tell the truth about their relationship with money. This is no small feat.

Stuart: I sell air time for commercials on a local radio station. My monthly take-home pay? Five months ago, I was supposed to get a 10 percent raise. Not looking at my pay stubs, I just assumed it had been added to my paycheck. Preparing for my taxes, I found that due to a computer error, I had not received the raise. In addition, there was an unauthorized deduction being taken from my check. This had gone on for seven months!

Miriam: I'm the day manager of a supermarket. I take home $2314 a month. For years, I've been avoiding balancing my checkbook by rounding up to the nearest dollar. That way, I know I'm not overdrawn. As part of this course, I balanced my checkbook to the penny. I was amazed to find $1123.00 that I didn't know I had! That is the good news. The bad news is that two months ago I passed up going on a cruise with my best friend because I thought I didn't have the money.

Carol: I'm a school principal. I make $3800 a month and I don't ever see it. It's gone after a few days and again I'm waiting for the first of next month. My credit cards are charged to the hilt. But I can't bear the thought of taking them and cutting them up. I know I'm using at least one-sixth of my income in interest payments alone.

George: I own a small gift and card shop. Somehow I manage to pay my bills each month, but when I do my taxes, I realize I haven't made a profit. In fact, I'm working for about $3.00 an hour when you add up all the extra time I've put in. I borrowed a lot of money to get into this. I don't see any way to get out.

Julia: I have to get my family expensive gifts at Christmas. It only comes once a year. I'll have a spending hangover in January and I'll promise myself to open a Christmas savings account. But I'm 45 and I haven't done it yet. When I get my paycheck, there always seems to be something more important to do with the money. Maybe I'm too old to change my ways.

These stories have one thing in common: each person is doing the same thing, over and over again, though it is obviously not working for them. You could probably suggest two or three solutions for each person that would get them out of their personal money swamp. Likely, they would not listen. You would end up frustrated, and so would they. If you are like me, you have been in that swamp a few times yourself, or you are there right now.

The Monkey Mind

Why do we keep repeating worn-out patterns of behavior, even when they are obviously not working? For the answer, let us take a closer look and compare ourselves again with other living creatures. There is one big difference between us and the rest of the animal kingdom. You can train a pigeon to peck at a bar for food pellets. Then you stop giving him food when he pecks at the bar. First, he will show an initial burst of pecking. After a while, he will stop pecking and do something else. No problem.

With people the story is different. We will not stop our behavior for a long, long time, even if there has not been a reward for that behavior in years. But we will put a lot of energy into the project and justify why we are "right" about doing it that way. The reasons are endless:

*   It was supposed to work this way.
*   It will work if I just try harder.
*   It works this way with other people.
*   It worked this way once. I know it will again.
*   I don't have the time to do it another way.
*   This is just the way I am, and there is nothing I can do about it.
*   If I just keep pushing through it, the pain of doing it this way will eventually stop.
*   This is how my mother/father always did it.
*   I don't want to do it like my mother/father did it.
*   This is the way I was taught, and I'm going to stick with it.
*   I have to analyze why I'm doing it this way before I can stop.

> "Insanity is doing the same thing, over and over again, expecting different results."
>
> Rita Mae Brown

This type of thinking makes no sense. Still, you know that this kind of self-talk is very familiar. Similar thoughts have kept us all from ending what does not work and beginning a new, ultimately more fruitful path. In the *You and Money* course, I began to see that we all have a Monkey Mind. The Monkey Mind concept is taken from the Buddhist principle that there is a part of our mind that chatters at us as it swings around inside our head.

It is particularly useful to know that this voice gets loudest as we approach the border. Monkey Mind calls at you to maintain the status quo: Stay in the tree you know, even if it is uncomfortable. That's much better than looking for a new tree. After all, there may even be more tigers around those trees you're thinking about.

So, it appears that we have a much louder, more active, or at least more distracting mind than other animals. Is that all we can claim for ourselves? Absolutely not! Did George quit his steady job to buy a gift shop so that he could earn $3.00 an hour? Did Miriam intend to punish herself by deliberately not seeing she had enough money for a cruise? Was Stuart happy to find he had a smaller check than necessary for seven months? Did Julia gleefully anticipate her spending hangover in January? Did Carol look forward to spending a sixth of her income on interest payments? No.

The truth about these people is that they have goals, dreams and a vision for their lives and the lives of those around them. So it is with all of us. Sometimes the monkey chatter distracts us, and we forget who we are and what we really want out of life. Sometimes we still remember our dreams but listen to that voice when it tells us, "Next year, when things clear up, then you'll go for it." In my work with people, I have found that things do not usually clear up. And, if they do, something else equally distracting takes their place. Nowhere does Monkey Mind get stronger than when dealing with our relationship with money.

Joseph Campbell, noted author and mythologist, suggested that one way to experience personal fulfillment is to look upon our life as an heroic journey. For me, that adventure has included discovering the aspects of my life that are meaningful and relevant and then maintaining that experience in the midst of whatever antics Monkey Mind creates. It is that clarity of *knowing who we are and what we want, no matter what* that we focus on next. That focus is important because without it our relationship with money gets downright crazy.

We start seeking the things money can buy as a way to satisfy inner promptings that cannot possibly be satisfied that way. Over time we discover that a dysfunctional relationship with money is usually the result of not remembering who we truly are or how to make the best use of our gifts.

It is Useful to Know Who You Are

Can you remember a period when you were having a hard time but you knew you would be okay? I remember coming home from a vacation in Hawaii to find that my house had been burglarized. As I walked through my home and saw what was taken, I was able to say to myself, "It's not so bad, I can live without that TV, stereo, ring ... *Ring?! That was my mother's amethyst ring! This isn't fair! The only valuable thing of hers I ever had ... why this?*" After my crying fit, I realized something that seemed to make no sense at that moment. I was okay. I was breathing. In fact, I was joyful and glad to be alive!

Since that time, I have talked to others who have undergone a similar crisis. In the midst of great loss they often became aware that there was something much bigger inside them than they had realized. There was an inner core that remained intact, even if everything else seemed to be falling apart. Accessing this core brought feelings of joy and liberation, even when they were grieving.

While leading the *You and Money* course, I realized that it is far more useful to discover one's core *before* a crisis.

Then, you can manage real or imagined obstacles within an empowering context. You can create a life that is a direct expression of the person you truly are in your heart.

You will discover who you truly are if you engage in the process described in Chapter 3. You may come to see what I have seen: that our lives are not only heroic adventures, but that we are all truly heroes! It is when we do not live within our inner standards and values that we grind ourselves up into small pieces.

The only thing that would keep someone from wanting to know who they are is the fear of who they might be. A teacher once explained to me how we live as though there are three aspects to our being:

1. Who we pretend we are
2. Who we are afraid we are
3. Who we really are

Who We Pretend We Are

The *pretend* us is what we try to show to the world. In the circle with two rings, this is the outer one. When it comes to money, pretending is expressed in the most interesting ways. In 1989, eleven hundred people responded to a survey I conducted with a metropolitan magazine. Many reported that they pretend to their friends and colleagues that they have more money than they really do. They want people to think they have their financial lives together, that their debts

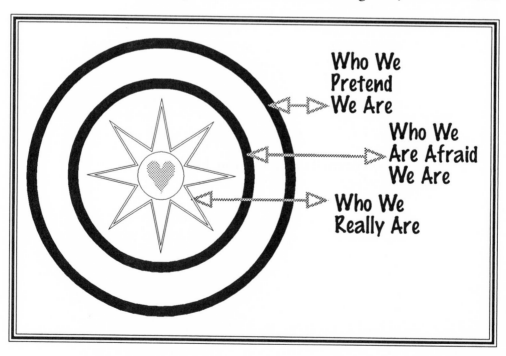

are under control and that their financial futures are secure. On the other hand, some wrote that they pretend they have less money than they really have so that others will not be envious or take advantage of them. Our pretend selves are crafted from what we *think* is expected of us, as well as how we *perceive* the norms in our culture.

It is not easy to be clear about who we pretend we are because we are the people most affected by the sham. We justify or ignore the truth of certain situations in our lives. For example, one participant in the course introduced herself as the owner of a gardening business. She maintained the business was doing well, in spite of a temporary loss of revenue because a few workers had just quit. The dialogue went something like this:

Me: Tell us about your business, Sylvia.

Sylvia: Well, like I said, it's successful. I was able to buy a great car this year, and I'm planning a trip to the south coast of Spain. We're just having a temporary downturn in revenue.

Me: How long has your business been losing money?

Sylvia: Not long.

Me: Do you know how long?

Sylvia: Look, do you want me to give you the exact figures?

Me: No, you don't have to. When was the last time you looked at your books with a friend or bookkeeper?

Sylvia: Now you want me to show my books to a friend? I could never do that!

Me: Well, how about a bookkeeper. Do you have one?

Sylvia: (softly) No.

Me: Okay, look, I know this is hard. Take a deep breath (Sylvia breathes). I am not saying that there is anything wrong with you. I know you want to be successful and I can tell you're capable of having a great business. You're smart and energetic. Still, something is not working here. You really know that yourself, don't you? Just take a look. You'll make it a lot easier on yourself in the long run. I know you're in pain about this, which is why talking about it makes you so cranky.

Sylvia: Yes. The truth is that I've been losing money in this business for a year. My dad gives me money, but I'm tired of asking him to bail me out. I hate this! I feel like such a loser! (She begins to cry but there is a great sense of relief in her tears.)

This story has a happy ending. Sylvia got through the pretense of being a "successful entrepreneur" and let herself be coached to see what was true about her circumstances.

She paid down her credit card debt, the interest of which was eating into her profit, and moved out of her big office to work out of her apartment. Today she is successful. With one trustworthy employee, she now supports herself consistently and has bought the home of her dreams.

who We Fear We Are

It is time to return to the circle diagram on page 28. The inner ring of the circle represents the person we are afraid we are. We get anxious even beginning to consider this part. All of us have incidents where we took actions of which we are not proud. We may have failed in a business because we were careless. We may have dropped out of school, stolen money, or intentionally failed to pay someone what we owed them. These acts, if not rectified, are harmful enough. What is worse is what we say to ourselves *about ourselves* for having done them and not cleaned them up. We may call ourselves lazy, crazy, a loser or undeserving of having what we want in life. This whole layer of self-recrimination seldom gets looked at because it is so painful. Sometimes this layer is covered over with blaming others for our predicaments.

This book will give you tools to visit the "shadow side" of your relationship with money. You will also look at your relationship with time, scarcity and driven behavior. This trip is absolutely necessary if you are willing to wake up and have goals that are a reflection of the person you truly are, rather than what you fear. Like Sylvia, there may be places where you have been fooling yourself which, when discovered, will give you freedom to have what you authentically want in life.

You and I know how distressing it is to look at our own shortcomings. On top of it all, there is that scathing inner voice that tells us how awful we are for having these shortcomings to begin with. This is who we are afraid we are. But consider this for a moment: if we are to be successful heros on our path, one provision we need to pack in our knapsacks is compassion. To be compassionate is to be charitable with ourselves and others.

Everyone suffers inner dialogues. They come and go like waves. When you fully realize just how true this is, you will see that what it takes just to be a human being *is, in and of itself*, nothing less than heroic. Your work in this book will teach you to observe your internal dialogues in such a way as to let them roll over you, just like a wave in the ocean.

who You Really Are

Inside the inner ring, at the heart of the circle, is who we really are. As you will see time and again in this book, the pain associated with the second ring is the result of actions that do not reflect our authentic selves. Remember, pain, especially if heeded before it knocks you unconscious, is a great teacher.

Perhaps the greatest teacher you will ever meet is your discovery of your true nature. This knowledge about yourself can help you face whatever discomfort arises as you look at how you have thwarted your goals and dreams.

Who are you inside? Are you willing to see? Marianne Williamson very profoundly noted, "It is not our darkness that we most fear, but our light."

What if you were to see clearly the strength, integrity, intelligence and wisdom that are inside you? You can discover this through the work you will be doing in this book. But consider the following, because there is a price you pay for this awareness:

When you become conscious of the person you truly are, you sacrifice your ability to stand in the dark about your self-limiting ways. This will be very clear where your relationship with money is concerned.

The Journey Continues

The next chapter addresses your craziness about money. And make no mistake, everyone is crazy to some extent when it comes to money. You will look at your own money story and see patterns and images about money you may not have known existed. You will also see how to use your own willingness to alter the course of your life. Please make sure you have a notebook for the work you will be doing.

Summary

✎   Successful people have no special attributes; they have just learned to use energy. They focus money, time, creativity, vigor and intelligence to bring their desires into reality.

✎   What is your relationship with money? When you know the answer, your path to a fulfilled life will be clear. It will be as if a guide has gone ahead in the forest, clearing the way for you.

✎   We are designed to bring elements from metaphysical reality into physical reality.

✎   You are invigorated when you know your life's intentions. But a life of unrealized intentions can be just as stale and frustrating as a life of no intentions at all.

✎   In order to manifest an intention, you have to do something physical. You must take action that focuses energy.

✎   Success is doing what you said you would do.

✎   People who get what they want have fashioned their dreams into measurable goals.

✎   In a paradoxical way, the easy life includes the experience of discomfort and pain. It is when we try to *avoid* naturally occurring pain or discomfort that life becomes difficult.

✎   The key to an easy life is to use pain and discomfort as teachers while using compassion with ourselves and others.

✎   Everyone possesses a deep inner core of strength and wisdom.

✎   Everyone has a Monkey Mind. It chatters at us as it swings from doubt to worry. It calls at us to maintain the status quo, it says to stay in the tree we know, even if it is uncomfortable, is much better than looking for a new tree.

✎   We often live as though there are three aspects to our being: who we pretend we are, who we are afraid we are, and who we really are.

✎   When we become conscious of who we really are, we sacrifice our ability to remain in the dark about our self-limiting ways. This will be very clear where our relationship with money is concerned.

CHAPTER TWO:
You and Money: A Process of Illumination

You and Money: A Process of Illumination

"The difference between transformation by accident and transformation by a system is like the difference between lightning and a lamp. Both give illumination, but one is dangerous and unreliable, while the other is safe, directed, available."

Marilyn Ferguson

Looking at our relationship with money is a little like asking a fish to look at the water he is swimming in. We are so deeply immersed in it, surrounded by it, really a part of it, that we can hardly imagine what we might do to stand back and get an objective view.

In our culture virtually everything is in some way affected by money. Choose a day to do the following experiment and you will get the point. For one day, take a small notebook with you and jot down every time you think about money. Include everything: the ads you read in the morning paper, the number of times you hear commercials on radio or TV, the times your attention turns to ads on billboards as you drive down the freeway. Jot down times that you think about your salary or income, the times you sell something to a customer, the times you make a purchase, the thoughts you might have about investing.

Try noting these money-related activities for an hour, because you might otherwise be writing in that notebook nonstop until you go to sleep that night. You will find that money is always right there in your face, or it is at least lingering at the periphery of your mind, demanding that you give it your attention. Doing this experiment was enlightening for me. Between reading about interest rates in the morning paper and watching my favorite morning TV show, I thought about money at least thirty times, including offers to buy about twenty different items, from a van to a special credit card, from joining a special CD club to signing up for a Caribbean cruise. Even more disconcerting was this tug I felt. It was like an urge to spend money I did not have to buy something I did not need. For most items, it lasted about one minute before an inner voice said, "You really don't need that." But the truth was, I had *felt*, for the moment, I needed something. This had happened at least thirty times. If you track the times you think about money in one hour, then multiply this by 16 -- the number of hours you are awake -- you can get a sense of how pervasive our thoughts are about money.

As you begin the process of examining your relationship with money, remember that money, time, physical well-being and love are some of the essential forms of energy we are here to learn about in life. With all forms of energy, we may:

* Confront the options of being thwarted or empowered, stressed or nurtured
* Face how we keep or break promises we have made in life, to ourselves and others
* See where our actions are guided by our heart or by our fears
* Experience that there is *not enough* in our lives -- not enough money, or enough love, or enough of whatever form of energy we are focused on at that moment.

Money is unique. The paper it is printed on, the plastic that represents it, or the computer bytes that move it around do not have inherent power as do other entities of value, be they gold, oil, coal, or food. When it comes to money, the energy it has is by agreement only: people say it is worth something, and so it is. Entire national economies can and do collapse when a majority of people suddenly agree that its money is no longer viable. On the other hand, seemingly inexpensive items can become priceless, as with the soaring cost of tulip bulbs many years ago in Europe, when they were rare. One bulb could fetch the equivalent of thousands of dollars today. And that was only for the *possibility* of the tulip, since there was no guarantee the bulb would bloom.

It takes skill and wisdom to handle any form of energy in a way that is going to be of benefit to ourselves and others. The early Greeks understood this principle. In their mythology, Icarus learns how to fly like a bird with wings constructed by his father. But in the flush of his newfound power, he flies too close to the sun; the wax on his home-made wings melts, and he plunges to earth. This happens right after his father (representing wisdom) warns him not to fly so high.

The present day equivalent of this story might be found in the lives of people who win the lottery, or inherit huge fortunes, only to find that the heat of this new energy is more than they can handle. Maybe they go on a buying frenzy that lasts for years, every new purchase only driving them to buy more but bringing no sense of real satisfaction. Or they give money away left and right, discovering after a year or two that they have no money left to pay their own taxes -- and the people they thought were friends have abandoned them now that they are poor again.

Can you be absolutely certain that given the opportunity you wouldn't fall victim to the *Icarus Syndrome*? We all read newspaper articles about families that are split apart when big sums of money are suddenly introduced into their midst. Without the wisdom and planning to handle this energy, there is always the potential for greed, anger, and resentment to tear to shreds even the most valued relationships. One man who inherited $750,000 from an uncle, told his story in the *You and Money* course:

Allen: I just went crazy. I bought all kinds of toys: a car, a boat, a jet-ski. You name it. I had huge, expensive parties and even gave money away in obviously bad business deals. I thought the money would never run out.

I finally came to my senses when I had about $200,000 left. I went to a financial planner and made some sound investments. It was like coming out of a nose-dive.

Allen's story may be extreme, but look at your own relationship with money. All of us, at some time in our lives, have acted in bizarre ways where money was concerned. In his book *Money and the Meaning of Life*, Jacob Needleman said: "Do you know anyone who is really normal with money? Nobody. We don't even know what it means to be normal with money."

Yes, We Are Crazy About Money

Many of us begin acting crazy with money when we are very young. For example, when you were a child, did you ever do something like eat a bug for a dollar? Steal money from your parents' wallets? Take candy, toys or comic books from the market without paying for them? In your teens, did you ever practice "mooning" from your friend's car, up and down your main street, because someone bet you $20 you would not do it? If these examples do not sound familiar, I bet you can find ones just as crazy that do! Just find that old video tape in your mind and play it back for a moment.

Even today, there may be something you would do for money that would be totally out of character for you. Try the following thought experiment and see. The only requirement is that you tell the truth.

If someone offered you $10,000,000 cash, tax-free, would you be willing to run down the main street of your city absolutely naked at high noon on a weekday? If you are tempted to say no quickly, wait a moment. Imagine a suitcase filled with one hundred thousand $100 bills. Think about what you could do with that money! Now answer the question. Okay, if you still answer no, then think about something that is totally out of character for you that you *would* do for $10,000,000 cash.

Taking this a bit farther, if you answered yes to running naked, or anything else, would you be willing do this if someone offered you $1,000,000 cash? $100,000? $10,000? Do you notice how your modesty and sense of reluctance increase as the amount of money decreases? You begin to regain a sense of sanity and proportion. It is the same with all of us.

Why do so many of us have such a peculiar relationship with money? We are vulnerable to it in the sense that we hope it will satisfy a number of needs. For example, we believe it will:

* Provide us with security and a future free from worry.
* Help us nurture our children.
* Help provide our children with good educations.
* Bring excitement or new experiences into our lives.
* Support us in our own self-development.
* Allow us to get what we really want in life.
* Help comfort us in our old age.

These are some of the same reasons that we want to be in close relationships with other people. In most personal relationships, we expect the other person to require our presence, too. Where money is concerned, this is not the case: money doesn't need us.

Of course, there are many things we would not do, no matter how much money we were offered. But there are many things that the promise of money, or the threat of losing it, could induce us to *tolerate*. Look at this for yourself. Are you presently hanging on to a job that is psychologically, emotionally and physically draining simply because it provides you with good health care or retirement plans -- both of which you will need soon if you continue too much longer at this job! Are you holding on to a relationship because it provides you with financial security, even though it is clear to both of you that separation would be the best for your emotional and spiritual well-being? Have you ever stayed awake at night, wondering where you were going to get enough money to pay the bills, only to go out on a buying binge when some money finally does come in?

These are tough questions to consider. It is a rare person who is drawn to considering them with enthusiasm and gusto. We would much rather ask ourselves other questions such as, "When am I going on my next vacation?" Or, "How can I get another credit card with lower interest rates?" So that there is no misunderstanding, let me clarify that those questions are also valuable. However, at times they distract us from answering the more important ones that could give us the power to alter our lives. Along these lines, I have found the following to be true:

People who are successful attend to the important questions that are before them, whether they like these questions or not. They may not want to look at them, they may be afraid of the answer, but they are willing to answer them nevertheless.

The operative word in this principle is *willing*. As we shall see, *to be willing* requires courage. We turn to this subject next, because *to be willing* is absolutely required if you are to accomplish the important, uncomfortable, yet liberating work in this book.

To be willing is your ticket of admission into the arena of creativity, power and fulfillment. It will change the course of your life.

Notice I do not use the word "willingness" here. That is because willingness is something you *have*. It seems to exist outside you. It is something you possess. To *be willing*, however, is a state of being. It is something that exists inside you, is a part of you. It is the difference between saying: I *have* this, and I *am* this. To be, rather than to have, is much more powerful in getting you across the border between the metaphysical and physical realms.

I am not merely playing with words here. To really get the importance of the difference between the two, ask yourself which you would choose: to *have financial success* or *to be financially successful*? Would you not choose the second statement, where you are owning the quality as something *you* generate? This is a part of who you are. It comes from your center, the inner core upon which your personal strength and ability are built. You can *have* financial success through little or no fault of your own, such as winning the lottery or pulling the handle of a winning slot machine in Las Vegas. But *to be* a financially successful relies upon drawing from your inner core to manifest your intention.

The good news is that you already are willing. You may not already know this, but it is true nevertheless. Let us revisit the diagram on goals and intentions that we discussed in the first chapter. Do you see the border between metaphysical and physical reality? If you will remember, that border is guarded by Monkey Mind. As you approach this border, Monkey Mind yells at you to turn back. One way to proceed is to try to overpower that voice with brute force, which is driven behavior. The most important thing to know about driven behavior right now is that it is repetitious, unsatisfying, and perfectionistic. It is also exhausting and a waste of energy. Too often we indulge in driven behavior not to accomplish our goals but to avoid our own unpleasant thoughts and feelings.

An easier, more effective way to proceed toward your goal is to make a distinction between the chatter in your head and *being willing*. You can be willing to do something you do not want to do. For example, I might suggest that you write down, and then clear up, your unfinished money business. This includes paying neglected loans, getting appropriate insurance, and making good on any promises you have made regarding money. Would you *want* to do this? Would you tell yourself it is make-work nonsense? But, in spite of not *wanting* to do this, are you willing?

Ernie thanked his monkey mind for sharing and then went about his business.

Being willing is a quality that transcends your doubts, worries and dislikes. That is, you can have all kinds of opinions and judgments about why you do not want to do something but still be *willing* to take action if necessary. A pregnant woman does not *want* to go through the discomfort of childbirth, but she is *willing*. When you are willing, you call upon something inside you that is bigger than Monkey Mind. You tap into the core of your being. For many, accessing this core is an empowering and sometimes spiritual experience.

Here is another trait of successful people:

Successful people are willing to challenge their assumptions in order to discover how they may have limited their own creative powers.

About now you are probably saying, "Okay, I understand all you're saying about being willing. And I'm willing. What do I do now to alter the course of my life? Just tell me: what do I need to be willing to do?"

My answer is going to seem pretty simple and straight forward. You take the following steps:
* You look
* You see
* You tell the truth
* You take authentic action

This looks easy enough. Your work in this book will be guided by those four steps. Familiarize yourself with them. Make them a part of your vocabulary. If you do, you will proceed along your path toward your goals with far more speed and clarity than ever before.

Let us take this one step at a time.

Step One: You Look

When you look at something, you are focusing your attention on it. For instance, I will ask you to track every penny you spend for a while and look at whether or not you leak money. To leak money is to allow it to trickle or seep through your fingers without knowing where it is going or even being aware *that* it is going. As an example, you may start out in the morning with a $20 bill in your wallet and at the end of the day find you have only $2.97 remaining. What is more, you do not even know exactly where the other $17.03 went.

So far, so good, as far as looking is concerned. But then Monkey Mind begins chattering away. I will bet that even as you turn your attention toward the question of leaking money, you will notice that garrulous little beast telling you things like:
* You really don't have to do this, you know.
* This is meant for other people. Your money situation is fine.
* You know you don't have time to do this work, even if you wanted to. What's the point, anyway?
* I'll tell you what, why don't we look at this when you're not quite so stressed out?

The question becomes: "Are you *willing* to look at how you leak money in spite of all this chatter?" Only you can answer this question. The moment you answer, "Yes," you place yourself at the next step.

Step Two: You See

"To see" means to notice, to examine or to discern. Once you look thoroughly at the money leaks in your life, and continue to look, you will see something about yourself. You may, for instance, see that you love to buy quick snacks on the way to work every morning, or that you have a "Velcro hand" every time you pass the magazines at a checkout stand.

Or you may see that you do not leak money. In fact, you do not spend enough money on yourself! Or you may not see anything at all about the way you leak money, but you do become aware of how you leak time instead. The point is, you are waking up, becoming more conscious about your relationship with money.

Step Three: You Tell the Truth

Let us begin this discussion with a special point. There is a difference between being honest and telling the truth. For our work here, consider that when you are *honest* about something, you are aware of your thoughts and feelings about it. To return to leaking money, you may notice thoughts and feelings like:

* I know I do leak a lot of money. But I work so hard, I need treats.
* I hate to leak money. I'm surprised at how much I do spend unconsciously.
* I probably learned this from my father/mother/brother/husband/wife.

These are honest responses. Nobody could argue that. After all, honesty is being candid, frank or sincere about your experience. It takes courage to be honest with ourselves, especially when owning up to thoughts or feelings we consider to be weak, silly or embarrassing.

But we must go a step beyond honesty. Honesty clears the way for *the truth*. As the word is used here, *truth* is the accurate fact or reality; it is *what is so*. The truth is measurable and objective, without embellishment. When it comes to emotionally-charged matters, telling the truth is definitely easier said than done. Monkey Mind goes wild. This is how a *You and Money* participant put it:

Ron: My son left his new, radio-controlled miniature race car in the driveway. I told him to stow it in the garage so it wouldn't get wrecked. Well, he didn't do what I said, and now it got run over when I backed the car out of the garage this morning on the way to work. I got out and told him what I thought of this: how careless he was, how angry he made me. When will he learn?

No one would fault this irate father for the way he felt. His thoughts and feelings are absolutely fitting. His son may need a verbal wake-up call. The only thing absent from the father's statements is the truth of the matter: *he* was the one who ran over the toy. Now, this does not excuse his son's

> "Recognize what is in your sight, and what is hidden will become clear to you."
>
> *Jesus of Nazareth*

carelessness. However, unless dad tells the truth, all he will get from this situation is a sense of righteous indignation. Telling the truth, at least to himself, might give him some breathing room. He could ask if maybe, just maybe, he has been in too much of a hurry lately to notice what he might usually see: in this case, a small race car parked on the driveway.

Honesty is sometimes confused with the truth. However, honesty does not, in and of itself, relieve a difficult situation. You know this instinctively when someone comes up to you and says: "Can I be honest with you about something?" You sense that they are about to tell you what they think or feel about you and that this will not be a pleasant experience. Sure enough, you often walk away from the conversation irritated, guilty or angry at the other person's honest opinions or feelings.

Honesty usually does not create breathing room for authentic action. Here is another example. In the Introduction to this book, I told you about the time I wrote a $35,000 check in exchange for an unsecured promissory note. I gave it to an "investor" I had known for only a few months. I felt angry, resentful, humiliated, foolish and guilty when I lost my money. I wanted to blame the other person for manipulating me into this position. But, even as I repeated this scenario to friends and family, I noticed that telling the story of what happened gave me no relief. I just got angry over and over again. What was missing? I was leaving out *my* part in the matter.

It was only when I told the truth, that *I* had written the check of my own volition--I and no one else--that I experienced some breathing room. I remember how my friend Rita helped me look at the truth. It went something like this:

Me: This guy, he just took my money. I could kick myself for trusting him.

Rita: He *took* your money? How did he *take* it?

Me: He had me write a check. He promised I would see 110 percent return on my money in three months.

Rita: *Who* wrote the check?

Me: I did! (Growing irritated.)

Rita: Are you sure?

Me: What do you mean, am I sure? Yes. I wrote it! (As you can tell, I wasn't defensive at all.)

Rita: Well, did he make you write it? Did he force you or something?

Me: Don't get cute. No, I wrote the check. I remember writing out thirty-five thousand and no-hundredths dollars.

By then I was starting to get the idea. *I did it.* I was not excusing the con man's actions, but the fact of the matter was that *I* had written that check. I remembered that my friends had counseled me against doing it. Instead, I had listened to Monkey Mind, which told me: "Don't pay any attention to them. They don't know what they're talking about." I even recalled having sensed at one point that this was a risky proposition. I had not even listened to myself!

It cannot be emphasized strongly enough that telling the truth needs to take place with a liberal dose of compassion and forgiveness for oneself. If not, you send yourself a message that looking at reality will only lead to a lot of grief. You risk remaining in the "comfortable discomfort" of blaming others, external circumstances, fate, or society.

Returning to the question of leaking money, telling the truth might be: "I spend seventy dollars a month on cappuccino and scones before work. I didn't know this." This is not an interpretation or a personal evaluation. This is a fact.

When it comes to truth-telling, people often ask me, "Can the truth really be stated so simply? Are there circumstances in which fact is difficult to separate from interpretation?" Yes, there are. However, I ask that you be willing to ferret out the simple truths about your relationship with money as you work with this book. This is empowering and will bring you the greatest relief.

Here is a chart to help clarify the difference between honesty and telling the truth:

Honesty	The Truth
I feel guilty about spending so much at the mall today. (Feelings)	I spent $45 for a scarf, $50 for a blouse, $10 for lunch -- $50 more than I should have spent.
I don't think I should have to pay so much in self-employment taxes. (Thoughts and Judgments)	I didn't pay all the taxes I owe.
I just don't have the money to open a Christmas savings account. (Justification)	I haven't opened the account.
It's your fault we don't have enough money for a vacation. (Blaming)	I didn't ask for your alignment on a savings plan for our trip.

Step Four: You Take Authentic Action

You take this step only as the result of genuinely looking, seeing and telling the truth. Authentic action takes you farther down your path toward being a financially successful person. All the insight and inspiration in the world means little or nothing if you do not take action. People who are successful take authentic action. In my case, when I told the truth that *I* had written the check, a number of options for authentic action became obvious. I would:

* Make arrangements to pay back the relative who loaned me that money.
* Make an appointment with a financial counsel.
* See where I was unconscious about money in other areas of my life and clean it up.

In addition I joined with other investors to see if we could recover our money. We got nothing. However, I had learned something that would help me in future financial transactions: get professional advice and *listen* to it.

There is an obviousness about authentic action that makes it unappealing to those who like to see their situations as being more complex. I call this the *Who's Buried in Grant's Tomb?* syndrome. It is really a very simple principle: Attend to the obvious. Avoid burying the simple truth just because you do not want to look at it, or do not want to do what must be done to correct the situation. For example, an authentic action for someone with a toothache would be to see a dentist. For the person who wakes up with a New Year's spending hangover, an authentic action might be to open an automatic-deposit Christmas savings account for this year. However, standing between the truth and taking action you will often find Monkey Mind, ready to tell you that you do not have the time or energy to do anything right now. After all, the toothache is not that bad; a few aspirin every hour or so will handle it. In the case of Christmas savings, "Just wait until you get your tax return in April."

The question that continues to stare you in the face is this: are you willing to take action, even if it seems obvious or simple? The woman who spent $70 a month on cappuccino saw that she had developed a habit of buying food whether she really wanted it or not. She decided to use $35 month for morning treats and put the other $35 into a travel fund.

Exercise: Your Money Autobiography

You now have the chance to look at your own relationship with money. This may be your first foray into this uncharted territory. But doing the following exercise will provide you with a personal context for the work you will be doing in the pages ahead.

It may seem odd to think of your autobiography in association with money. However, your experience with this form of energy began when you were very young. When do you remember first hearing about money? Who was it from? What was the emotional climate at that time? When did you first earn money? Lose money? The answers to these and other questions in the exercise will give you a picture of the associations you bring to any discussion of your personal finances, goals and dreams.

What You Will Need

Get out the journal you purchased to record the exercises in this book. Label this exercise, My Money Autobiography.

Time For This Exercise

Give yourself at least forty minutes for this exercise. You can divide this time into ten minute sections. Make sure you are in a place where you will not be disturbed. You can do this at your computer, but I strongly recommend that you use pen and paper because they are portable and accessible. Most of all, just do at least some of this.

The Exercise

Tell the story of your life using money as the central theme. Begin with your earliest childhood memories. Write in narrative form, like, "I first learned about money when I was ..." Let the following questions spark your recollections. You do not need to answer them all in your money autobiography. They are listed here to make your task easier. However, should you wish to skip over a question, it is probably one worth serious consideration.

1. What were your family's financial circumstances when you were born?

2. When did you first learn about money? How old were you? What were the circumstances?

3. Did you have an allowance? Did you have to work for it, or was it given to you without your having to do chores? If you have children, how does your own past experience with allowances affect how you handle allowances with your kids?

4. When was the first time you bought something with money you had saved?

Where were you? What did you buy? Was it money you earned or money someone gave you?

5. Do you remember your first paycheck? How did you earn it? How much was in it? What did you do with it?

6. Do you remember ever losing money? When was the earliest time? What happened? Has this happened to your children? How did you handle it?

7. Did you dream of one day having a particular job or career? Have you achieved this? Why or why not? Was the amount of money you could earn a factor in your choice of careers?

8. If your relationship with money was a personal relationship, how would you describe it? Do you fear, love, hate, depend upon, feel possessive of or generous with money? Just write whatever comes to mind.

9. How do you relate to people who have more money than you? Less money?

10. Do you recall your mother's or father's relationship with money? If you did not live with one or both of them, pick people who were your primary care givers for this question.

11. How did the above person's relationship with money affect you? Did this person have particular financial expectations of you? What were the expectations? Were there some aspects of money that were not discussed? Even though they were not discussed, you may have known what they were. If you have children, do you have similar expectations of them? Do you treat them the same way you were treated? If you are married or in a committed relationship, do these expectations affect your partner?

12. Have you ever accomplished an important task or project involving money. What was it? What did you do that made you successful?

13. Was there a time when you tried but did not accomplish an important task or project regarding money? What was it? What did you do that made you unsuccessful?

14. Have you ever given or received gifts of money? If yes, how much? For what reason(s)? How did you feel about this?

15. If you were to characterize your own brand of money madness, how would you describe it?

16. Where do you want to see yourself ten years from now regarding money? How much in savings? How much in investments? How much money do

you see yourself making ten years from now?

17. Regarding money, for what do you want to be known? If people were to speak about you regarding you and your relationship with money, what would you want them to say?

When you are finished writing, give your autobiography an appropriate title.

Discussion

Having written your money autobiography, no matter how long or short, congratulate yourself! You have begun some important work. You are allowing yourself to see facets of your relationship with money that will begin to inform you about your present decisions in life. It is useful to recognize money themes that are important to you, and how they recur.

Regarding the title of your story: what is the emotional tone? Is the title a theme that is echoed in your relationships with love, time, physical well-being and creativity? If so, where?

This exercise is designed to get you to examine your own perspectives about money. Is there someone with whom you can share this information? Talking about this exercise with other people you can process the results of your money autobiography on a verbal level. Even though there are differences among people's stories, you will see how potent a subject money is for most of us. Some emotions may have surfaced as you wrote your autobiography. It is useful to talk about what they are. Were some questions more difficult to answer than others? What do you suppose accounted for this?

Please remember to have compassion for yourself as you do this work. It will allow for a free flow of information, images and memories from the past.

Who Are You Really?

In Chapter One you looked at how we live as though there are three aspects of ourselves:
1. Who we pretend we are
2. Who we are afraid we are
3. Who we really are in our hearts

When you first look at your relationship with money, important realizations may surface about who you pretend you are and who you are afraid you are regarding money. This can be uncomfortable and could discourage you from continuing your work in this area. What will help is to know who you *really* are. That knowledge will give you the fortitude to *clean up your act* and see your true goals and dreams.

The next chapter helps you discover your magnificent qualities. I say this because there is a certain shyness or even cynicism that attends any discussion on one's own extraordinary qualities. Do the work that is there. It will provide you with a framework for the rest of your journey.

Summary

✎   Money, time, physical well-being and love are some of the essential forms of energy we are here to learn about in life.

✎   With all forms of energy, we may:
*   Confront the options of being thwarted or empowered, stressed or nurtured
*   Face how we keep or break promises we make in life
*   See where our actions are guided by our heart or by our fears
*   Experience that there is not enough (of whatever type of energy) in our lives.

✎   Many of us have a peculiar relationship with money. We are vulnerable to it in the sense that we hope it will satisfy a number of needs, the same types of needs that enter our personal relationships.

✎   People who are successful attend to the important questions that are before them, whether they like these questions or not. They may not want to look at them, they may be afraid of the answers, but they are willing to answer them nevertheless.

✎   *Being willing* transcends your doubts, worries and dislikes. That is, you can have all of your opinions and judgments and still be willing.

✎   Successful people are willing to question their own assumptions in order to discover how they may be limiting their own creative powers.

✎   Four steps are required to change the course of your life:
*   You look
*   You see
*   You tell the truth
*   You take authentic action

✎   The definition of "honesty" is "to be candid, frank or sincere about one's experience." Honesty clears the way for the truth.

✎   The "truth" is the accurate fact or reality of something, best expressed as *what is so.*

✎   Telling the truth needs to take place with a liberal dose of compassion for oneself and others.

✎   Authentic action furthers you down your path. All the insight and inspiration in the world mean little if you do not take authentic action as a result.

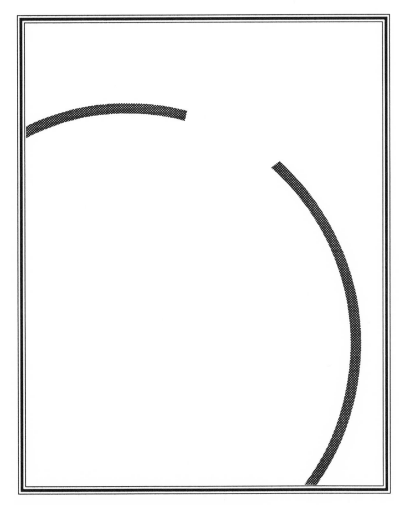

CHAPTER THREE:
Integrity and Intentions --
The Sources of Your Personal
Power

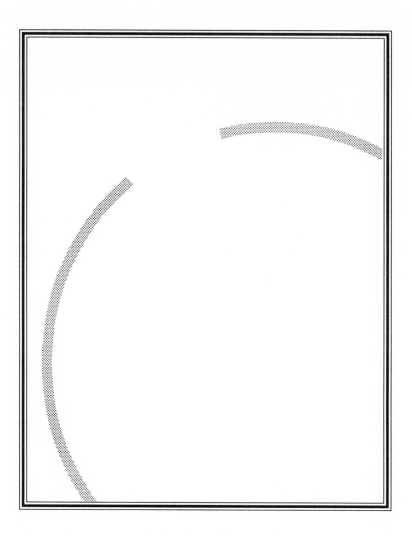

Integrity and Intentions -- The Sources of Your Personal Power

"This is the true joy in life: being used for a purpose recognized by yourself as a mighty one. Being a force of nature instead of a feverish, selfish little clod of ailments and grievances, complaining that the world will not devote itself to making you happy ....

"I rejoice in life for its own sake. Life is no brief candle to me. It is a sort of splendid torch, which I've got to hold up for the moment, and I want to make it burn as brightly as possible before handing it on to future generations."

George Bernard Shaw

A simple principle can become the cornerstone for being financially successful and powerful, with new freedom to manifest what you truly want. That is what this chapter is about, the hidden magic that awaits you when you know and exhibit your Standards of Integrity and your intentions.

Consider again how we operate as though there are three aspects of our being: who we pretend to be, who we are afraid we are, and who we really are.

Who you really are, to quote Deepak Chopra in his book *Creating Affluence* is "true potentiality." Note that the root of potential is "potent," which means being vigorous, capable, powerful and effective.

If you consider the principle of potentiality, you see that it refers to power that may not yet show up in the present. When we say, "She has great potential," we are usually referring to someone who shows the signs of doing great things in the *future*. In fact, we never reach our full potential. If we did, it would no longer be potential, but *actual*.

Your true nature exists as potential. This potential resides in the metaphysical realm. It is formless. However, you can describe and measure some of its properties by exploring how you hold that potential within yourself as your hopes and dreams, your intentions and your joys. I will explain how you do that in a moment. At the point where you have identified your potential, you have the opportunity to show these properties, *who you really are,* in physical reality. This is, to quote George Bernard Shaw, "the true joy in life!"

How can you see who you really are? How do you identify a potential that is not yet fully realized? Let us look at this for a moment. In quantum physics, we see that getting an exact measurement of quantum particles is impossible. These particles are so small that it is hard to tell whether they have mass or are really just vibrations of energy or both. One way to get a bead on them is to watch for their reflections on highly-sensitive photographic surfaces. Quantum particles: the extent to which they are nothing more than energy vibrations may be the bridge between metaphysical and physical reality.

"All the goodness, beauty and perfection of a human being belong to the one who knows how to recognize these qualities."

Janet Flanner

Now let us apply this metaphor to you. If who you really are is formless, pure potentiality, *seeing yourself exactly is impossible*. You can, however, see the *reflections* of your self. To borrow a metaphor from our quantum physics example, what is the photographic surface upon which your true self is reflected? The answer may surprise you. It is your heart. What it reflects are the feelings of joy and inspiration that you experience when you think about or do certain things in your life.

When you experience joy, inspiration, or gratefulness, you are in contact with the core of who you really are.

Take a moment and think about someone whom you admire. What are the qualities you prize in them? By qualities, I am not referring to physical attributes or the number of material possessions they may have collected during their life. Look for more enduring traits, ones that reflect their basic goodness. Do you admire their courage, loyalty or creativity? Do you honor their love, compassion or truthfulness? Even as you are thinking about this person, do you notice a certain warmth in your heart?

Your heart warms to certain qualities in others because they are inside *you*. If you did not have them yourself, you would not be able to see them in others. Let us look at this for a moment. To value loyalty, you must know what loyalty is. You must sense what it means to be dependable, steady, faithful and dedicated. You know the pain of *dis*loyalty. This is true for any other attribute to which your heart responds. To use a physiological metaphor, if you respond to the trait, you must have a *receptor site* for it. That is, a location in your heart that recognizes and reacts to the quality when you see it in others. That is what we mean by having the quality inside you as a possibility, a potential.

Let us now take this a step farther. You possess the possibility, the potential, for a host of attributes or characteristics that *you* consider to be special and admirable. When you see them in others, your heart lights up, like the heart light in the movie character *ET*. When you act according to these qualities, you experience a sense of well being. You feel whole and complete. It is a feeling that you experience only when you are acting in integrity, that is, acting according to the standards that are most important to you, the standards that, finally, express who you are.

The Integrity Factor

You may not be aware of all the admirable qualities that exist as possibilities for you. In fact, you may cringe whenever you hear the word "integrity." Aieee! Not the "i" word! When we put that word next to money, it can lead to many reactions:

Marlene: Integrity? Hardly anyone really has it anymore. Just look at what you read in the papers. It's everyone for themselves out there!

Albert: Integrity is all relative. Sometimes you have to bend the rules. It's all about knowing when and when not to cross the line.

Mel: Now we start talking about what I should and should not be doing with my money. This is going to be a lecture on morals, isn't it?

Everyone has their own particular gut reaction to the subject of integrity and money. In the *You and Money* course, this is the part where people get a pinched look on their face. Nevertheless, before you throw this book across the room, let us back up and examine more closely what integrity means. Integrity has come to stand for decency, honor, principal and virtue. The original meaning of the word is simpler than that, less value-laden or judgmental. Integrity is the state of being whole and complete. According to most dictionaries, integrity is the "entire correspondence with an original condition."

Integrity, your original condition, is who you really are in your heart.

So without further ado, let us see if we can reveal your personal Standards of Integrity. In the next exercise, you will uncover the traits you most admire in others. Nevertheless, remember: These are reflections of you. As you get in touch with these qualities and feel them as a part of you, you may have an experience that is like coming home to what has always been true about you. If you give yourself fully to the exercise, you will create a blueprint or guide that will fully unveil the source of your own greatest personal power.

> "The first attitude or belief necessary for being is integrity, which centers around truth and honesty. The closer the outer expression and inner feeling are to being the same, the more we can say that the person or organization has integrity."
>
> *Mark S. Guterman*

When you act from your standards of integrity, you increase your capacity to bring goals and dreams from the metaphysical into the physical. You can transform your heart's desires into authentic action, and do so efficiently and effectively. No energy is wasted. You drag no extra baggage ponderously along behind you on your hero's journey.

Exercise: Identifying the Attributes You Admire: Preparing to Unleash and Focus Your Greatest Power

This process requires you to be quiet and contemplative, going deep within yourself for greatest accuracy. In doing so, you are giving yourself the gift of discovering who you really are. You will see the pattern of your potential.

What You Will Need
Take out your notebook or journal. Have at least four clean pieces of paper handy.

Time For This Exercise
You will need about forty minutes for this process. Doing it all at once is fine, or divide the time over two sessions of approximately twenty minutes each. Make sure you are not distracted during your work periods.

The Exercise
Take out your notebook. Turn to a clean piece of paper.

1. On the left side of the page, list all the people who have qualities you admire. Write their names. Use the following checklist to spur your memory. Take your time and reach back into your past. The lists of possibilities include:

    a. Your family, such as your mother, father, sister, brother, aunt, uncle, grandfather, grandmother;

    b. School, such as teachers, principals, custodians, classmates;

    c. Religious teachers and leaders, ministers, priests, Sunday school teachers;

    d. Friends from school, work, home, social clubs or any other source;

    e. People in the healing professions, such as doctors, nurses, therapists, alternative medicine professionals;

    f. Sports figures, whether from professional or amateur sports and the Olympics;

    g. World leaders, spiritual or political;

    h. People in the arts and entertainment industry such as actors, directors, singers, dancers, artists, musicians and composers;

    i. Biblical figures, people important to your religion;

j.   Mythological characters, from Greek, Native American, Indian, Egyptian or other cultures' myths;

k.   Anyone you have ever read about, whether real or fictional.

2.   Survey your list. Look at each name, starting with the first and working down the list. On the right side of the paper, record the qualities or traits you most admire in the person. A quality is something that is inspiring to you. They may be loyal, intelligent, adventurous, courageous, creative, truthful, and so on. Go to the next person on your list. If that person shares qualities with the first, simply put a check-mark next to that attribute. List any additional traits not found in the first person. As you proceed, you will develop a list of qualities, with check-marks that indicate when that quality was noted more than once.

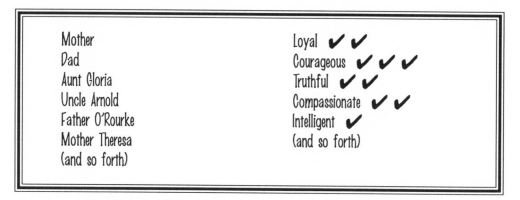

Mother   Loyal ✔ ✔
Dad   Courageous ✔ ✔ ✔
Aunt Gloria   Truthful ✔ ✔
Uncle Arnold   Compassionate ✔ ✔
Father O'Rourke   Intelligent ✔
Mother Theresa   (and so forth)
(and so forth)

Bear in mind that your lists can be as long or short as you like. However, give yourself enough time to compose an inventory that is as complete as possible. This process is vital to the rest of your work.

3.   Now we are going to revisit your list of qualities. Take out a clean piece of paper. Starting from the top, look at each trait. Spend a few moments contemplating each attribute. Ask yourself the questions, "When I read this word, aloud or to myself, does it warm my heart, if only for a moment? Do I like being in the presence of people who have this quality?" You could think of your heart area as a little lantern that lights up when it encounters certain traits. If that warmth, light, or sense of well-being is present, write that word on this new piece of paper.

Repeat this process until you have contemplated each word on your list. You may find you have transferred all or just a few of them. This is not important. What does matter is that you are willing to see what touches your heart.

4.   Take the new list and place it in front of you. Each trait has significance and meaning for you. That is because you possess the receptor site for it in your heart. If you did not know what each quality meant, it would not have the

power to evoke a response from you. To put this another way:

If you see these qualities in others, if your heart resonates with them, it means they exist within you. If not, you would not be able to see them.

5. Take this list and print it on a 3"x 5" card. At the head of this list, put **These are My Standards of Integrity**. On the bottom of the list, write, "I know these are mine, because I see them clearly in others." Keep this card with you. Having it with you will be useful for this work.

Discussion

What you have before you is the blueprint for your personal power, your Standards of Integrity. You are a human being who possesses the qualities you listed. They are part of your nature. You can do nothing to get rid of them no matter what you do.

What do you feel as you read all the words you wrote on your list? Sharing your reactions with a friend is useful. If couples do this exercise together, the discussion can lead to profound insights and understandings. When you do this exercise in a group, you might have each person stand and read his or her standards to the group. For some people, this can be an emotional moment, as they begin to realize the possibility that they really do possess these qualities. While they read these standards aloud, you will notice that *they are obviously describing themselves!* You will have a window into their heart. You may recognize that they are naming the precise traits you have also seen in them.

Take your integrity card with you and read it at least once a day for one week. After a week, ask yourself if you have noticed any changes in your relationships. You may see a subtle shift in your behavior, mood and conversations.

Record your observations about yourself in your notebook. When you are aware of your Standards of Integrity, is it easier to talk with others? Do you think before you speak? Do you let them in a little closer? Observe yourself. If you do, you will be practicing a skill that is essential to the hero's journey.

Coming Full Circle with Integrity

Many people consider it a mixed blessing to discover their own Standards of Integrity. You pay a price for the awareness of who you really are.

Maxine: At the very moment when I read the word *honest,* I saw all the times I have been *un*truthful lately. This is not fun. Am I supposed to feel good about this? I really feel guilty.

Jordan: I *know* I have not been acting courageous and trustworthy at my job, and these are two of my top standards. In fact, my gut feels tight right now as I talk about it.

These people are describing the phenomenon I call the *Impetus toward Integrity*. We look at this now. It will help explain the tension you may experience as you go over your

Standards of Integrity.

Study the figure below for a moment.

What do you see here, a circle with a piece missing? It is not a true circle, but your mind wants to turn it into one. That is because you recognize the possibility of its being a full circle if that piece were added. Take this one step farther. Do you notice that your eyes keep going to the area that is

missing? They are drawn there by the tension of the incompletion. If the part were added, it would restore the circle's integrity.

The above is an example from the psychology of perception, called a *gestalt*. A gestalt is a perceptual whole that we recognize even when part of it is missing. We are born with that ability. We also come "hard-wired" with the need to correct obvious incompletions. This explains the tension we experience at the point where we see that the circle's edge is missing.

In my experience working with all kinds of people, I have found that the need to recognize and maintain integrity is a driving force in most of life's arenas. This impetus to maintain or restore the "whole," as we see it, is an automatic response. We perceive ourselves in the same way. When we see what is really true about ourselves, we become aware of areas in our lives in which our behavior does not correspond with this perception. Sometimes, we have that bittersweet experience of feeling great about ourselves but not so great about our behavior.

Look at it this way: your discomfort about your own behavior is a validation of who you are, not a condemnation. The discomfort you feel is an expression of your awareness of your integrity and your urge to attain wholeness.

Think about this principle as you contemplate your Standards of Integrity. You will naturally and automatically come up with memories of situations in which you acted outside these standards. This is a normal process. It is human! Everyone has such memories. You may feel tense, sad, guilty or regretful. Allow yourself simply to experience this tension. *Do not do anything about it at this point.* In a later chapter, you will see a method to deal with areas in your life in which your integrity is incomplete. Nevertheless, for now, just look.

If you have done the work suggested so far, you will have seen at least two things that are true about you:

*   You have Standards of Integrity.
*   You have a basic need or impetus toward achieving and

maintaining alignment between these standards and your own behavior.

virtue-al Reality

Whenever the subject of integrity comes up, it is not long before another term enters the conversation. The word is "virtue." What does this word mean? How does it apply to the idea of integrity that we have been examining here?

Virtue is the result of displaying your Standards of Integrity in physical reality.

Synonyms for "virtue" are excellence, worth, value, merit, potency and power. As you can see, these words connote something that you can see or measure. You see *excellence* in an athlete's winning performance. You see *worth* in a service you buy from a doctor or other professional. You find *value* in working with a person whose skills augment your own. You find *merit* in a person's very best efforts to accomplish a particular challenge in the workplace. You see *potency* or *power* in a speech that a person delivers from the heart.

This brings us again to a major theme of this chapter: whatever exists as a possibility is useless unless you display it in physical reality.

The virtuous life is one in which you actively display the attributes you cherish in others. It begins when you ask yourself the question:

How would an honest, intelligent, creative (fill in the qualities that appeal to you) person handle this situation?

This question directs your attention away from yourself and your purely self-serving needs and toward making a real contribution to others. Remember, you already know what your highest qualities look like, or else they would not be on your *medley of greatest hits.* Here is the way one person processed this challenge:

Arnold: I admire people who are kind. Yesterday I had a talk with one of my salespeople. He has not brought in one client to our computer training company in two weeks. Normally I would have had his head on a plate within ten minutes. This time, I asked myself: "How would a kind person handle this situation?" Just asking the question gave me ideas. I began by letting him know that *I* knew he wanted to be successful, and that this period of non-productivity was probably hard on him. The result? We had a good session on what to do next, and brainstormed some ideas that could help him get out of his slump. I felt great. This morning he called me. He had just landed a new contract for us. It was a win for all of us, all the way around, because we will all end up benefiting from that little talk he and I had.

"I felt great." These three words epitomize the experience that comes from putting into practice what is in your heart. Your Standards of Integrity are your guidelines for leading a healthy and productive life. Do not take my word for it. Look again at the meaning of the word *integrity*. Integrity means *to be whole*. The root word of whole is *heal*. When you are healed, you are healthy.

I recommend you spend a week with your Standards of Integrity card. *Notice specific cases where you actually do show these qualities or attributes.* How do you feel at those times? What is your experience of yourself? Pay very close attention to these inner messages. Your real power, the personal power that comes from living within your Standards of Integrity, is the wellspring from which your success will come.

Practice living what you consider to be the virtuous life. It is well within your grasp. After all, you are following no one's rules but your own. Remember, *you* are the one who identified these guidelines of personal excellence. I promise that if you do this, you will connect with the hero within in a powerful, indelible way. You will equip yourself to attain your goals and dreams with ease.

Intentions Dig: Unearthing Your Treasure

An "intention" is a direction, aim or purpose that comes from deep within you. Just like Standards of Integrity, your intentions are a mirror of who you are in your heart. You can tell this because discovering them evokes the same response in your heart as your Standards of Integrity.

Albert Einstein once said:

"All means prove but a blunt instrument, if they have not behind them a living spirit. But if the longing for the achievement of the goal is powerfully alive within us, then we shall not lack the strength to find the means for reaching the goal and for translating it into deeds."

Your intentions are the *living spirit* behind your goals and dreams.

Never doubt that the spirit of intentions can fuel your goals. For example, who can watch the Olympics without being moved by the pure, clear, focused intentionality of all the athletes as they strive for excellence?

The movie *Rudy* is another example. This man wants to be a football player for Notre Dame. He is not very athletically talented. However, he insists upon spending time with the team, carrying towels and playing on the practice squad. The football players run all over him, but he keeps getting up. He gets to suit up along with everyone else at the last game. Inspired by his courage and persistence, his team lets him play in the game, and then carries him off the field in triumph.

You could say to yourself that people who have intentions like that are lucky. They know what they want. Well, you have intentions, too. If you are willing, give yourself the gift of discovering exactly what they are by doing the exercise below.

Your life's intentions, like Standards of Integrity, live in the metaphysical domain. They represent ways of being. That is why they usually start with the words: *To be*.

To be:
* An adventurer
* Physically fit and healthy
* Artistic
* A contributor to my community
* A great mother (father, brother, sister, etc.)
* Creative
* A successful entrepreneur
* Financially successful
* Spiritually developed
* Well-educated
* A great entertainer (host, hostess)
* A well-respected professional
* A good friend
* Surrounded by love and beauty
* A good provider
* A generous, charitable human being
* An author, poet or playwright

There are infinite possibilities for who you can be. Everyone has a different blend of intentions. They reflect the unique contributions you are here to make. As far as I can tell, there is no correlation between your Standards of Integrity and your intentions. You cannot predict one from the other. However, taken together, your intentions and your Standards of Integrity provide the cross hairs that allow you to hit the exact bullseye of who you really are.

The true wealth in having intentions is that they provide a way to channel energy from the metaphysical into the physical realm.

Swami Yogananda, a man of compassion and vision, explained the principle in this way:

"The world is nothing but an objectivized dream. Whatever your powerful mind believes very intensely instantly

> "Our brains are made of matter, but our minds are made of a nonmaterial "intent". This intent acts like a laser beam. It shines through our material substance and gleans information."
>
> *Fred Alan Wolf*

comes to pass."

You actually gain both mental and physical power when you focus on realizing your intentions. Intensity and intention have the same root: *to stretch out*. One purpose of this book is to encourage you to stretch out and make your goals a reality. For example, you are learning consciously to direct your energy rather than leaking or wasting it. What is great about this is that it is easy to concentrate upon what brings you joy and meaning. To paraphrase the earlier George Bernard Shaw quote, *the true joy in life is being used by a purpose that you consider to be important.*

You will soon have the chance to see your life's intentions. If you are worried that you presently do not know what they are, and that you will never know, or that you simply do not have any, take heart. Your intentions already exist. The next process will help you uncover what may have been unclear or just simply hidden from you.

As you continue your hero's journey, having tools that empower you is important. You will need them to help you maintain courage in the face of everything you consider to be your dark or "shadow" side regarding money. By the end of this chapter, your tools will include:

*   Knowing your Standards of Integrity
*   Knowing the power of intentionality in focusing your energy
*   Knowing your life's intentions

So, let us now get to the business of unearthing your treasures.

Exercise: Your Intentions -- A Treasure Hunt

You are about to begin the search for your personal treasure: your life's intentions. You can discover hundreds of intentions. It is all up to you. In fact, when you see your intentions, you will have a rich experience of who you really are.

What You Will Need
Make sure you have your notebook with you. You will want to be in a quiet, undisturbed place for this exercise.

Time For This Exercise
As with the integrity exercise, you will need about forty minutes for this. You can do it all at once or in parts. Just make sure each segment is at least twenty minutes long.

The Exercise
1. First, you are going to empty your mind. Pretend that you have found a magic lamp. As you rub it, a genii appears and offers to give you anything you want. All the money, time and talent that you need is yours for the asking.

   On a clean piece of paper, list all the things that you have always wanted to do or have in life. Write down whatever comes to mind. You have all the freedom in the world. You will not be held to this list. It can be pure fantasy, not necessarily based upon the reality of your current circumstances. This is just to get out of your mind and onto a piece of paper everything that has captured your interest over the years. Write it down even if what you want to have or do seems outrageous. In fact, the more audacious the better. Just make sure it is something you really want. The list may look like this:
   * A new car
   * Writing a best-selling novel
   * Having a home with a swimming pool
   * Being hired to direct a motion picture
   * Learning how to scuba-dive
   * Having my own yacht in the Bahamas
   * Going on a picture-taking safari to Africa
   * Swimming with the dolphins
   * Having a brand new wardrobe
   * Taking my kids to DisneyWorld
   * Giving one million dollars to the community food program
   * Running a marathon
   * Going on a trip around the world
   * Having enough money for my daughter's education
   * Taking art lessons and painting a picture
   * Eating at all the best restaurants in Paris, New York, and San Francisco
   * Becoming a pediatric physician and healing all the children in the world
   * Becoming an astronaut

2. Look at each item. Ask yourself the questions: "Why do I want this? What need will it satisfy?" When you discover the underlying reason for your choice, write it down on a separate piece of paper. For example, you may want to take your kids to DisneyWorld because it would satisfy your desire *to be a good parent*. Similarly, writing a best-selling novel would make it possible for you *to be a well-respected author*.

    Take other examples: you may discover that the reason you would want to become a pediatric physician is *to be a healer with children*. Or, traveling to Africa, or around the world, would satisfy your need *to be an adventurer*. Remember, by writing these down you are not committing yourself to actually doing these things. It is a way really to get to know the desires that influence each of your choices. Upon completing this phase of the process, you will have a list of intentions. Put this list aside for the moment and go on to the following.

3. For the next phase of this exercise imagine a group of your friends, family and co-workers at a party honoring you on your eighty-fifth birthday. Everyone is there, still alive and in good health. You, too, are in perfect health. A group of these people has prepared an acknowledgment of you, for all you have done in your life. They have jotted down what they have observed about you and are about to read what they have written. You will be taking notes on what they say, so have your pen and notebook ready.

4. Write the list of who is there at this party to honor you. Put their names down: husband, wife, children, teachers, colleagues, friends, parents, co-workers, bosses, minister (rabbi, priest), students, neighbors, committee members, aunts, uncles, cousins.

    Picture each person getting up and speaking about you. What do you hope, in your heart of hearts, that they will say about you? Boil what they say down to two or three sentences. This is what two people, Alex and Mary, reported in a recent workshop:

    Alex: The first person to stand up is my best buddy Dave. He starts to roast me, but soon he settles down and gets to the heart of things. He says I have always been a good friend. He compliments my sense of humor and says I always watch out for other people to see that they are okay.

    Mary: My sister says that I am a great mom and that I was always taking her and everyone else on adventures. She remembered the time I took some friends petroglyph hunting in Hawaii.

5. Distill to an essence what the people at your gathering say about you, pre ceded by the words *to be*. For example, Alex wrote the following statement: "To be a good friend, to be humorous, and to be kindhearted." Mary wrote this: "To be a great mom, and to be an adventurer."

    You may have to use your best creative abilities to turn the words of your imaginary gathering of friends, relatives and associates into *to be* statements. Stick with it. Add these phrases to the list you began earlier.

6. At the conclusion of this process, you will have a list of *to be* statements. Look at them. This is the fun part. Which ones do you really hope are true of you? Circle them. Never mind if you do not feel you have fulfilled any of

them lately, or *ever*, for that matter. Do you want *to be an artist* or *to be a healer*? Give yourself the gift of choosing what sings to your heart. Transfer everything you have circled to a clean piece of paper.

Discussion

You now have a preliminary catalog of your life's intentions. Live with this list for at least one week. During this time, go back to it and notice how you feel when you read it. After a week, you may add or subtract any item you wish. After all, this is *your* list.

Sharing these intentions with another person is useful. If you do this in a group, have each member stand and read his or her list, much like you did with the integrity process. The group offers support and helps the person clarify items as necessary.

You may find that doing this work is both emotionally satisfying and draining. Many people feel this way. You are taking a different view of yourself and your life. As with the integrity process, you will likely notice a bittersweet reaction when you encounter the intentions that you have not yet manifested in your life. This discomfort is a signal that you are on the right path. Your work in this book is specifically designed to assist you in bringing your intentions from the metaphysical into the physical.

Take yourself and your intentions seriously. They are your reasons for being on the hero's journey. If seeing this in yourself is difficult, ask your friends or loved ones to help. They may see your intentions long before you can see them in yourself.

The Road Ahead

You now have a picture of who you are in your heart. Your Standards of Integrity and your intentions are the reflections of your inner self. The recognition that you have not fully manifested them in physical reality tempers this view. It is part of the cause of *trouble at the border.*

In the next chapter of this book you will pinpoint the exact nature of this border problem. You know that it is impossible to clear away barriers unless you see what they are. So *gird your loins* with your integrity and intentions, and set out to take a little trip to the shadow side of your relationship with money. You will encounter the experience of scarcity and the Land of the Driven. You will look at what you have feared in your relationship with money.

When you finish that work, you will be ready for the next part of your journey: how to have your goals and dreams come true with ease. I will show you how to clear away whatever has kept you from fulfilling your life's intentions and dreams.

So, take heart and continue. You will be following in the footsteps of thousands of others who have shifted their relationship with money from scarcity to abundance.

Summary

✎   Your true nature exists as potential. Potential resides in the metaphysical realm. This potential is formless. However, you can describe and measure some of its properties. At that point, you have the opportunity to demonstrate those properties, *who you really are,* in physical reality. You are well on your way to crossing the border into the physical realm.

✎   When you experience joy, inspiration, and gratitude, you are in contact with the core of who you really are.

✎   Integrity, your original condition, is who you really are in your heart.

✎   If you see great qualities in others, if your heart resonates with them, it means they exist inside you. If not, you would not be able to see them in others.

✎   When you act from your Standards of Integrity, you increase your capacity to bring goals and dreams from the metaphysical into the physical with ease.

✎   Your intentions are the living spirit behind your goals and dreams.

✎   The true wealth in having intentions is that they give you a way to channel energy from the metaphysical into the physical realm.

CHAPTER FOUR:
Driving or Driven -- The Hidden Dynamics

Driving or Driven -- The Hidden Dynamics

"I am an old man, and I have lived through many trials and tribulations, most of which never really happened."

Mark Twain

How long has it been since you let yourself relax? I mean really relax, not collapsing on a couch at the end of the day, too exhausted to do anything else. When was the last time your mind slowed to notice the season, trees, birds and other signs of life in your neighborhood? How long since you last walked barefoot on the lawn, feeling the moist grass tickle the bottom of your feet? When did you last sit on a hillside and watch the kaleidoscopic colors of a summer sunset?

Amazingly, these questions have everything to do with money, your goals, and your dreams. When worry, doubt and fear drive you, there is no time to cool your mind. It becomes frenzied and overheated. You do not appreciate what is happening in the moment. You imagine everything that could go wrong if you just let go and breathed. That little voice inside you says the world will surely fly apart if you were to relax! One thing is certain, when you are driven, you are too tired for the hero's journey. In this state, getting in touch with what you really want out of life is almost an impossible thing to do.

Driven behavior wastes energy -- such as time, physical energy and money -- that you could focus to make your dreams a reality.

I suggest keeping your written Standards of Integrity and your list of life's intentions by your side as you go through this and the next two chapters. Doing so will remind you of who you really are and what you have come to life to accomplish. You are about to look at the dark side of your relationship with money. Do not be put off. You will begin to see where you have been getting in the way of having your goals and dreams.

Please remember that we are using the word "dark" in the sense of that which is obscured or hidden from view. Once you look, see, and tell the truth about these matters, clarity and ease come through. You get the breathing room to have what you genuinely want in life. You are no longer running around looking over your shoulder or around every corner for everything that could possibly go awry.

It is great to do this phase of the work with a group. If you are not working with a *You and Money* support group try to find at least one close friend with whom to share your observations. While some of this material can be difficult to look at, the point here is not to wallow in it, but to awaken your hero.

Our goal here is to uncover where your own driven behavior has kept you from focusing energy effectively. We want to find where behavior of this kind has dissipated energy and perhaps even left you depleted. The clearer this becomes, the quicker you can do something about it. You can then make choices about how to use energy in the future.

The following diagram is an example of how it looks to have your energy dispersed, rather than focused.

Note that you may spend the same amount of energy in both cases. However, in the balloon on the right the energy bolts are unfocused and so there are no results for all your effort.

Consider the following:

Your experience of an abundant life is the sum of your authentic choices minus the sum of your driven behavior.

You can only make authentic choices when you are not driven. Driven behavior occurs when you are trying to avoid fear. You become rigid and fixed in your ways. Your thoughts capture you, blinding you from seeing what has real meaning for you. You *must* have, be or do something to survive. This approach to life is costly with time, money, love, physical well-being and virtually every other form of energy.

These are some examples of how being driven can cost you money:

* Taking on too much overhead -- big offices, secretaries, support personnel, phones. So that you spend most of your energy just trying to keep your business afloat.
* Accepting so much business that you have difficulty making good on your promises to your customers.
* Being so tired that you end up making costly mistakes.
* Being so tired that you deliberately cut corners which affect the quality of your work.
* Taking unnecessary or unwise risks in the hopes of making a quick profit.
* Having too much work, but refusing to hire someone to help, though it is affordable.

All of us fall prey to driven behavior at one time or another. It is a normal consequence of listening to Monkey Mind's chatter. How do we distinguish between an authen-

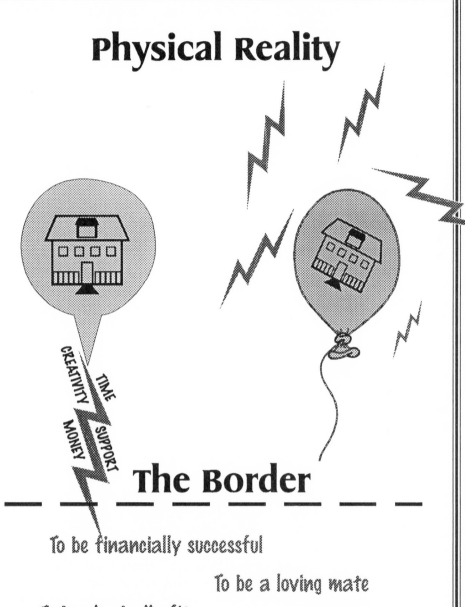

tic choice and one *driven* by Monkey Mind? To begin with, the authentic choice reflects your deepest intentions and brings you a sense of joy and accomplishment. When you have made an authentic choice, it just seems right. You know you are furthering yourself, moving in a constructive and creative way down your own path. You are having what you really want. This is an example of what happens with an authentic choice:

> "Why is life so speeded up? Why are things so terribly, unbearably precious that you can't enjoy them but can only wait breathless in dread of their going?"
>
> *Anne Morrow Lindbergh*

Walter was a successful carpenter. He wanted a forest green Jaguar XJ6 convertible with tan leather upholstery. As he described this goal to his *You and Money* team, he appeared both nervous and excited. Then, four weeks later, he rushed into the team's meeting, a gleam in his eye. "I just got the car I really wanted," he whooped.

Everyone rushed out to the parking lot to see. They looked for the Jaguar. Not there. Some joke! Walter led them over to a red Volkswagen Rabbit convertible and patted the hood. Was there some mistake? "Nope," he said. "I just learned something very valuable. When it came down to the wire, I didn't really want the Jaguar. It was more like what I used to want. What I thought I should have as a mark of success."

"If I had bought the car, I could have made the payments, but it would have been hard. Instead of me having a car, the car would have had me! When I saw what it really would cost me to do it that way, I decided to buy this car instead. You know what? I love it. I even bought a red jacket to match. Anyone want a ride?"

With that, seven people stuffed themselves into the car. Off they went, tooling around the corner, laughing like a bunch of teenagers.

Looking at your own driven behavior, however subtle or obvious it may be, will help you answer the following questions:

* Why don't I feel satisfied with what I have?
* Why haven't I gotten what I want in life?
* What do I want for myself and my loved ones?
* Why do I feel tired and uninspired about how my life is turning out?
* Why do I have the experience that time is passing me by?

When you tell yourself the truth about where you are driven, and start making authentic choices, your goals undergo some changes. They are no longer just attempts to plug up the holes created by frantic activity. Instead,

they are reflections of what you really want out of life.

For example, what would you rather do? Take a trip to Hawaii because:

1. You really wanted to go and have fun swimming, laying on the beach, sightseeing, etc.
2. You were so tired that you needed to rest and get away from work. Just crash for a while.

When it comes time to choose goals, the aim here is to increase the likelihood that you choose for reason "1" rather than "2."

Driven, or in the Driver's Seat?

When you are driven, your behavior can border on being obsessional or compulsive. Obsessions are recurring thoughts. They get in the way of accomplishing things with ease. These thoughts take up energy. They divert you from your path rather than help you along.

Suppose you worry about finding the job you want. The worry by itself is not an obsession until it is nearly the only thing you think or talk about. An obsessional thought takes up all your energy. It does not necessarily motivate you to solve the problem. In fact, obsessional thoughts can immobilize. They can prevent you from taking constructive action. Also, in hopes of alleviating your fears, they can lead you to take actions you really know are inappropriate.

Compulsions are a little different. They are actions that you become convinced you must just perform, again and again. These actions continue even when the behaviors themselves are tedious or even painful. For example, you have a need to check your house before leaving. You do so over and over again, to make sure the stove is off, the iron unplugged, the windows closed, and the doors locked. Perhaps you insist on Christmas dinner being prepared a specific way, year after year, without any deviations. You feel that having large amounts of cash in your purse or wallet is absolutely necessary, just in case. Or, you go to the race track every week because you "just know" you are going to win this time, despite consistent, serious losses.

We pride ourselves on our accomplishments. We work in production-driven workplaces where we have to meet deadlines. With tightly-controlled routines such as these, obsessions or compulsions can easily go unnoticed, or seem acceptable behavior. Yet, if we observe ourselves, we really

> **Question:** What is one way to tell if you are being rigid and driven?
> **Answer One:** If you get defensive or sarcastic when your friends and loved ones tell you they are concerned about your behavior.
> **Answer Two:** If you feel you do not have enough time even to consider this matter right now.

do know when our behavior is edging toward these counter-productive patterns. We can see behaviors that seriously drain our energy, making it harder to realize our goals.

Obsessions and compulsions act like blinders on a horse. Narrowly focused, you have little chance to enjoy the present. Frustration becomes a way of life. Sorting out these driven behaviors starts with telling the truth about what you think you *must have* to feel secure. Examples of *must have* thoughts are:

* But I really do need a new car every three years.
* I work hard. I deserve to eat at the best restaurants.
* We know the children are gone, but we have to keep this big house. What if they want to come back for a visit in a few years?
* I must have that speedboat. I don't care what it takes.
* I always go to the local bar to blow off steam on Fridays.

One thing you are sure to discover when looking at your *must haves* is an endless stream of internal arguments, perfectly good reasons, rules and stories for what you need. All will be very convincing. We are all driven at some time in our lives. So for most of us, the question is not *whether* we are, but *in what ways* are we driven by our worries, doubts, fears, needs and *must haves*?

Many experts say that very strong parallels exist between driven and addictive behavior. If you think about it, you will see the logic behind this. Addictive behavior can be measured by the extent to which it interferes with our lives. It leads us further away from our authentic choices and goals.

Driven behavior and addictions can link in the following way. Driven behavior overheats your mind. You begin to use drugs, alcohol, shopping, gambling, work or sex to feel better. These can all be forms of self-medication. Soon, you become dependent on them, then addicted. The addiction, in turn, interferes with how you function. You become more stressed, needing more of the addictive substance to handle it. Soon, the addictive spiral begins. The "medicine" that dulls your symptoms has become the problem rather than the solution.

The first sign of an addiction is "withdrawal symptoms" when you try to control it. You may be familiar with the withdrawal symptoms from alcohol and drug abuse. Let us look at how withdrawal from other addictions can affect us at a mental and emotional level:

Maureen: Just the thought of cutting up my credit cards leaves me nauseous! I break out in a cold sweat. I can't imagine living without them. What if I have an emergency? What if I see something I just have to have? I don't know how people got along without credit cards fifty years ago.

Symptoms of Being Driven

You may feel uneasy thinking about discovering your own driven behavior. People seldom wake up one morning and say, "It's a beautiful day outside. I'll just go out and confront my self-limiting habits." We usually wait until something big happens, like losing $35,000 in an investment scam.

To make this as quick, easy and painless as possible, I have put together the following list of driven symptoms. Go through the list now. Identify any items that apply to you. Keep your notebook handy. Take notes as you go along.

Repetition: You do or think something over and over again, even if it causes you trouble or needless effort. Even when you get frustrated, angry or sad about it, you continue the behavior or thought.

Frank: I wait until the last minute to pay my bills. I have the money, but that doesn't matter. Last month I waited too long. They cut off my phone. It embarrassed me. Some clients called and got that recording about me being no longer *in service*. This is the third time that's happened.

Jane: I know I can't afford it, but I have to have cable television with all the channels. There's no time to watch TV, but when I think about not being able to see what I want, when I want it, I get frustrated.

Michael: It's always the same. I go to the supermarket with a list of what I need, and come back with all kinds of stuff I never use. Walking the aisles, I scoop up items on sale, just in case they might come in handy. Waiting in line for the cashier is bad news. Ten minutes, three magazines, four packs of gum and a bag of pretzels later, I push my bloated cart to the parking lot.

Look now at yourself. See where your thoughts or behaviors are repetitious. Write down what you discover in your notebook. Do you overeat, overspend, get parking or speeding tickets regularly? What is it that you promise yourself never to do again, only to catch yourself doing it yet another time? Look at what you do or think during Christmas, Hanukkah, Kwanzaa, birthdays or other regular events. Do you buy presents you really cannot afford? Are you driven to explain yourself?

> "The sin of perfectionism is that it mutilates life by demanding the impossible."
>
> Jerome Frank

Unpleasant though it may be, cough it up! Tell the truth to yourself. Take notes on how you feel as you look at repetitive or driven behavior. Are you embarrassed, humiliated, annoyed, bored or overwhelmed? Remember, this is part of the hero's journey. We are facing the dark side here.

Limited satisfaction: You find the satisfaction in doing things is either fleeting or nonexistent.

Sylvia: I'm glad my daughter's wedding is finally over. I worried about the plans for the reception. Athough we hired someone to take care of everything, I worried about the money. I knew we were getting a good price from the caterer, but I just wasn't used to letting someone else be in charge. All day I just waited and watched for something to go wrong. It didn't, but I was a pool of nervous exhaustion by the end of the day.

Fred: I remember standing with my diploma in hand during graduation last summer. My parents and friends were in the audience. There I was with my B.A., ready to go on for my teaching credential. I know I should have felt proud, but this song by Peggy Lee kept going around in my head: "Is That All There Is?" I thought: "I've graduated. So what! Now I've got to bust my butt to get the credential. Then it's off to work."

Return to your notebook. Consider times you were too hurried, worried or distracted to enjoy the satisfaction of a job well-done. Is your pleasure short-lived? Are you focused on the next task? Do you approach celebrations, vacations, or family outings thinking, "Just let me make it through this?" Think about these experiences and be specific. Recall names, dates and places.

Perfectionism: You almost never feel that you do anything well enough. You do not feel you have done enough to justify a rest or some acknowledgment. Included here are any patterns of not completing projects.

Patricia: So what if I graduated cum laude from my college. Why didn't I graduate summa cum laude?

Alice: I didn't enter my photo in the local competition. I didn't think it was good enough. My friends all encouraged me to do it, but I wasn't 100 percent satisfied with it. Last week I saw the photo that took first place. Mine was just as good. I've always wanted to be a professional photographer. But what if I'm not good enough? Besides, I hear there's no money in it.

Jorge: All right! I have two days to do what I want. I could finish the cabinet I started six months ago; make the doll house I promised my daughter last year. Maybe I should start building the work table in the garage that I've always wanted. So many projects, so little time!

Sharyn: I almost stop breathing at the end of each month when I look at my billable hours and commissions. I set income goals that are a stretch for me. If it doesn't look like I'm going to make them, I get really nervous and irritated. I yell at my husband and the children for no reason. Since I'm a Certified Financial Planner, you'd think I'd be calmer about money issues. Guess again!

Consider the following as you write about this in your notebook:
* After you start something, do you quit when it is almost finished?
* When working on a project, do you hold onto it even when you have done all that is necessary?
* Is there an unfinished final report, master's thesis, or doctoral dissertation between you and getting that certification or degree for which you have studied long and hard?
* Are you delaying an interview for promotion because you worry that you are not prepared enough?

Let us look at perfectionism more closely for a moment.

Perfectionism is an inability to arrive at closure. It masquerades as virtue. It is really an explanation for nonproductivity.

Think about this a moment. Do you often use being a "perfectionist" as the reason for not keeping your word or finishing a project? Is the term used as if it were a virtue instead of an excuse? Ever heard someone use it to explain why they got a project done early?

Other reasons exist for perfectionist thinking, of course. The person who feels they are "not enough" can get into this pattern of thinking. They may use "perfectionism" to justify not finishing a task.

The purpose of these and the following examples is to

make it as easy as possible for you to identify where you are driven in your relationship with money. You can substitute other forms of energy, such as time, physical well-being and love in this equation. Do that later. For now, concentrate on money. Your Monkey Mind will want you to turn your attention away from this topic. Nevertheless, listen to your higher purpose here. Clarify what changes are called for.

The Rut Syndrome

A rut is a habit, or pattern of action or inaction, that blocks your progress. Although repetitious, it may be so automatic that it escapes your awareness. When you are in a rut, the pattern blocks your goal or vision. You feel uncomfortable, frustrated or resigned.

Assess the following true scenarios. In each case, the person relies on old, familiar ways of coping, even when those coping mechanisms stand in the way of achieving goals and dreams. Note, too, that the excuses for staying put usually seem very "reasonable."

Ray: I know I'm in a rut. At least it's familiar! It's not like stepping out into the unknown. There's nothing worse than that. I am 47. I work for the state. For three years, I've been trying to decide whether to leave this job and open a combination book store and coffee house. It's something I have always wanted to do, but I am seven years from retirement. The money is very good at my present job. Maybe I should wait before I contact the Small Business Association. Besides, I know I can put up with seven years of anything. Even this nowhere job.

Frank: I hate to stay in one job for more than about a year. Last year I sold computers at a retail outlet. I was the best salesperson there. I know how to talk to customers. Everything goes just fine. Then the manager starts to bug me. It's always the same, no matter what job I'm in. So what if I'm a few minutes late or take a longer lunch hour? I'm still the best producer in the place! The manager kept bugging me. Now I'm working for another store. But it won't be long before this gets on my nerves.

Shawn: Yes, I know I'm 83 pounds overweight. My husband and I have dreamed of going trekking in Nepal, but I'll never make it this way. I've joined the same weight-loss program eight times. It costs a lot of money. Come to think of it, maybe enough money to have paid for the trek. Each time, I promise myself to work with the weight counselor. After one month, I start cheating on the program. Why? Maybe I want to see how much I can get away with before the counselor notices. Maybe I don't want to lose the weight. I really don't know.

To look at the Rut Syndrome and how it may be a factor in your life, ask yourself the following questions and note the responses in your journal:

*   Are there specific ruts I am in right now? Ruts in my physical well-being, or in personal, financial, career and social arenas?
*   What reasons do I use for staying this way?
*   What has it cost me, or is it continuing to cost me, to stay in this rut? Look first in the area of money. Can you specifically calculate what staying in the rut costs? Go on to areas such as time, goals, dreams, well-being, and creativity.

> *"I used to think I had ambition ... but now I'm not so sure. It may have been only discontent."*
>
> *Rachel Field*

The Spendaholic -- Obeying the Call of of the Sirens

The Sirens were mythological women with beautiful and compelling voices who lured Greek sailors to dive from their ships onto jagged rocks. We have the modern day equivalent of this in all the sirens that lure us to spend. Whether we tumble on the rocks from a great height, or merely stumble and fall on our rear ends in the pebbles, the sirens still pull us off our main course.

Christina: I wander around shopping malls a lot. Their bright lights are especially great in the winter when it gets foggy outside. Inside the mall, the color, glitter and wonderful smells boost my mood. I can easily drop $20 on yogurt and assorted knickknacks in the first fifteen minutes I'm there. Usually, I stay a couple of hours.

Denise: My friends call me bookwoman. I don't spend much on clothes or eating out. I've promised myself a great vacation to Europe for the past five years. I put it off because I don't have the money. But, put me in a bookstore, any bookstore, and let me loose for less than an hour. I'll crawl to the cashier's counter, my arms filled with books I know I'll probably never have time to read. I just want to have them with me in my home, just in case I *do* have time to read them all someday.

Mark: My wife and I fight about money. She says I spend too much on my toys. But I figure I'm old enough to decide what I want. I work hard enough as it is. Last week I bought some great software for my PC. The week before, it was a portable CD player. She's right about one thing. Sometimes the stuff sits in boxes for weeks before I unpack it. There's a relaxation machine I bought six months ago that I haven't learned to use. Every time I see one of those slick new catalogues in the mail, I know I'm a goner.

When caught in a pattern of behavior like this, the thought of *not having* what you want, at the moment you want it, can be frustrating. You feel deprived, and experience moments of sadness. Check on this by answering the following questions and noting them in your journal. Tell the truth.

* When I get it in my mind that I deserve something, like new clothes, books, toys, or collectibles, do I usually find some way to buy it, even if it might get me into financial trouble?
* If I do not get what I want, when I want it, do I feel sad, angry, bored?
* Does the thought of being on a budget send shivers down my spine?
* Have I created a budget, only to fail at following it, repeatedly?
* Do I ever get home and discover that I do not really want what I have bought, yet I never take it back?
* What has doing it this way cost me? Look again at money. Then think about what it costs you in time, relationships, stress, the fulfillment of your long-term dreams or sense of well-being.

Binge-ing and Purging with Money

You can have a relationship with money that looks very much like a food addiction. This is most true with entrepreneurs who have times where there is lots of money, followed by times in which money is scarce.

Phyllis: As a real estate agent, it's either feast or famine for me. Some months I don't bring home anything, and then in one month, three escrows close. I'm flush. I know I should put some away so I'll have a steady income, but by the time the money comes in, I'm so starved for things, that I buy, buy, buy. Then it's back to a strict financial starvation diet for a while.

Ned: I have myself on a strict budget. For weeks, I live within it. I'm careful to track every penny I spend. Then, something will come over me. Last time, a friend called me about a real estate venture, asking me to join him in it. Without learning much about the details, I ran to the bank and withdrew $10,000. Didn't even tell my wife until it was a done deal. She was pissed off. Meanwhile, I'm sweating it, hoping I didn't make a stupid move. Then, promising myself I'll never do it again, I go back to the strict budget.

Periods of abstinence, with little or no spending, followed by intervals of intense spending, create a kind of emotional rush. You feel as though you are living on the edge. To put it mildly, this does not promote stability. While the lifestyle can be exciting, it diverts you from pursuing goals that have real meaning and substance.

Look at the following questions and be truthful. What are the obstacles on your hero's path?

* Do I secretly, or not so secretly, think that having a predictable relationship with money would be boring?
* When I have closed a deal, do I count on the money as a sure thing, even before I receive a check?
* Do I feel guilty about how I handle, or fail to handle, money?
* Do I get a thrill at receiving an enormous amount of money after a particularly lean time?
* Do I create that thrill by waiting until my accounts receivable are large before I try to collect on them?
* Do I believe that money in accounts receivable is money in the bank? (Did you know that the more these accounts age, the less likely the money owed will be collected?)
* What has it cost me to do things this way?
* How long has it been since I kept my word to myself or someone else, about attaining a long-term financial goal?

Gambling

The main hook with gambling is the risk involved. It is exciting to beat the odds. When it is a casual pastime, gambling can be fun. When you become driven about gambling, the results can be very painful.

Some people report they experience a sort of ecstasy when they win. They also say the biggest rush comes when they win after they have been losing for a while. This brings us to a critical question: What is the veteran gambler playing for -- the big win, or the big loss?

Will: I live close to Lake Tahoe. On weekends, I like to go and play blackjack. I get there Friday night and I don't move from the tables until Saturday evening. Everything goes okay until I start losing. I'll do anything to get more money to keep playing. I get desperate. Last time, I maxed-out my credit card and came home $2500 in the hole. I keep telling myself it is the last time I will go up there with credit cards. But I always manage to forget to take them out of my wallet before I leave.

Julie: We have a new kind of lottery in our state. It's like

Keno. You sit at tables, pick numbers, and wait for them to come up on the screen. I've lost $500, so far. Every time I go into the liquor store and see the screen flashing numbers, I'm hooked for at least an hour.

What is fascinating about gambling is the way money is stripped of its intrinsic value. Sitting at the table, losing $600, you rarely stop and think what could be done with this amount of ready cash.

As with everything else in this chapter, the only thing you need to do right now is look. Ask yourself if what you are doing is getting in the way of attaining the goals that really mean something to you? Is it possible that you have been shooting yourself in the foot? Check out the following questions:

* Do I know, or suspect, that I have wasted time and money trying to beat the odds in life? (Look at areas like high-risk investments, lotteries, gaming, consistent wagering at office jackpots, etc.)
* Are my friends, family or co-workers concerned about my gambling? Has a loved one openly complained to me about it?
* If I were to add up all the money I've lost in gambling over the past ten years, what is the estimated figure?

Information Addiction

In their book, *Creating a New Civilization: The Politics of the Third Wave,* Alvin and Heidi Toffler observe:

We are creating new networks of knowledge. Businesses, governments and individuals are collecting and storing more sheer data than any previous generation in history. Never before have we had such access to information as we have now. The easy availability of the PC is giving rise to a new class of addiction. It is one that was almost unheard of only fifteen years ago; information addiction.

Jeff: I can spend an easy eight hours every day at the computer. I log onto the net, find a chat room, or go in search of great web pages. I've got a good modem, but it still isn't fast enough. I'm thinking about getting one of those ISDN lines, dedicated to my Internet connection. It's expensive, but what the heck? I work hard. I deserve it. My wife gets upset with me. She doesn't see enough of me, she says. So, I wake up at three a.m. to get a few hours on the net before work. It's great then, because there's not much traffic on the lines.

With access to information comes the opportunity to use it compulsively or addictively. The questions to ask in exam-

ining whether or not you are an information addict are:
*   Does my recreation time with computer software, in-
    cluding games, the Internet, and information managing
    programs, exceed two hours daily?
*   If the above is yes, do I see where this interferes with my
    relationships, goals, health and peace of mind?
*   Can I lose myself at the computer, without noticing that
    I need to eat, sleep, or attend to biological needs?
*   What could I do with my time and money if I did not
    spend so much of either on my PC?

Is There a Positive Addiction?

I call the following example a "positive" addiction. It can
still cost time, money, and intimacy; particularly if you need
it for comfort or relief from an overheated mind.

Jack: I jog ten miles a day. Rain or shine. If I don't do it
for more than two days in a row, I get nervous. Snap at
everyone. I used to be 50 pounds overweight. I took the
weight off by jogging, and that's how I intend to keep it off.
Once, I pulled a tendon. The doctor told me to rest for three
weeks. I thought I'd go crazy. So I tried to jog after ten
days. Pulled the thing even worse. More doctor bills. People
say I should swim. It's not the same.

Look at the next questions to see if you have a positive
addiction.
*   Does this activity take up most of my free time and money?
*   Does this behavior allow me to become isolated from
    family and friends?
*   Does what I do pose a threat to my physical well-being?
*   Does the thought of not doing it make me nervous?

Is There Life After Driven Behavior?

Yes, there is! Allen, who was an example of the Rut Syndrome, is now the proud co-owner of a coffeehouse/ bookstore. He was on 60 percent time with his former job until
the business could support him.

Carol, the real estate agent who was caught up with
binge-ing and purging money, went to a financial counselor.
She has paid off all her bills. She also has a bookkeeper who
gives her a predictable monthly draw, no matter how much
money has come in. Within a year, she saved enough money
to take her mother to visit their family in England. It was a
lifelong dream come true!

The Journey Continues

The next chapter takes a deeper look at driven behavior, some

of it life-threatening. Compulsive behavior is such an intimate part of the modern lifestyle! These patterns clearly interfere with our ability to experience what it is to be truly
alive.

The road to achieving your goals and dreams begins with
this visit to the dark side of your relationship with money. It
is not the fun part of the hero's journey, but it is absolutely
necessary. Courageously looking at these hidden truths can
liberate you from their negative impact. It will pay off in
creating the freedom to bring your dreams and goals into
reality. It will make life easier for you, and those who love you.

Summary

As we bring this chapter to a close, let us take a last look at the points we have been discussing:

✎   Driven behavior wastes energy, whether in the form of time, physical energy, or money. Your energy could be more powerfully focused on making your dreams a reality.

✎   Your experience of a satisfying and abundant life is the sum of your authentic choices minus the sum of your driven behavior.

✎   When you tell the truth about where you are driven, and start making authentic choices, your goals undergo some changes. They are no longer attempts to plug up the holes created by frantic activity. Instead, they are reflections of what you really want out of life.

✎   The symptoms of being driven are:
1. **Repetition:** You do or think something over and over again, even if it may cause you trouble or needless effort. Even when you get frustrated, angry or sad about it, you continue the behavior or thought.
2. **Limited satisfaction:** You find that the satisfaction in doing things is either fleeting or non-existent.
3. **Perfectionism:** You never feel that you have done something well enough, or that you have done enough to justify a rest or some acknowledgement. Included here is the pattern of not completing projects you have begun.

CHAPTER FIVE:
Busyholism and Money --
Don't Just Do It!

Busyholism and Money -- Don't Just Do It!

"Active laziness ... consists of cramming our lives with compulsive activity, so that there is no time at all to confront the real issues ... Our lives seem to live us, to possess their own bizarre momentum, to carry us away. In the end we feel we have no control or choice over them."

Sogyal Rinpoche

You may not be aware of it, but a particular slogan greets you in the morning as you snatch ten minutes for the newspaper and your first cup of coffee. It is implied in almost every ad you read or radio commercial you hear as you head for work. It walks with you during the day while you check off items on your *to do* list. It waits for you as you take your tired body and mind to the bookstore to buy the latest primer on peak performance. It is as ubiquitous as the refined sugar found in snack food. It is a phrase that three words and an exclamation point best capture: Just do it!

Think about it. For most of us, peak performance means doing more, better and faster. A recent billboard ad for physical fitness shows a woman hitting a punching bag. The caption reads: "You can rest when you're dead!"

In the last chapter you examined driven behavior in its many shapes and sizes. Here we graduate to the higher school of driven behavior, where you get a Ph.D. in "busyholism." **Busyholism is activity in the physical domain that is not anchored to anything in the metaphysical domain.** Let us look at this more closely.

Purpose, direction, aim, dreams: these exist in the metaphysical realm. When your actions are "on purpose," you are doing what has meaning for you. Your energy is focused and you are moving forward. Busyholism is unattached to any intention. Like flies buzzing in fast circles on a hot day, there is a lot of noise and activity, but nothing of substance gets done. Busyholism distracts us, and it is seductive. You know the phrase you hear inside. It goes something like this: "I will rest and figure out what I really want some day -- when I finish everything else I have to do."

We are all tired. Recent studies have shown that many of us are suffering. We get between sixty and ninety minutes less sleep at night than we need for optimal health, productivity and creativity. Even while you read this, you might be experiencing conflicting thoughts or emotions: a sense of longing to get some rest, coupled with the worry that you will not get enough done if you do. Perhaps you are even worrying that reading this part of the book is taking you away from another, more important activity.

How does all this connect to money? In this chapter you will look at *busyholism-deprivation* cycle, and how it affects your relationship with money and other forms of energy. This is important since, oddly enough, to have goals because you feel deprived only increases your sense of deprivation later. I promise this will become clearer to you as we go on.

The whole purpose of this book is not just to "fix" something that you perceive to be broken but to take the step beyond fixing. It is about wisdom. Wisdom comes when you clearly see and tell the truth about where you have been making your life harder than necessary. Then you have some breathing room to take authentic action, rather than hasty action aimed only at getting you through the day. Focusing upon your busyholism may be uncomfortable for a little while. So, having your Standards of Integrity and life purpose statements with you will be very useful. It will allow you to compare your busyholism to the person you really are. Be patient. We are not looking at solutions yet. That would be premature. Let yourself engage with this material so that the hero can observe obstacles that have always been there.

> "Of all the unhappy people in the world, the unhappiest are those who have not found something they want to do. True happiness comes to him who does his work well, followed by a relaxing and refreshing period of rest. True happiness comes from the right amount of work for the day."
>
> *Lin Yutang*

Workaholism and Money in the Motivated Society

We live in a highly motivated society. Our heroes are men and women who are champions of *doingness*. We are chock full of sayings exhorting us to produce, grab for the gusto, and exceed our personal best. By now, we know all the motivational slogans by heart. This is no surprise. They are on television every time our favorite show goes to a commercial break. Hundreds of motivational tapes, lectures and workshops exist. The American public spends hundreds of millions of dollars to be prodded on with essentially the same messages:

* Take control!
* Get off your butt!
* You can have it all!
* When the going gets tough, the tough get going!

Mottoes such as these are useful, especially in moderation. However, it can be like sugar for someone who is addicted to it. We can use motivational expressions to keep ourselves hyped, active and on the go. We can pack more activities into every second of our waking lives. One more item to complete from our daily planner, another errand to run before we rest. Rest during the middle of the day? Are you joking? Flying to the moon would be easier!

It is no secret that we work longer and more strenuously than we did twenty years ago, just to maintain the same lifestyle. Few would argue that this way of life takes a toll on our health. Most of the adult population suffers from stress-related illnesses brought on by pushing themselves too hard. The list of these illnesses includes: headaches, insomnia, back pain, heart disease, cancer and respiratory problems. Many experts suggest that our high divorce rates are the direct or indirect result of our society's emphasis on *doing*. Health experts have identified a heart-attack syndrome called "Black Monday." More fatal heart attacks occur Monday mornings around 9:00 a.m. than at any other time of the week. Japan suffers from a high incidence of *karoshi*, death from overworking. Employees literally keel over at their desks after working long hours under pressure.

> "What counts is not the number of hours you put in, but how much you put in the hours."
>
> *Theodore Roosevelt*

Workaholism is one form of busyholism. We deal with it now because it is more common than you may think among high achievers. Putting in long hours of work is integral to corporate and institutional cultures. In addition, if you are a small business owner, salesperson or trades person, this behavior is not only condoned, but required. While addiction to drugs or alcohol is getting attention from employee assistance programs around the country, workaholism is not. If you were to survey corporate or institutional human resource departments, you would find few people get referred for counseling because they are working too hard. In fact, few Workaholics Anonymous (WA) groups meet regularly. They definitely do not meet within corporate facilities during work hours!

In 1994, staff writer, Bob Walter, wrote about workaholics in *The Sacramento Bee*. He reported that only three WA groups existed in the greater Los Angeles and the San Francisco Bay areas.

"Let's face it," a well-known workaholic once told me, "If people from other companies knew I worked this hard, they'd all want to hire me. I get lots of praise and perks for what I do, especially since I'm on commission. It's like getting high."

The competitive climate we live in puts a premium on go-getters. With downsizing, corporations continue to escalate standards for performance and results, getting fewer and fewer people to do more in less time. As one highly intelligent corporate attorney put it:

Ruth: I'm an associate for a corporate law firm. They expect everyone to bring in forty-five billable hours a week. Know what that really means? I don't just put in nine hours and then go home. I spend time talking with prospective clients, attending staff and professional meetings, reading business mail, answering interoffice memos, and preparing reports that account for time spent on each project. Before I'm finished, I've put in at least sixty hours. Sure, the work is exciting, but it's taking up my whole life right now. From what I hear, it's not much different at other firms around here.

Yes, sometimes hard work and long hours are a necessary part of completing a project. In addition, not everyone who likes to work hard is a workaholic. However, certain people know when to work, when to relax, and when to play. Certain people do not.

A few years ago, the Extension Program at the University of California, Santa Barbara coordinated a conference on excellence. Experts focused on peak performers and the traits they share. After all the presentations and discussion, only one common factor consistently distinguished peak performers from everyone else.

Peak performers take time for complete rest every day!

Rest. The taboo, four-letter word for workaholics. To which peak performers were they referring? Some examples were John F. Kennedy, Winston Churchill, Albert Einstein and Thomas Edison. Typically, they took naps every day, if for only twenty to thirty minutes.

Let us consider rest and play for a moment. They are not the same thing. One highly-driven person in a *You and Money* course said:

Paul: I work hard and I play hard. That's my rest and relaxation. If I sit still too long, I get antsy.

Rest means letting your body and mind slow down and become replenished. There is no such thing as resting hard.

Take out your notebook. Write your answers to the following questions, much as you did in the previous chapter. Remember, this is primarily to help you further identify the places where your driven behavior interferes with your goals and dreams.

*   If I were to give myself time to rest, would I feel guilty

or edgy because I would be thinking about all the things I need to do?
* What would I do with my life if I did not work so much?
* Who am I, under the flurry of all the activity in my life?

workaholism is an Addiction

Working hard with no rest may put you into the money-sapping cycle of busyholism/deprivation I mentioned earlier. It goes like this:

Look at the rationalizations in the diagram. They usually precede your spending money on something, not necessarily because you genuinely want it, but because it makes up for the deprivation. You have worked so hard, and had so little rest, that a reward is needed.

Brian: I get caught up in *I deserve it* thinking when I'm not careful. When I'm tired and stressed-out, I get this idea that I deserve a good meal at an expensive restaurant. There I

Doing/Working Hard

Feeling Tired, Deprived

Rationalizations:
a) This has been one killer week. It's time for a pick-me-up.
b) I *need* a new outfit, a great meal, a new toy.
c) After all, I work hard for my money. I *deserve* it.

Spending Money

was one night, staring into a $25 plate of food. I asked myself: "Am I working hard so I can afford to spend money on spaghetti arranged on a Southwestern landscape, with basil leaves for a cactus? Is this really what I want?" Don't misunderstand me. I love good food. Still, sometimes I know I've bought the notion that a pricey meal at a trendy place is the best reward for hard work. It's a knee jerk response to stress. Spending my money that way is one reason I end up working harder.

The *I deserve it* thinking expressed by this person provides a reason to buy almost anything. This is why some of the most effective ads around begin with the words: "You deserve a break, a car, a vacation, etc."

Costs are incurred when you consume out of a sense of deprivation. You have probably read that 20 percent of the world's population consumes 80 percent of the world's resources. As consumers, we buy goods, use them, wear them out, and replace them. The faster we use them up, the more we buy. The more we buy, the faster the economy grows. At least, that is what we think happens. However, we reach a point of diminishing returns. What if you were to discover that you personally use twice as much energy as people in Europe and Japan? Further, that you consume 100 times more of our planet's resources than those who live in developing countries. What if you found that what is fueling all of this is your hard work? It allows you to earn, and then spend money on gadgets that monitor the gadgets you bought before.

You have undoubtedly noticed the call to buy a better way to grind your coffee or more sophisticated VCR. When it comes to computers, a new generation of them will be built before the ink has dried on the most recent computer ads.

Joe Dominguez and Vicki Robin, in their book *Your Money or Your Life*, put forth an interesting premise about all of this consumerism. They suggest that we are not appreciably happier than our parents or grandparents because we have more material goods than they did. They make the case that our current philosophy, *more is better,* sets up a chronic sense of dissatisfaction with life as it is now. We are caught in a deadly *more* trap: The more we have, the more dissatisfied we become, thus, the more we spend, and the harder and longer we work to get money to spend.

Take a moment to get in touch with what is of real value to you. Try this experiment: imagine a fire in your home. Your family and pets get out safely. You have two minutes to remove your possessions. What do you take? For me, it would be the photographs of my family and the other people I love. I think those would be the most difficult to lose. Next, maybe some art objects and computer discs full of my writings. My VCR and coffee grinder? Way down on the list. Even if they were not insured.

I have talked with people who suffered through the Santa Barbara fire of 1989. Hundreds of homes were destroyed. Many lost everything they owned. It was awful for them. At first, many went deeply into shock. Two years later, I talked with a woman who had lost a valuable weaving loom and rugs to the flames:

Laurie: After grieving over the loss, I felt kind of free at not having all of my possessions. People came to help me with what I needed. I got another loom. Now I'm weaving, giving lessons and selling my work. The tragedy also knocked me off my treadmill. I'm traveling in a month on a grant to research for a book about weaving methods in Third World countries. I guess I've reworked my priorities.

Let us return to workaholism. We are not looking at whether you work diligently. We are concerned here with the extent to which you:
* Work without rest;
* Spend money because you are tired and therefore *deserve* to fill the internal hole created by stress;
* Allow work to interfere with other areas of your life, such as intimate relationships, creativity, leisure time and physical well-being. Consider the following:

If you are a workaholic, pursuing more money and more goals can be like cocaine for a cocaine addict. It just increases your craving and your need and you end up doing whatever you can to get more.

> "For workaholics, all the eggs of self-esteem are in the basket of work."
>
> *Judith M. Bardwick*

As a workaholic, you can use a goal to prod yourself into action, no matter how tired you are. A certain "high" can result from this process. You escalate standards for success. You create goals that guarantee you will be working hard for too long a time, until the work strikes you down. In this way, the goal is not really authentic. It is not feeding you. It is feeding your addiction.

Here is an illustration. Jim, a very bright sales representative for dental equipment came to the *You and Money* course with the goal of retiring by the time he was forty-five. At the time, he was thirty-eight and working very hard. Our talk went something like this:

Jim: I figure if I can save up enough money, I can retire.

Me: What does retirement look like to you?

Jim: I can work at something I love. I'll rest, have fun, see more of my friends and family.

Me: What if you could work at something you love, get the rest, enjoy yourself right now? Would you choose to withdraw, resign, or retire as your goal?

Jim: No, then I could start doing what I want with my family and friends instead of waiting another seven years. Maybe if I have fun, I won't want to retire. Maybe I'll stay at this job or quit it and go back to school. Come to think of it, I could go back to school right now. Oh, oh! (laughter) This is getting too easy!

Jim's solution may seem obvious to the onlooker. However, when you are caught up in working hard, missing the logical flaw in your thinking is easy. Errors like this are often the product of that overheated mind we visited in the last chapter.

If any of this sounds even remotely familiar to you, take heart. Your job here is to wake up to what you are doing. Ask yourself the following questions. Let your mind get quiet and listen, really listen. Let the true answers come from deep within you. Write down your discoveries in your notebook. Share your answers with a friend or loved one, as a way of bringing this to your consciousness.

*   What would I find inside if I were to slow my drive for working for several hours?
*   Am I willing to see whether I need the money or possessions I think I need?
*   What is more precious, my time or my money?

These questions may lead to important answers. The last one, looking at time and money, is particularly important. Consider the fact that it costs time out of your life to make money, even if you do love what you are doing. With that in mind, you can see very clearly how spending money is dispersing a form of your life's precious energy. You want to make sure that how you spend your money has true value and relevance for you. The choices you make about how much to earn and spend will be what determines the quality of your life.

A Closer Look

What follows are more scenarios from the lives of workaholics. They are designed to help you look at how you spend your life's energies. As you read these anecdotes, substitute your own profession or other details for what they are saying. Do not let differences between their stories and your own stop you from looking at the underlying themes that have taken over too much of your life. Only you can see where your energies are going.

Daniel: (A real estate agent) I've got to close three escrows a month, no matter how hard I have to work. I'm successful. A top producer in the region. I made it into my agency's Golden Circle Club. But I spend lots of time with it. My wife and kids feel like strangers to me. I've taken a course called *How to Set Priorities and Take Control of Your Time and Your Life.* I even have a daily planner notebook that helps organize my days down to the minute. One day I misplaced it. Almost had a heart attack on the spot. I took a course called *Working Smarter, Not Harder.* Give me a break! Now I'm working harder in a smarter way!

Laura: (Public relations officer) I've got a beautiful time share at the lake. Do I ever get to use it? No. I've given the time slot to friends for their vacations. Last week, I finally decided to take two weeks off and go there myself. One problem: there's a big publicity party for our top clients during a weekend I'll be gone. Everyone will be there. I tell myself I can just go and not get caught up supervising the event. But that's not true. I'm kidding myself. What if something goes wrong? I'm good in an emergency. I don't know what to do. Why does this have to happen, just as I was trying to break free for a while?

When you are addicted to your work, there are always work-related issues that interrupt your plans for rest or recreation. You find compelling, even irrefutable reasons to keep working. Or, you bring work with you wherever you go. At the very least, you feel pulled by last minute crises that come up and beg for your attention. You are convinced that you are the only person in the world who can handle them.

Here is a sure sign of workaholism: you consistently leave for vacations exhausted because you have been working so hard to tie up loose ends before you go. Another sign is if the thought of leaving your work behind makes you feel uncomfortable or anxious.

Elizabeth: (A pharmaceutical sales rep) I feel naked without my briefcase. Last summer, my husband and I had a really big fight. He didn't want me to take the briefcase on our vacation. I did anyway, packing it with only one report. I didn't get to it. But I felt guilty every time I came into our cabin from a day of snorkeling or shopping. I'd see the black briefcase on the floor near our bed and feel pressure to work, though I didn't want to.

A workaholic finds it difficult to develop a personal identity away from the work he or she does.

This aspect of workaholism is addressed by Judith Sprankle and Henry Ebel in *The Workaholic Syndrome: Your Job is Not Your Life*. Sprankle and Ebel maintain that workaholism is endemic to our society. We use our jobs, rather than our families and interests, to define who we are. We use them to avoid looking at what troubles us, or what we feel we cannot control.

Observing how we use our jobs to create our personal identities is easy. What happens when you first meet someone? One of the first questions one of you will ask is, "What do you do for a living?" If you have just been laid off, anxiety arises when someone asks you that question. It is bad enough saying that you are not working right now. Even worse is trying to figure out what to say about yourself.

Until 100 years ago, the work someone did was just about

the only thing that identified who they were. People were often named according to their work or profession. People were called Smith, Carpenter, Baker, Taylor, Hunter and so on. Now the circumstances are different. We can say much more about ourselves. For the most part, we just have not developed the way to say it. For example, what if we were to introduce ourselves by talking about our goals and dreams, favorite charities, inspiring books we have read, qualities we admire in people, or places we want to visit? It might be awkward until we got the hang of it. Yet it would provide us a way of really getting to know each other.

Traditional psychiatry has given us a precedent for putting a very high value on work. Sigmund Freud's notion was that the purpose of life was to work and love (*arbeiten und leiben*). Notice the absence of the word "play." However, even putting play aside, we often get too carried away with work. We sacrifice love, family and friendships:

Steve: (A building contractor.) Two years ago, my wife left me for my best friend. I went into a tailspin. I was pissed, all right. Soon the truth hit me. I drove her away. I'd been working fourteen hour days, six days a week to build this business. I told myself I was doing it for her, and that we would iron out our difficulties later when I'd made some big bucks. Three years ago, she asked that we go to a marriage counselor. I said no, because I didn't have the time. So she left. I haven't been seeing other women. But, I've sure been working hard. Sometimes, when business is slow, I worry about what to do with my free time.

Steve's last sentence is a real giveaway. It reveals his workaholism. The following question expresses it best:

If I were to have some free time, would I know what to do with it or myself?

The inability to cope with free time is not only true of workaholics. Free time is a challenge for Busyholics. One way of solving this dilemma is to keep busy so you will never have to confront the above question. Another way is to face the compulsion and tell the truth about it. This leads to wisdom, and a way out.

To Do or Not to Do -- That is the Question!

Busyholism is even harder to nail down than workaholism. That is because of the way we lend it respectability. Remember the saying about idle hands and the devil's workshop?

Dennis: I play hard. For me, resting at a vacation resort means getting up at seven to jog, eating breakfast at eight, then snorkeling until ten, horseback riding until lunch, read for twenty minutes after eating, and then swimming until sundown. I have to stay in motion. It drives my wife crazy. She wants me to sit and talk to her. But sitting too long drives me nuts.

Rudy: I have all these catalogues and financial magazines piled up for when I take a vacation. My wife and I took our two kids to the grandparents. I lugged all the junk with me. I read most of it, even though it cut down on play time with the kids. But then I get home and find a whole stack waiting for me at the post office. It never ends.

Margaret: I go on binges where I have to do things perfectly. At Christmas I have to make sure the tree is done just so. The decorations are put around the house, and then I start baking cookies; from scratch, none of this premixed stuff. By the time I've shopped and wrapped presents, it's time to occupy the kids, who are on vacation. To make matters worse, I usually get sick. It's like the flu and it knocks me flat. Then I have to go to bed and rest for a few days. One of my friends told me that I don't have to get sick in order to allow myself some down time. She may be right.

> "It is not hard work which is dreary; it is superficial work."
>
> *Doris Fielding Reid*

If you are a busyholic, you do not need to get more motivated to do things. On the contrary, you need to know that you can relax and savor life.

When I work with busyholics, I often suggest that they reduce their goals (gasp!). This can be very distressing for the busyholic. Nevertheless, too many goals can eventually drive a person to illness or exhaustion. This is especially true when you become addicted to the rush that goes along with frantic activity.

Armando: I love the adrenaline rush at my work. I'm a stockbroker. Need I say more? Every morning, things heat up when we get our market data. I have a cellular phone and a fax in my car. I read three newspapers a day. I want to know what's happening at all times. For me, a day without the news is a day wasted. Everything's great except for my lower back, which hurts most of the time. I go to a chiropractor every week. He says it's stress and that I have to rest. But the thought of rest makes me nervous. I'll miss out on something. I just know it.

Exercise: Am I or Am I Not a Busyholic?

By now, you have read numerous examples of busyholism. The next step is to look at its role in your own life. I suggest you go a bit more slowly than usual with the following inventory. Be careful not to skip over subjects you find uncomfortable.

It is useful to talk about these items in a group. Each person speaks about that which most concerns them. A supportive atmosphere gives you breathing room to acknowledge publicly what you might dismiss privately.

What You Will Need
Your notebook and a pen or pencil are all that are necessary. Record your responses there.

Time For This Exercise
Most people take forty minutes for the entire exercise; twenty minutes for this inventory, plus some discussion time.

The Exercise
Each item below is presented as a statement. Write it down. Next, assign a number, from 1-5, to the item, showing how true the statement is for you. The number 1 means "not true"; 2 means "sometimes true"; 3 means "do not know"; 4 means "somewhat true"; and 5 means "true." There is no score to add up at the end. The scale makes it easy to discern the degree to which each item relates to your life.

After rating each item, take a few moments to write about what you thought, especially if an item rated "true" for you. For example, do you recall the last time this happened? Who was there? What did you do? What does it cost you to do things this way, in terms of time, money, love and health?

Busyholism Inventory
Rate each of the following statements according to the scale I just described in the paragraphs above.

1. I am tired most of the time.

2. I always seem to be in motion.

3. I get anxious even thinking about leaving the work in my briefcase at the office.

4. Most of the people in my life (spouse, friends, family) do not understand why I need to work so hard.

5. I get very frustrated when I cannot finish a task or an interruption occurs so that I have to complete it later.

6. Sunday (or my day off) I have a list of things I must do before I can play or rest. I rarely get through the list to the rest and play part.

7. I feel isolated from those I love.

8. By the time I do something I like, I am too tired to really enjoy it.

9. I feel guilty or anxious when I am resting or just taking it easy.

10. When I am doing something (such as watching a son or daughter play soccer) I often miss out on the fun because I am too preoccupied with what needs to be done next.

11. I use substances to prod myself into action during the day. They can be caffeine, sugar, or drugs. Or, to relax in the evening, I use alcohol, marijuana or other drugs (prescription or over-the-counter).

12. I feel deprived because I am not doing the things I really want to do.

13. I feel that I have more responsibilities than most of my family or friends.

14. I have irrefutable reasons for why I need to bring my work home at night or on weekends.

15. I usually do things in a hurry, like gulp my food or throw on clothes.

16. I forget to take care of myself (do not eat, drink water, or use the restroom) for long periods.

17. I do pleasurable things, such as going on trips, buying a new car, or eating sweets, because I work so hard I feel I *deserve* them.

18. My friends and family tell me they are not seeing enough of me. When I am with them, they tell me I seem withdrawn or emotionally removed.

Discussion

This is not a cumulative scoring evaluation. It does not matter whether you rate yourself at "5" on one or all of them. What matters is the self-awareness that comes out of the process.

When we start looking at our own busyholism, most of us will discover that Monkey Mind is aroused. It will do everything in its power to avoid the truth, to protect its own selfish interests. You can be assured that Monkey Mind has something invested in keeping you addicted to the busy life. By its very nature, the "inner busyholic" does not want to be exposed, and Monkey Mind wants to protect itself. Your inner busyholic will do everything in its power to convince you that all this busy-ness and work that fills your life is absolutely and unequivocally justified. Our inner busyholics can be like very slippery fish that we are trying to grasp with our bare hands.

Based upon what you have already read, coupled with the above questions, is there just a slim possibility that you are a busyholic? Or, at the very least, are you maybe, just maybe, leaning in that direction?

If you still do not know, for certain, we have a sure-fire way to find out. It requires courage, but it is a way of getting more than your money's worth out of this book. It is going the extra mile. *Ask your family and friends.* Do not rely on the people who work with you, because they may be caught up in the same system you are. Or, they may have an interest in your staying the way you are. For the most trustworthy answers, turn to those who know and love you outside work. Be prepared to look, see, and tell the truth!

The Journey Continues

The next chapter will take your hero's journey along a path where you will confront the fearsome, fire-eating dragon called "scarcity." Scarcity is the experience of not having enough. It follows at our heels, not only when we look at money, but all forms of energy. You will need to have a deep understanding of scarcity and its purpose. This will help you manifest authentic goals, not ones born of the need to escape scarcity.

Summary

✐   Busyholism is any activity in the physical domain that is not anchored to anything in the metaphysical domain.

✐   Peak performers take time out for a period of complete rest in the middle of their day, every day!

✐   If you are a workaholic, pursuing more money and more goals can be like more cocaine for a cocaine addict.

✐   A workaholic finds it difficult to develop an identity away from the work he or she does.

✐   A way to begin an inquiry into your own busyholism is to ask yourself: If I were to have some free time, would I know what to do with it or myself?

✐   If you are a busyholic, you do not need to get more motivated to do things. On the contrary, you need to know that you can relax and savor life.

✐   For the most trustworthy answers about your busyholism, ask those who know and love you outside work. Be prepared to look, see, and tell the truth!

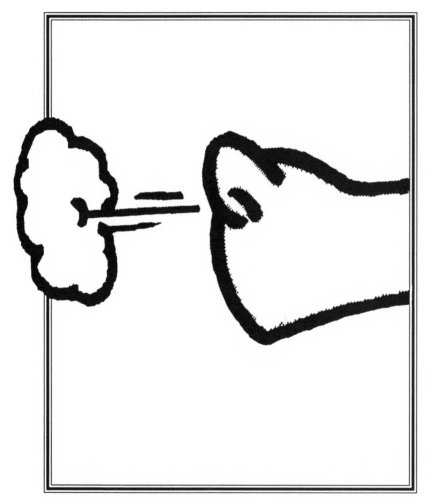

CHAPTER SIX:
Scarcity, Scare-city or Scar-city --
Getting to the Heart of the
Problem

Scarcity, Scare-city or Scar-city -- Getting to The Heart of the Problem

"Heroes take journeys, confront dragons, and discover the treasure of their true selves."

Carol Pearson

Abundance and peace of mind are the dreams that fill the hero's castle. A forest lies just beyond the castle. Lurking in this forest is the dragon whose name is "Scarcity." It scavenges all forms of human energy. Its fierce reputation is legendary, causing trembling in the hearts of even the most courageous warriors. Or, is it a magic dragon?

So much drama in life revolves around the theme of scarcity. Scarcity is your subjective experience of an objective fact, interpreted by Monkey Mind. Limits, borders or constraints are a part of physical reality. It can be uncomfortable to face a limit. In fact, you first experienced scarcity at the moment of your birth, as you drew your first breath. Initially, limits could seem scary. Monkey Mind can make a circus out of this.

Is the dragon really a monster in the dark? What you fear may hold your greatest lessons. Those lessons may ultimately fuel your wisest choices. Something lives in the forest, but what is it? Is it our nearest resource, or something to fear? Scarcity is our interpretation, what we draw from our discomfort of encountering a limit. How do we learn from it? First, we must face our fear.

The experience of scarcity occurs naturally for all of us, no matter how enlightened or conscious we may be. Running from it, or trying to hide it behind a smoke screen of positive thinking will not stave it off. There will come times it must be faced. Doing so will lead to your personal transformation.

The moment you face and tell the truth about your experience of scarcity, it loses its potency. Then you can move on to its lesson of the limitation it represents.

This is why scarcity is such a common experience in our lives. Recall the diagram depicting the physical and metaphysical realms. One aspect of physical reality is impermanence: virtually everything comes and goes. Rocks, people, oceans: all are born, all exist and then disappear. Everything has its own limited time span. Impermanence and limit therefore, go hand-in-hand in this domain. Limit is a necessary condition of the physical realm.

Take a moment to do this experiment. Pick up a pen or pencil. Get the feel of the object in your hand. Next, imagine the pen or pencil getting bigger, its boundaries streching out ten feet in each direction. Continue to expand the boundaries of that object, pretend that the limits of the pen or pencil stretch out for a thousand miles in each direction. Now have the limits stretch into infinity in all directions. Infinity means it goes on forever. As it expands infinitely in all directions, what happens to that object? It *disappears*. Do you see that it becomes everything? That is because it expands to fill all available space. At the same time, it becomes no single *thing* in particular. Or, you could say, it is now everything, and nothing!

Hold on to that observation as you look further at scarcity. This is not a philosophy lesson. It is a pragmatic demonstration of the necessity for limits in physical reality. We need limits to carry out actions in the physical domain. No limits, no form. No form, no pen. No pen, nothing to play with. It is just that simple, joyful, and painful.

Joy and pain figure prominently in physical reality. For example, upon receiving a beautiful bouquet of flowers, what is one of the first things you worry about? How long they are going to last. In the middle of a joyful moment, a pang may arise at the thought that it is only transitory.

The human condition is filled with lessons about living in a finite physical universe. Most lessons in this lifetime seem to have some form or substance as their theme, and all form, all substance, has limits and boundaries. The limits distinguish one thing from another. The minute we come up against these limits, we have a perception of scarcity. That is just the reality. It causes us all a great deal of discomfort, like having to pass the dragon's lair every time we leave or return to the castle. Still, there are ways to placate this dragon, even befriend it. We need not allow our lives to be run by the fear he triggered in us.

We are here to learn from the limits and boundaries we perceive. For example, if food grew wild and was plentiful throughout the world, cultivation would not have been needed, nor would storage and transportation of food. If some regions did not have more food, minerals or fabrics than others, no reason for trade would exist. All the people of the world would thus have remained quite separated. Each time we confront scarcity we learn something from it. This prompts us to develop, or evolve, our human potential and our consciousness. What makes money, or anything else for that matter, valuable? Scarcity. If gold and diamonds were as common as sand, they would lose their distinguishing features and become valueless. The same would be true for money in its other forms. Consider the following:

You are here to learn from scarcity. It is not your enemy. It is one of your greatest teachers.

What do we know about lessons in life? We know that the more you ignore or try to run from them, the more they persist. When you finally turn and face them, what has seemed to be your enemy can be transformed into your ally. This scenario is at the heart of the hero's journey.

We all have a limited time here on earth. We all have limited energy. The question for many of us is *not* "how can I get more?" Instead, the question is: What miracles can I perform with what I have? In later chapters, we look very closely at miracles, and how to bring them from the metaphysical into the physical. The first step, however, is to recognize that scarcity is a reality in the physical domain.

> "I could never work with great spirit in any material unless I knew the amount of it was limited. I had to be hedged in by a boundary of either space or material, in order to awaken the feeling of creative excitement."
>
> *Katherine Butler Hathaway*

A minister friend of mine once told me: "It's as though we got bored living without limits. We decided to incarnate -- which means, literally, to turn into meat. We further chose to work with the limits of form, time and finite energy. This was to see how much of the divine we could bring into the mundane before it was time for us to leave."

Buddhists suggest that we try to live as though we were going to die within the next ten minutes. In our own country, in the last months of his life, actor Michael Landon said: "Somebody ought to tell us, right at the start of our lives, that we are dying. Then we might live life to the limit every minute of every day." The conscious limits we place upon existence allow us to see that which is unlimited. But, make no mistake. We reach the infinite through living fully in the finite. The infinite is not reached by trying to ignore limits, as many of us do.

Scarcity Unconfronted

Monkey Mind hates scarcity and constantly tries to manipulate us through our fear of it. We drive ourselves half crazy with our avoidance of what we fear. This reminds me of a joke I heard long ago in college:

What is the difference between a psychotic and a neurotic? The psychotic thinks that two plus two equals five, and is fine with it. A neurotic knows that two plus two equals four, but *hates* it!

The neurotic's dilemma is at the heart of most of our struggles.

What does Monkey Mind hate about scarcity? Monkey Mind, above all, is adamant about the survival of the physical form. It wants to keep things the way they are at any cost. It plays the role of obstructionist wherever change raises its head -- and, of course, that is everywhere. What a losing battle! In Monkey Mind are found conversations about the terrors of growing old. Monkey Mind wants to live forever. It will do anything it can to ensure this happens, even if the results paradoxically endanger the body:

Rena: I don't care what anyone else says about being forty. I weighed 115 pounds when I was eighteen years old, and I want to weigh that now. I've put myself on a diet, and exercise two hours every day, rain or shine. I'll lose those last twelve pounds if it kills me!

Edward: There's still so much I want to do with my life. I don't have time to slow down. These vitamins keep me going. I can get by with much less sleep. About five hours a night is all I need.

Neither Rena nor Edward looked in great shape as they spoke these words in their *You and Money* course. Both seemed tired and on edge. Their bodies were being left behind in Monkey Mind's quest for survival.

I have asked more than two thousand people what they most fear when it comes to scarcity. Many say that not having enough money is close to the top of their list. It is hard to even think about. Money is so tied into our feelings of safety and well-being that we will do anything to avoid talking about it, even when it is causing us great discomfort.

Robert: The last thing I want anyone to know is how much money I *don't* have. I spend too much. I can't hold onto my money. I know something's wrong with me. Some nights, I worry a lot about growing old and poor.

Robert's predicament is not at all unusual. On one hand, he fears not having enough money. On the other hand, he hates the idea of facing that fear and doing something about it. He tiptoes past Scarcity, the fire-breathing Dragon, and sneaks off to spend everything he has, keeping himself in poverty. This makes no sense at all. Yet fear often magnetizes us to the very thing we most abhor. On our circuitous route to avoid the dragon, we end up at the dragon's door!

While we are looking at scarcity and money, let us tackle a universal misperception:

Contrary to popular belief, the way to deal with scar-

city is *not* by amassing more. This can actually make scar-city grow!

John Maynard Keynes offers a wonderful quotation that plays on this theme, putting it into perspective: "The love of mo-ney as a possession -- as distinguished from the love of money as a means to the enjoyments and realities of life -- should be recognized for what it is, a somewhat disgusting morbidity, one of those semi-crimi-nal, semi-pathological propensities which one hands over with a shud-der to the specialists in mental disease."

People have all kinds of thoughts when they first hear this:

* Sure, sure; just let me win the lottery and I'll show you how to handle scarcity!

* I absolutely know that having more money would get me out of this funk.

* Here we go with more metaphysical dou-ble-talk. Let's get real! I want more money. I know it will solve the problems I'm facing.

Reflect upon the following scenario. It has been echoed hundreds of times in the *You and Money* course. Can you see yourself here?

Esther: When I was a student on scholarship, I lived on $500 a month. I remember saying to myself: All I need is another $100 per month and I'll have it made. Sure enough, I got a part-time job and started pulling in an extra $120 a month. Three months later, it was the same thing: If only I had another $75 a month! I could take myself out to the movies and buy some extras. Then I got my first full time job for $2500 a month. It was heaven for about six months. Then the old voice came back: Just give me $500 a month more, and I'll be on Easy Street. That was six years ago. Today, with my MBA, I'm earning $5000 a month, and I still wish I had more money. What's weird about this is that I am more in debt now than I was five years ago. I worry about money a lot more now than when I was in school.

The above is not just a case of poor money management. It is a reflection of *scarcity unconfronted*. Does more money fill the hole created by your experience of not having enough? No, it does not. You have undoubtedly heard of millionaires who pinch every penny they earn. I remember one very wealthy man with whom I had lunch. He took sugar packets out of the restaurant's sugar bowl so that he would not have to buy sugar for home. Similarly, a very wealthy couple I met used to go to the movies and linger in the restrooms for a while. Then they would enter a second movie without paying.

An extreme example of scarcity in the face of plenty is the story of a small business owner in Sacramento who lived alone in a shabby two-room apartment. After his death, distant relatives found $200,000 cash in shoe boxes in his closet.

> "We cannot escape fear. We can only transform it into a companion that accompanies us on all our exciting adventures."
>
> *Susan Jeffers*

Look again at Esther's story. You may remember a time when you had less money. Life may have seemed a lot easier and simpler. Rest assured that the purpose of this book is not to force you to be content with less money. There are those who have lots of money who can live easily and without worry. They do not fall prey to the *Icarus Syndrome* mentioned in an earlier chapter. That is, they can harness and use this energy wisely to benefit themselves and others. You can, too!

By doing the work here, you may genuinely discover contentment with what you have. You could begin to enjoy the abundance that you so desperately seek. Perhaps, you will see that you could be happier making less money than you presently do. You may find that you are willing to have more money and are up to the challenge of using the energy that it represents. The point is, these alternatives are only possible when you are willing to face and resolve your lessons about scarcity. One thing we know for sure: **the experience of scarcity will arise again and again, as long as you are breathing.**

Esther saw how her fear of scarcity influenced her relationship with money. A subtle shift occurred in the way she viewed her life, goals and dreams. One year later she bought her first home, began working with a certified financial planner, and was saving money rather than incurring more debt. More important for her was the experience of ease. She was no longer running from her dread of not having enough. She had confronted these fears and they had lost their influence.

Here is guidance for your hero's journey: when you are

afraid, look boldly into the face of whatever you fear. It is not necessary to try to escape the discomfort. You can handle it. Use the support of your friends. Pema Chodron, in her book, *The Wisdom of No Escape and the Path of Loving-Kindness,* describes the importance of both pleasure and pain in becoming conscious:

"There's a common misunderstanding among all the human beings who have ever been born on earth that the best way to live is to try to avoid pain and just try to get comfortable ... A much more interesting, kind, adventurous and joyful approach to life is to begin to develop our curiosity, not caring whether the object of our inquisitiveness is bitter or sweet ... we must realize that we can endure a lot of pain and pleasure for the sake of finding out who we are and what this world is ..."

Waking up to your relationship with money will become easier and easier if you are willing to face the initial discomfort. As Talulah Bankhead so wisely said: "There may be less to this than meets the eye." Relief is on its way.

I'll Show You Mine if You Show Me Yours

One way we experience scarcity is through the scale of comparison. We compare our lives to others. Everyone does it, from the time we are old enough to compare body parts, to the time we are old enough to compare retirement plans. Look at these examples and see where you fit in.

Jorge: I don't talk about my commissions and how much I bring home every month. It's nobody else's business. The real truth is that I think I make less than most of the insurance agents in my company. I'd never want anyone to know that!

Marge: I felt just wonderful about my new 4x4 truck until I found out a girl friend got the same one at a much better price. Now I feel stupid because I didn't go to the other dealership. I'm angry that my dealers took advantage of me.

James: I'm really mad! Last week, I sneaked a look at the salary structure in my firm. There are some attorneys here making a lot more money than I am. They don't work half as hard as I do. I got my yearly bonus check yesterday for $25,000. Ordinarily I'd be overjoyed. But looking at the amount just made me even more resentful. I know that others are getting more than I am. It burns me up!

A few years ago, I conducted a survey on "Money Secrets" for a local magazine. One of my favorite questions was, "What is one thing you would never want anyone to know about you and money?" Out of the 1,100 people who responded, the majority answered : "How much I have." The implication was that they did not have as much as others.

When you compare yourself to others, do you usually get the short end of the deal? That is just the way your mind works. Even when we compare ourselves to those who are less fortunate, our minds usually jump to those who are better off than us.

This feeling of being one down is especially powerful when you compare yourself to people you think are barely ahead of you. I conducted my dissertation research on this phenomenon in young children. I have found it to be true of adults as well.

In my study, when young boys played pinball, they became most competitive when they were just slightly behind their partners. Boys who were way ahead, slightly ahead, or way behind could be more easily induced to stop the game and donate their playing marbles so others could play.

A good place to observe or experience the process of comparison is at work, with people who operate at about the same level of responsibility. This process is most noticeable with people whose salaries are based on individual effort, as in sales or the legal profession.

Comparisons are knee jerk responses. Trying to stop them is useless. On the contrary, it is important that you recognize and identify these responses. Make them conscious. **The comparisons you make between yourself and other people often reflect your current life's lessons.**

Take James' story for example. There he was, angry because others were making more money than he. Was that really the source of his suffering? No, his foremost fear was of being overlooked. He hated that. Just telling the truth gave him some breathing room. Our exchange in the *You and Money* course went something like this:

Me: What do you hate about being overlooked?

James: I work so hard. I deserve respect.

Me: Does everyone else work this hard?

James: Yes.

Me: Okay, look again then. What do you really hate about being overlooked? What is the fear?

James: It's more like I don't fit in. They don't even acknowledge all the business I've brought to this firm over the past two years.

Me: Let us look a little deeper. How do you know they don't recognize all the work you've brought to the firm?

James: Well, I've never heard any of the partners say anything about my contribution.

Me: When was the last time you really talked to any of

them? You know, taken at least one of them out for coffee? You could talk about how you feel.

James: I don't have time.

Me: Not enough time for relationships? This has all the makings of a good lesson.

James: Yeah. I haven't been spending enough time with my wife and family lately, either. I'm working long and hard hours.

Me: You're lonely, aren't you?

James: Okay, I know where this is leading. Your next question will be, *have you had enough of doing it this way?* You're so predictable! Yes (laughs) I have had enough. Tomorrow I'll take one of the partners out for coffee. I'll tell my wife how much I've been missing her lately. Satisfied? (Laughs again).

Me: And, while you're at it, think about asking for a raise if it's appropriate!

> "You gain strength, courage and confidence by every experience in which you really stop to look fear in the face. You are able to say to yourself, 'I lived through this horror. I can take the next thing that comes along.' You must do the thing you think you cannot do."
>
> *Eleanor Roosevelt*

Facing your discomfort opens the door to personal transformation. It creates an opportunity to put scarcity in perspective. Carefully look at how fending off discomfort affects your daily life. Do you try to avoid scarcity? Do you manipulate yourself into thinking it does not exist by rationalizing away your feelings: "I'm being overly sensitive?" Do you misuse positive thinking strategies or affirmations? Unfortunately, the more you run, and focus attention on avoiding your feelings, the faster the fire-breathing Dragon of Scarcity catches up with you.

You have the capacity to know yourself better by looking at the ways scarcity works in your life, and at how to live more fully as a human being. Your life will become full of adventures instead of defenses.

If I Don't Think About It, It Doesn't Exist

Have you ever wondered why affirmations do not always work? Shakti Gawain, author of the book *Creative Visualization,* has the answer. She says that when people complain that their affirmations do not work, it is usually because they are trying to use them to suppress negative thoughts or feelings. Affirmations work best when you use them to affirm the truth about yourself. They help to focus on a thought or image that will help you to fulfill your goals and dreams.

For example, you can use your Standards of Integrity to affirm who you really are in your heart. They become like a shepherd's rod and staff, gently prodding you to take authentic action. The following illustrates how affirmations are misused to suppress or cover up negative thoughts and feelings:

Harold: I've gone to lots of prosperity workshops. I heard that if I hold the right thoughts, my outward reality will begin to reflect my new thinking. Still, nothing has changed in my life over the past year. I still don't have the job I want. I'm even deeper in debt. Maybe there's still something wrong with me or my way of looking at things.

Paul: I just joined a network marketing system to make more money on the side. I've seen videotapes of people who are successful at it. They're sitting on the beach in Hawaii or in their beautiful homes, telling me to think positively and expect the best. They say it's important to work hard and have a winning attitude. But how can I have a winning attitude when I get so anxious about my finances? I try not to worry. It doesn't work.

Unfortunately, Harold and Paul are trying to use positive thinking to avoid their honest thoughts and feelings. They are trying to control what they do not want to look at. But thoughts and feelings need an outlet. They need to be expressed, not allowed to fester and undermine our whole outlook on the world. The effort to make them disappear with positive affirmations is as futile as trying to stop the waves from lapping along the shore of a lake.

We will now do another experiment. This time, about thought suppression. For the next ten seconds, do *not* think about a hot fudge sundae with whipped cream. *Do not* think about the rich chocolate topping, the cool, sweet taste of the ice cream, the smooth whipped cream and chopped nuts.

What do you notice? Your mind may be saying something like this:

Okay, now I'll stop thinking about a hot fudge sundae with whipped cream. This is easy. I'm not even thinking about a hot fudge sundae with whipped cream right now. See? A hot fudge sundae with whipped cream is the last thing on my mind. Let's see ... what else can I picture in my mind so that I don't have to think about a hot fudge sundae with whipped cream?

You can see from this how your mind is drawn to the very things you tell it to avoid. So, is it possible to cover over your negative thoughts? Perhaps, but remember the example of trying to control the waves on a lake? The entire lake would have to freeze to do that. In the same way, you would have to freeze huge areas of your life experience to block your thoughts. Frozen with the parts you do not want to think about would be your enthusiasm and joy for life.

It takes a lot of energy to suppress your thoughts. This energy is better spent in pursuing your goals and dreams.

You have met people who maintain that everything is *just fine*, *just wonderful*, no matter what! You sense that their bright-eyed smile and firm handshake are not real. Although they appear outgoing, cheerful, full of energy and enthusiasm, connecting with them is difficult or impossible. In a very real way, it is like trying to connect with a person who is wearing a mask. Who they really are is hidden behind their plastic exterior.

Floyd: I'm a minister. In the past, I refused to acknowledge to myself that I had negative thoughts about other people. I would insist I only had positive thoughts. But something strange happened. I developed negative judgments about myself every time I had an unkind thought about someone else. Then I started feeling righteously indignant toward those in my congregation who I thought weren't trying to think positively like me. One thing that's good about the ministry is that the bottom line can measure your effectiveness: Sunday contributions. Mine were going down. I talked to some parishioners I knew well. The consistent feedback was that I didn't seem like a real human being any more. That was my wake-up call. I'm starting to relax. I see that everyone has negative thoughts from time to time. I have more compassion for myself and others.

> *"If you bring forth what is inside you, what you bring forth will save you. If you don't bring forth what is inside you, what you don't bring forth will destroy you."*
>
> *Jesus*

Here is another experiment in trying to control your mind. Think about someone you dislike or who irritates you. Get a picture of them in your mind's eye. Now, find ten positive things to say about them. What happens? Some confusion may enter your mind as it searches for a positive thought about this person. Tension may rise as the positive thoughts battle with the negative ones. Most likely you are not feeling very joyful doing this experiment. Does it feel phony, like you are trying to pull one over on your mind? That is because you *are* trying to pull one over on your mind. Guess what? It will not work.

Sheryn: My ex-husband and I divorced three years ago. We're still fighting about how much child support he owes me. After we separated, I tried hard to let go of my resentments toward him. A friend taught me a way to visualize. I put all my feelings in a bubble and watched it sail away into the blue sky. I have done that technique repeatedly. It only works for a little while. Every time I hear Sam's voice on the phone I get pissed-off again.

Using positive thinking in that way is a kind of superstitious thinking. You are engaged in superstitious thinking when you use positive thoughts like a talisman to ward off negative emotions or circumstances. Our mythology is full of examples of heroes facing their dark side to become truly powerful. In *The Return of the Jedi,* the hero Luke Skywalker faces a Darth Vader-like figure in the dark forest. Upon vanquishing it, he throws open its helmet. It is himself.

Carl Jung, noted psychotherapist and thinker, spoke of this dark or "shadow" side. He talks of the consequences of not facing it:

"Everyone carries a shadow, and the less it is embodied in the individual's conscious life, the blacker and denser it is. At all counts, it forms an unconscious snag, thwarting our most well-meant intentions."

Let us look at your intentions. There are grand reflections of your hero's heart. You have come to life to manifest them through your goals. The root of the word "manifest" is "hand." You are here to grasp your dreams. Before you can do so, you must be free. Seeing what you currently hold in your hand that is obstructing your power will allow you to release it. Then your dreams can take its place.

Exercise: Encounter with a Dragon

You are about to read some questions that will help clarify how scarcity operates in your life. Allow yourself to answer them. Bring your Standards of Integrity and your life's intentions with you. Keep them by your side. Look at them frequently. They reflect who you really are.

There are a number of parts to this exercise. Each section uses a different format to help you arrive at a picture of your relationship with scarcity.

What You Will Need
Use your notebook to record your responses to the following questions.

Time For This Exercise
Take your time with each part. Do not rush your answers, even if you are tempted to do so. Respond to one or two questions at a sitting. The benefits you reap from this experience will be in direct proportion to how truthful you are with yourself. You may find some similarities between these questions and the ones in the first chapter. However, the work here approaches scarcity and money more explicitly. After doing this exercise with money, you may want to substitute another form of energy, such as time, love or physical well-being. Would there be a similarity in your answers with these forms of energy? It might be interesting to find out.

Part I: An Overall Picture of the Dragon

1. **What issues, problems or concerns do I have about money?**
   Guidelines for answering: Look at all your worries regarding money. Even if it seems petty or silly. Do you have overdue bills? Do you worry about your children's education or your own retirement? Does it seem like you never have enough, no matter how hard you work? Have you been the victim of fraud, theft or deceit regarding money? Do you envy people who seem to have more than you? Who are they? Look at all of your negative feelings about money as you respond to this item. Do you hate money? Fear it? Fear not having it? Let yourself write about this until you are emptied out. Write for at least ten minutes without a break.

2. **What do I say to myself *about myself* for having these issues, problems or concerns?**
   Guidelines for answering: Do you have judgments about yourself because of your money concerns? Do you think you are silly, incapable or irresponsible? Do you hope no one finds you out? We all have some of these thoughts and feelings about ourselves. This is especially true when we have been doing the same things, over and over again, expecting different results.

Keep listing until you get at least six statements.

3. **What were my major blunders regarding money?**
   Guidelines for answering: What have you done in the past regarding money that you would be ashamed to tell anyone? Have you gambled and lost large sums? Have you signed leases without reading the fine print? Have you made calculation errors that caused you to become seriously overdrawn at the bank? Have you invested and lost money you could not spare in ventures that were very risky?

4. **Who have I blamed for my difficulties with money?**
   Guidelines for answering: This is the opportunity to really let loose. Who are they, and what have they done to you? List all the funky things you think about people who have *done it* to you. This is no time to be quasi-enlightened. Do not fall into the: *But they didn't do anything to me. I allowed them to do it* trap. Just cough it up. What happened? How did it feel? Another hint: do not list yourself. Look for the culprits outside yourself.

Write what you feel as you answer these questions. Do you feel angry, sad, frustrated, bored, irritated? Many who go through this inventory find it stirs up many feelings connected with scarcity. It is a very rare person, rich or poor, who has nothing to get off their chest. On the other hand, you may be surprised or feel relieved just telling the truth. Everyone who takes the time to confront their feelings and concerns in this way benefits greatly.

As you face your experience of scarcity, you prepare the way to have a relationship with money that is fulfilling. This relationship will no longer be merely the extension of past upsets.

Part II: Dragon Prints in the Sand

In this next part, you will find a list of words. Each one is followed by a definition. These words represent how we often deal with scarcity when we are trying to get away from it. Write each of the words in your notebook. Then list incidents regarding money that are examples of that word or concept. Draw from real experience in your own life. For instance, look at the word "greed." Here you might write something like: "I sold sodas at a softball game for much more than they were worth. I knew people would pay that much because it was a hot day." It does not have to be a long description. In fact, the shorter the better. Do your best to cut out rationalizations or justifications for the event. Get right down to the essence. List everything you can recall under each word. I promise the list will not go on forever, even if Monkey Mind is telling you the opposite of that right now. You may find that an incident can be listed under two or more words. Some lists may be short and others long. Write whatever comes to you. Be as complete as possible.

Greed: The desire for more than one needs or deserves, especially without consideration for the needs of others.

Dishonesty: Lying, cheating, stealing.

Guilt: Feelings of self-reproach resulting from a belief that we have done something wrong or immoral.

Regret: A troubled feeling over something that one has done or left undone. Feeling it should not have happened as it did.

Unconsciousness: The state of not being aware, as with having made a mistake because we were not paying attention. Acting without the knowledge or preparation we should have had.

Manipulation: Managing or controlling by a shrewd use of influence, threat, or power. Often in an unfair or fraudulent way. Done for one's own gain or profit. Getting others to act against their will or best interests for your selfish gain.

Resentment: Feelings of displeasure and indignation, from a sense of being injured, offended or used.

Error: The state of believing something that is not true. Doing something incorrectly because of ignorance or carelessness.

Fear: Anxiety, agitation, or a sense of foreboding caused by the presence or nearness of a perceived danger or pain that is real or imagined.

Self-deception: To mislead oneself into believing something is true when it is not.

Yeah for you! This has been a difficult process, and you have completed it. Like a dragon fighter removing heavy armor that is awkward and bulky, you will now feel lighter and more agile.

Part III: Discovering the Magic in the Dragon

The next questions ask you to look at how your life would be if you allowed scarcity to be your ally. Take your time to move through these questions. Know that you are firmly establishing your way on the hero's path. You are joining the thousands of others who have gone on to thrive after fully examining the role of scarcity in their lives.

5. **What choices would I make if I no longer held scarcity at bay?**
   Guidelines for answering: What dreams would you follow that you have put on the back burner? What relationships would you pursue or enhance?

6. **Recall a time you faced and learned from a limitation. What was it?**
   Guidelines for answering: Were you pleasantly surprised from the outcome? What were your thoughts about your initial assessment? What new, creative ideas came from that encounter?

Discussion

Congratulations! You have done more to understand your relationship with scarcity than most people do in a lifetime. If you are doing this exercise with others, take time to share your answers. You may find their answers similar to yours. You may notice more awareness of the role that scarcity, or the avoidance of it, has played in your relationship with money.

When you have thoroughly shared your answers to these questions, I want you to do something special with Parts I and II of this exercise. Take them out of your notebook. Crumple the papers in your hand, one at a time, and drop them into a paper bag. Take this bag and throw it away in the trash. Notice if you feel uneasy about letting the pages go. Do it anyway. You are giving yourself the message that it is all right to let go of these thoughts and feelings. They may come up again. They will probably come up again. When they do, simply write them down and throw the pages away again. Notice if your thoughts and feelings shift.

The Journey Continues

Your hero's journey includes stretching beyond your customary ways of seeing the world. In the next chapter, you will learn to dismantle old thought systems about money. You will go beyond scarcity. You will see new ways to relate to money and other forms of energy in your life.

Summary

✎   Scarcity is the experience that there is not enough to go around. Limit is a fact. Scarcity is Monkey Mind's interpretation of that fact.

✎   The moment you face and tell the truth about your experience of scarcity, it loses its potency. Then you can move on to the lesson of the limitation it represents.

✎   You are here to learn from scarcity. It is not your enemy. It can be one of your greatest teachers.

✎   Scarcity is *not* relieved by amassing more of that which is scarce. This can fuel your perceptions of scarcity.

✎   You can learn about yourself from scarcity. Your life will become full of adventures instead of defenses.

✎   It takes a lot of energy to suppress your thoughts. This energy is better spent in pursuing your goals and dreams.

✎   As you face your experience of scarcity, you prepare the way to have a relationship with money that is fulfilling. This relationship will no longer be merely the extension of past upsets.

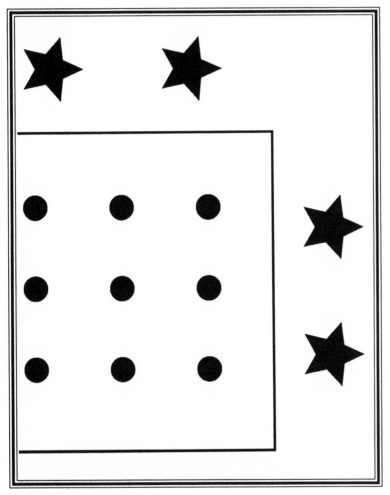

CHAPTER SEVEN:
Beyond Scarcity: New Ways to Relate to Money

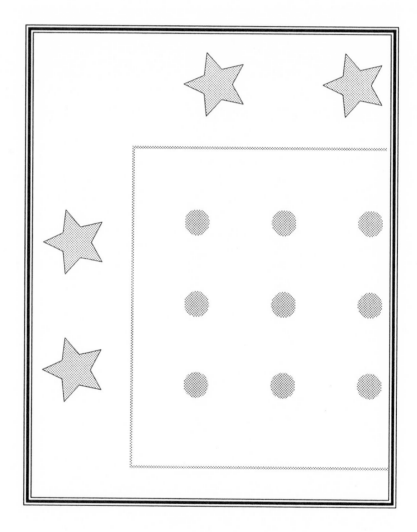

Beyond Scarcity: New Ways to Relate to Money

"Fortunate, indeed, is the man who takes exactly the right measure of himself, and holds a just balance between what he can acquire and what he can use, be it great or be it small."

Peter Mere Latham

Now you have explored scarcity, and can see it in your relationship with money. You may have discovered the following:

Telling the truth about where scarcity troubles you is powerful and enlivening. Having seen the truth, you can identify what you genuinely want in life, separating it from what you thought you *must* have.

In his book *The Enlightened Mind: Anthology of Sacred Prose*, author/editor Stephen Mitchell relates the following story, a teaching parable of the Buddha:

"A man walking a high road sees a great river, its near bank dangerous and frightening, its far bank safe. He collects sticks and foliage, makes a raft, paddles across the river, and reaches the other shore. Now, suppose that, after he reaches the other shore, he takes the raft and puts it on his head and walks with it on his head wherever he goes. Would he be using the raft in an appropriate way? No; a reasonable man will realize that the raft has been very useful to him in crossing the river and arriving safely on the other shore, but that once he has arrived, it is proper to leave the raft behind and walk on without it. This is using the raft appropriately. In the same way, all truths should be used to cross over; they should not be held on to once you have arrived. You should let go of even the most profound insight on the most wholesome teaching; the more-so, unwholesome teachings."

The lesson the Buddha offers here is that life will become easier and simpler as you disentangle yourself from old comfort zones and paradigms. Their weight, like a raft, can be lifted from your shoulders. You can disengage yourself from old thoughts and fears by seeing they are no longer useful. That is the purpose of this chapter, to free yourself from useless weight by discerning outmoded perceptions and beliefs. Doing so increases your power and speed.

Observing the Structure of Your Mind

As you wrote about scarcity in the previous chapter, themes

occurred throughout your answers. You may have discovered thoughts and feelings that repeated themselves and formed patterns. These patterns are called "structures of knowing." This is how they are formed:

Your mind makes sense of the stimulation that confronts it by forming mental models, or paradigms, of reality. This process helps the mind sort out incoming, sometimes unintelligible, information. The patterns your mind creates give you the experience of "understanding" your world.

We have structures of knowing about every aspect of our lives, including money. These structures include thoughts, feelings, beliefs, body sensations, attitudes, points of view and associations with the past and future.

Structures of knowing operate in your everyday decisions. Let us begin to unravel the nature of these structures, using your relationship with happiness.

Exercise: Your Happiness Structure of Knowing

What You Will Need
You will need your notebook and a pen or pencil.

Time For This Exercise
Take at least twenty minutes for this exercise. You may divide it into two ten minute sessions if necessary.

The Exercise
Step One: In your notebook, write the word "happiness" at the top of an empty page. Now begin to write down everything you think about happiness. Let all your thoughts and feelings about happiness pour out on the page. Jot down any body sensations you feel while writing. Is there a lump in your throat? Warmth in your heart? Feel tense in your neck or back? Is there a smile on your face? Remember those moments when you were most happy. Who was there? What were you doing? Do this for at least ten uninterrupted minutes. Fill as many pages as necessary.

Step Two: Look over what you have written. What might, at first, seem random thoughts and feelings are part of a structure. This system contains what you know about happiness. You have memories about when you were happy. You might have written about other people who seem happy. What beliefs are reflected in your notes? Are they based upon decisions you made when you were young? Many people have reported beliefs such as:
* A day for myself is true happiness.
* A loving family is the source of a happy life.
* Good health, good food, and a good partner are ingredients for happiness.
* I'm generally a happy person.
  Were there a few downbeat thoughts?:
* I'm too busy to be happy right now. That will come later.
* If I could just make a little more money, I'd be happier.
* Going to work is not happiness.

Discussion
If possible, share the results of your writing with someone else. If you do this with a group, have everyone share what they wrote about happiness. It is usually a very interesting discussion. It reveals our judgments, assessments, emotions, body sensations, memories, predictions and decisions. What is your structure of knowing about happiness?

   Anna: I see that I have a lot to be happy about, and the real sources were everyday events. I expected them to be the big promotion or the new car.

Raul: I feel I've got to *earn* happiness. What's so funny is that none of my happy moments have anything to do with *earning*. It's kind of nice to see.

Theresa: I got sad writing about happiness! I don't really know what that means right now, but it sure was an eye-opener. I'd like to pursue that and shake it loose.

Mike: This is great! I see there's a lot for me to be happy about right now. To tell the truth, I was worried about doing this exercise. I'm surprised at what I found.

No need to analyze your responses. You could be thrilled and delighted, or surprised by nostalgia or concerns. You are practicing the ability to observe what is there. Reasons *why* you answered what you did are more of your structures of knowing!

Unexamined Structures of Knowing

You and I have structures of knowing about everything we experience. They are at conscious and unconscious levels. You could write a 200-page thesis on what you consciously know about happiness. There would still be times when unconscious memories or decisions guide your responses to new situations.

How structures of knowing work can be described in different ways. For example, you could picture it as a grid that sits over your face, like a fencing mask. The grid is between you and your world. It keeps certain information out and lets other information through.

Some structures of knowing work for us. In ancient times, we had to be on constant lookout for danger, undistracted by details that were not relevant. Your structures of knowing can still have value for you today. They allow you to learn. They can serve as stepping-stones, allowing you to move from one place to another. Or, as the Buddha shows, they can serve as rafts, taking you over dangerous waters and onto safer shores. What would your world be like if you were unable to form lasting structures of knowing? Not so much fun. All we need to do is observe a person with neurological impairment to see the disorientation that would be created.

As useful as these structures are, the challenge for you is to recognize when they have become limiting. Once you discern this, choices can be made in your best interest. Look at examples of the restrictions placed upon us by unexamined structures of knowing.

Blair: I've already gone to a financial planner. He didn't seem to know what he was doing. Look, I've tried it that way once. I just need to make my own financial decisions from now on. I know now that nobody really knows that much about investments. It's all a crap-shoot.

Karen: There are lots of jokes about it, but I *know* that you can't trust lawyers. My sister had trouble with her attorney when she was getting a divorce. So, why should I give mine all the reasons my landlord is suing me for damages? He doesn't need to know.

Where are these people off-track? In both cases, they decided on the basis of a single negative experience. As a result, they have unnecessarily narrowed their options. Are their current structures of knowing restricting, or empowering their ability to take authentic action? Obviously, it is time to dismantle them so they can move beyond. They can leave their rigidity behind.

People who are successful are willing to discern and expand, beyond their structures of knowing.

It is possible. The best signal that you are being limited is when your structure of knowing seems irrefutably correct. Monkey Mind says: "This *is* the reality of the situation. Don't even question it!"

If Blair or Karen were to challenge their own thinking, they might come up with new and creative ideas. If not, they will get only reasons, facts and figures to justify their stand. It would be a poor trade, instead of a move in the right direction.

All structures of knowing have a developmental life-span. Each has a period of usefulness. Keep them past their time and you experience stagnation. Release them, and you create the future.

The following stories illustrate holding on too long:

Greg: I can't bring myself to throw things away. My garage is full of old books, papers, and exercise equipment. I've even rented storage space to hold more things. I mean, what if I need them some day? Even my rusted Volkswagen from college days is in my garage. My friends joke with me about it. They ask if I'm going to use it for a planter some day. I just remember what it was like when I was a starving student. I didn't own much then. I'd save everything. I'm still doing it.

Alicia: I've been going to Alanon for three years. It's been great. But, when I went to a therapist, he suggested to me that I look at my gambling. I was shocked. I told him that my gambling couldn't possibly be the problem in my marriage.

What does it take to dismantle a structure of knowing? The definition of dismantle is: to take the cover off. One person called it "removing the mask I've been hiding behind." Dismantling occurs when you look, see and tell the truth. A structure of knowing is like a fine old wristwatch. When it does not work, you take the cover off to see what is going on inside. You simply take a good look to discover what to exchange for a working part.

So, the first phase in dismantling a structure of knowing occurs when you step back and observe. The following questions will help you observe the content of your happiness paradigm:

*   Are there any patterns that limit my happiness options?
*   Do any outmoded thoughts or themes about what is necessary to be happy stand in my way?
*   What structures might I be willing to give up to find unexpected sources of happiness?

Notice your answers. They could be the beginning of a dismantling process. It takes flexibility, and sometimes courage, to dismantle what you have created. We have examples of heroes from everyday life who take apart what they have built so that progress can be made. Ytzach Rabin, for example, was a warrior who gained territory for Israel in 1967. In 1995, he realized it would have to be returned to have a chance for peace.

It is time to dismantle and expand beyond your present structures when:

1. Your reluctance and fear block the desire to follow your hero's path.

Phoebe: I don't know how to balance my checkbook to the penny. I have never done it, and I can't do it now. I don't care what effect it has on my future wealth. There must be some way around this.

2. You use the structure of knowing as an excuse for not keeping your promises.

Terry: I'm a busy man. I don't have time to train for that 10K run. I know I promised to raise money and do the run, but I'm just swamped. Maybe next year. Besides, I have a hard time asking people for money.

Mark: Yes, I've promised myself to do something creative. But, given my money situation, taking an art class right now would be totally irresponsible of me. Besides, I know I don't have any talent for it.

3. You use the structure to keep open old upsets.

Ed: Me, talk to my brother about the loan? What would I say? We haven't spoken since I missed my payment. He's

> "It was as if I had worked for years on the wrong side of a tapestry, learning accurately all its lines and figures, yet always missing its color and sheen."
>
> *Anna Louise Strong*

probably really angry.

4. The same thing goes wrong, over and over again.

Maureen: Borrow my lawn mower if you want. But, it may not start. It's sort of hit and miss. You can try kicking it. That may work. It's been that way for years. I'll get it fixed one of these days.

5. Circumstances have become predictable in a stifling way:

Bob: I know this financial seminar is going to be like all the rest: I'll get excited, but I won't end up doing anything with the information.

Doris: I'm always broke after Christmas. But, hey, I don't want to be stingy with my family and friends. This is just one of life's trials and tribulations. If I made more money, it wouldn't be so bad.

6. There is no joy or satisfaction in everyday events:

Ellen: Just another birthday party for my daughter! I'm really too tired for all of this. Kids, cake, ice-cream, presents: it's always the same. At least it's only for two hours.

7. The future just looks like more of the past:

John: I can't even think of taking a trip to Hawaii for at least two years, given the way business is going now. Yes, I know I've been saying that for at least three years already. But it's true!

Regina: I've got too much to worry about right now. When my life calms down, *then* I'll consider if I really want to go back to school. And I can't see things clearing up for at least a year.

> "Experience is not what happens to a man. It is what a man does with what happens to him."
>
> *Aldous Huxley*

Look carefully at what these people are saying. The part of the structure of knowing that *really* trips them up is often the parenthetical statement at the end. For Terry, it is: "I have a hard time asking people for money." For Mark, it is: "I don't have any talent for it." That is his main showstopper. What are the tripping-points for the rest of them? Go back and re-read them. See if you can spot what stops them.

Taking a structure of knowing apart is sometimes difficult. This is true even when staying in the same place is uncomfortable, because it is a way to organize your experience. It helps make sense of your world. In fact, the older you get, the more complex, finely-tuned, and rigid your structures of knowing can become. You simply develop more sophisticated evidence to support your view of the world!

As you begin to observe and examine old structures of knowing, you will notice Monkey Mind becomes loud and demanding. It insists that your thoughts, feelings and evidence are correct. It may even screech in your ear: "Turn back, turn back! You're sure to get in trouble." You may become convinced that it is a matter of survival to keep things the way they have always been.

One goal of being a human is to create, learn from, and then dismantle structures of knowing at increasingly complex levels. This is what we call growth.

Let us turn now to your structure of knowing about money. This exercise is similar to the happiness exercise. However, here we go more deeply to observe and dismantle what no longer works for you.

Exercise: The Money Structure of Knowing

This exercise is designed to clarify your structure of knowing about money. Remember, conscious observation is the key to going beyond your current structure of knowing. To continue your journey, where you stand now must become clear.

What You Will Need

Get several poster-size pieces of paper. Find some colorful felt-tipped markers or pens and a smooth surface upon which to work. As in the earlier exercise, do this in a place where you can concentrate.

Time For This Exercise

Give yourself forty minutes for this process. Or, break your sessions into no less than twenty minutes each.

The Exercise

Take one of the pieces of paper and lay it on a flat surface. Imagine that this paper forms the edges of a large box or structure. You are about to reveal your structure of knowing about money. You will use an adaptation of the mind-mapping technique that Gabrielle Lusser Rico describes in her book *Writing the Natural Way*.

Put the word "money" in the middle of the box. Now, using one consistent color throughout, start writing down your associations with this word. Do this by drawing lines moving outward from the word "money." An association is any word or phrase that pops into your mind when you think of money.

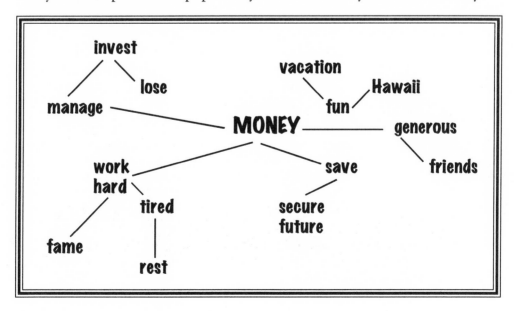

You might find that these words also have associations or connections with other words. Write those down as well, allowing one idea to flow freely into the next. When you run out of associations, return to your base word, money. See if anything else comes up. Do this quickly. This is no time for analyzing or editing. If you run dry, see if the following phrases stimulate any more material:

1. What it will take for me to have all the money I want

2. What I know I am right about, regarding money

3. Why I want money

4. What I must give up to have money

5. What I think and feel about others who have lots of money

6. How having more money will change my life or the lives of loved ones

7. What I can do with more money that I cannot do now

You may recall poems or sayings about money. Books or movie titles may come to mind, quotes from the Bible or a literary source. Put them on this structure of knowing map. Attach them to any item that seems appropriate.

When you are finished, it should look like a big web or net. There will be some associations clustered with lots of descriptive language. Others will stand alone.

Get out the other felt-tipped colored pens. Select another color. You are going to observe your structure of knowing more closely. Look throughout this network of words. Using one new color, circle words that get repeated or are similar in tone or mood. For instance, are there some that point to how hard it is to make a good living? Are there themes of excitement or pleasure? Use a different color for each theme. Do other kinds of energy, such as love, health, creativity, self-expression and spiritual well-being get mentioned? If not, could they easily be substituted for the word "money" in the middle of the page?

Discussion

This picture, with all of its associations and colors, is a graphic illustration of your current structure of knowing about money. It is your personal model of how money operates in your life and the way you see it in the world. You could list many more associations if you had more time. However, the work you have done here is sufficient to give you a handle on what money means to you. This structure affects you every time you read an article on money, go to an investment course, or listen to a lecture on prosperity. It serves as a grid as you try to make authentic choices about your goals and dreams.

Place this map, with all your work on it, where you can see it for at least three days. This is part of the observation process. If a few more associations occur to you during this time, add them. If you see more themes, circle them with a colored pen. Show this structure of knowing to a friend or someone else who knows you well. Talk with them about it as you point out the patterns. This will also aid in your ability to observe the way your mind has designed your relationship with money.

Note what you discover. Try standing back at least ten feet from this map. Does this shift your experience of the structure of knowing? Does there seem to be a lot of energy coming from your creation? Notice if the energy dissipates as you look at the structure over a period of three days. Write down what you notice. Place a red dot next to any items that continue to make you feel uncomfortable or anxious. We will use these items later as we continue the dismantling process.

Paradox Regained

To move beyond your structure of knowing about money requires confronting two phenomena: paradox and confusion. Two stone dogs guard the doors to many Buddhist temples. They represent paradox and confusion. This is done to illustrate that paradox and confusion are the sentinels we must pass through to gain enlightenment.

A paradox is a statement or thought that is self-canceling. Greek philosophers were fond of paradox. That is because it has an unusual effect upon the mind. It forces the mind into a logical gridlock. In this state, something outside the logical system, or structure of knowing, has the chance to appear. A typical paradox would begin with a simple statement like this:

My name is Maria. I live in Sacramento, California. Everyone who lives in Sacramento is a liar.

Now, here is the paradox: am I lying about this, or am I telling the truth? How would you know? Wrap your mind around that for a few moments. Gridlock? You bet!

Zen Buddhist koans produce a similar effect. These are teaching phrases, designed to produce a state of mind conducive to enlightenment. Remember the famous question: "What is the sound of one hand clapping?" There *is* an answer, but it lies outside the logical structure that created the question.

Confusion is a state in which, for the moment, nothing is clear. Discomfort often accompanies this condition. That is because Monkey Mind insists upon clarity. Even if it needs to manufacture that clarity out of incorrect "facts." When circumstances are cloudy or unclear, Monkey Mind does not know what to do. It feels that its survival is at stake. That is one reason we are often driven to have our questions answered in life. Hanging out with a question is hard. We feel unfinished or incomplete with the issue. Nothing is distinct.

The poet, Rainer Maria Rilke, wrote a lucid statement on the importance of questions in his book, *Letters to a Young Poet*:

"Have patience with everything unresolved in your heart and try to love the questions themselves as if they were locked rooms or books written in a foreign language. Do not search for the answers, which could not be given to you now, because you would not be able to live with them. And the point is, to live everything. *Live* the questions now. Perhaps then, someday far in the future, you will gradually, without even noticing it, live your way into the answer."

Some work you do here will cause questions to arise. For example, later you will engage in a process that further dismantles your structure of knowing about money. At first, you may not see how the things I ask you to do will accomplish this. You may have questions or feel confusion during the process. Allow yourself to stay with your confusion. Develop your ability to experience paradox and confusion. It will give you breathing room to get beyond the thoughts and feelings that have gotten you this far. Some of them cannot take you farther on your hero's journey. They may need to be left behind.

In observing heroes on their journeys over the past years I have learned that:

Successful heroes develop the capacity to encounter paradox and confusion. They do not jump to premature conclusions. They allow the amorphous space, the gap ... to be there ... and do not try to put something in its place. In this space, they can journey beyond what they currently know.

A Shift in the Space

So, what if you found that your mind chatter will never go away?! What if you found that 90 percent of what you think is, after all, not in the least relevant to your circumstances? What if you discover it is just a mental burp?!

One paradox in life seems to be that the harder you try to make your doubts and worries go away, the longer they stay around. I once heard an interview with the brilliant teacher Ram Dass. He was asked how life was different for him now that he had changed his name from Richard Alpert and had decided to follow a path of enlightenment. His answer warmed my heart. He said that he still had difficult or upsetting thoughts. They just didn't stay around as long, but came and went.

So, if thoughts and feelings will always come up, what happens when you dismantle your structure of knowing? The answer is that your *relationship* with these mental productions shifts. They are there, but they do not compel you to do anything to make them go away. Instead, they can be used as wake-up calls on your hero's journey. You see that these experiences are *your personal interpretation* of the situations in your life. You become curious about your experiences, no matter whether they are joyful, painful, hard, or happy.

Want to prepare to open some breathing room in your relationship with money? Let us take on your fears, worries, dread, doubts, and a host of difficult thoughts about the role of money in your life. Everyone has them. It is the nature of our relationship with energy and the scarcity that it evokes.

When you dismantle your structure of knowing about money, these experiences may not go away. Instead, you will be uncovering the structure that has held them in place. Then you can expand beyond that structure to encompass more experiences.

The following diagram illustrates what I mean:

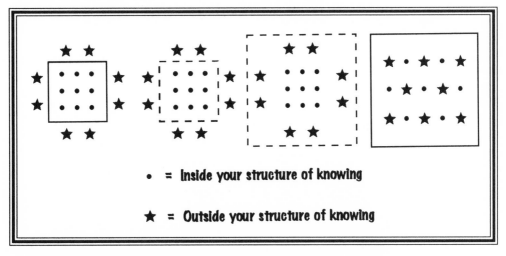

The following diagram illustrates what I mean:

• = Inside your structure of knowing

★ = Outside your structure of knowing

As indicated earlier, one goal of being human is to wake up as we travel the hero's path. This expanded awareness gives us more options. We are not tied to the same patterns and compelled to repeat them. We more fully integrate our life's experiences.

Be sure to discuss with a friend what you discovered by doing this process. Hearing yourself talk about what you discovered is important. It will also help to refine your observations further.

Have you learned something about yourself from this experience? If so, what is it? If not, are you willing to be with the question for a day? Remember what you read about confusion and paradox? Are you willing to learn something from this? When you begin a process, you sometimes do not get the answers you expect. Look at it this way: if you got the answers you expected, they would still lie within your structure of knowing.

Exercise: Dismantling Through Authentic Action

There is a way to shift your relationship with your money structure of knowing. It consists of deliberately doing something that runs counter to how you know you usually operate. Your mind chatter may get loud even contemplating the actions below. But, if you are willing, proceed. Do not wait for Monkey Mind to stop.

What You Will Need
Take your notebook with you to jot down what you discover.

Time For This Exercise
As you will see, this varies depending upon what you choose to do.

The Exercise
Choose one or more of the following actions. Take them within the next seventy-two hours.

1. For three days, resolve to pay for everything you buy with cash. Do not select those days when you pay your monthly bills. Is there a shift in your experience of money? What is it? Do any new thoughts or feelings arise?

2. Put all your credit cards (including gasoline cards) in a place where you cannot easily get to them for one week. What do you experience as you think about doing this? Is Monkey Mind chattering? Are your teeth chattering? Do it anyway and write about what you find.

3. If you drive through a toll booth, pay for the person in the car behind you. Do this three times. What thoughts or feelings arise from this act?

4. The next three times you go grocery shopping, put 10% of what you spend into the charity box that is usually at the checkout counter. Write about your reactions to doing this.

5. Tell someone you know and trust how much money you make each month. Make sure it is someone who does not already know. This need not be someone with whom you work. The norms in your organization may prohibit this sort of disclosure. Whoever you talk to, tell them you are doing this as an experiment. What do you experience?

These are not trivial acts. They are designed to help you pass the boundaries of what you know about money in your life. Write your reactions in your notebook. You are increasing your ability to observe how your relationship with money is wired up.

Discussion

A paradox occurs when you consciously observe your experience. Whatever you look, see and tell the truth about begins to lose its emotional charge. This is what clearing away your thoughts, beliefs and ideas means. David Cooper alludes to this in his book, *Silence, Simplicity and Solitude: A Guide for Spiritual Retreat*. He talks about the beginner's mind. This is a mind unfettered by old, worn-out structures of knowing:

"Most people think of enlightenment as a kind of magical attainment, a state of being close to perfection ... but for most of us, enlightenment is much more in line with what Suzuki Roshi describes. It means having a quality of being, a fresh, simple unsophisticated view of things."

To approach our lives with beginner's mind is a major breakthrough in how we experience our relationship with the world around us, and this certainly includes our relationship with money. In this respect, we are working toward a certain level of enlightenment. We are clearing away the thoughts, beliefs and ideas that cloud our ability to see things as they really are.

The Journey Continues

You are preparing yourself for miracles that transcend the predictability of your money life up to now. Know that many people have traveled this road. You have been observing the dark side of your relationship with money. The next chapter reveals more behind-the-scenes knowledge of how Monkey Mind preserves the *status quo*. You will also begin to look at a decision you made about life many years ago, called your Basic Assumption. It is a prime factor affecting how you view yourself, your goals, and your dreams. Keep going!

Summary

✐   Telling the truth about where scarcity troubles you is powerful and enlivening. Having seen the truth, you can identify what you genuinely want in life, separating it from what you thought you *must* have.

✐   We have structures of knowing about every aspect of our lives, including money. These structures include thoughts, feelings, beliefs, body sensations, attitudes, points of view and associations with the past and future.

✐   People who are successful are willing to discern and expand beyond their structures of knowing.

✐   All structures of knowing have a developmental life span. Each has a limited period of usefulness. Keep them past their time, and you experience stagnation. Release them, and you create the future.

✐   One goal of being human is to create, learn from, and then dismantle structures of knowing at increasingly complex levels. This is what we call growth.

✐   Successful heroes develop the capacity to encounter paradox and confusion. They do not jump to premature conclusions. They allow the amorphous space ... the gap ... to be there, and do not try to put something in its place. In this space, they can journey beyond what you currently know.

✐   When you dismantle your structure of knowing about money, these experiences may not go away. Instead, you will be uncovering the structure that has held them in place. Then, you can expand beyond that structure to encompass more experiences.

CHAPTER EIGHT:
The Border Patrol -- Monkey Mind and Your Basic Assumption

The Border Patrol -- Monkey Mind and Your Basic Assumption

"Whoever you are, some night step outside the house which you know so well ... enormous space is near."

Rilke

Why do poets find it so useful to remind us to step outside the confines of what we know? Why, instead of springing to the opportunity, do we slow our pace to the door leading to that enormous space? If we knew, would we use this awareness to ease our hero's journey? Yes. A thousand times, yes! The purpose of this chapter is to cultivate your ability to get what you want with ease.

Where do you start? You visit the *loyal opposition:* Monkey Mind and your Basic Assumption. These border guards jump into action every time you venture forth to explore possibilities beyond the safety of what is familiar to you. In this chapter, you will learn to identify the signs of Monkey Mind, so as to be aware of their presence. You will take a deep look at the concept of Basic Assumption. It is a decision you made about the world, based on your earliest experiences of life. The Basic Assumption surfaces whenever you are about to do something new, different, or innovative. It defines and patrols the border between what you know and are familiar with, and the unknown and unfamiliar. Here you will learn to use it as a validation of your courage, instead of as an interpreter of reality.

You will examine what "the border" means. You will look at two examples of the border. The first is the one between metaphysical and physical reality. If you recall from Chapter 1, you looked at the challenges that arise as you go from the metaphysical into the physical. The energy requirements shift. Your intention excites you, so you begin to manifest it through a goal. Immediately the energy demand increases. Monkey Mind starts chattering away with warnings to turn back. Now you have two things to deal with: your goal, and the thoughts that are getting stirred up by Monkey Mind.

Another border occurs between your structure of knowing and the possibilities that exist beyond it. On one side of the border everything is predictable. On the other side -- open space. You can access that open space by dismantling a structure. Every time you do, the borders become more permeable, providing more comfortable routes through them. This opens new vistas. Having open borders is the essence of Beginner's Mind. Of course, Monkey Mind is always in there, chattering away, trying to intervene to protect the status quo. In this chapter, you will learn how to handle that "border protection" chatter.

Think of these borders as similar to the membranes you penetrated at birth. In a sense, each time you go outside these boundaries, you are giving birth to a different aspect of yourself. People who accomplish their heart's desires often report this perception of being "reborn." We see this more clearly in a later chapter when we discuss how your goals in life shape your way of being.

Success and the Easy Life

One theme throughout this book is that successful people do what they say they will do. Not only that, they do it with ease. What do we mean by ease? We first look at what it is *not*. The opposite of ease is stress, aggravation, irritation, and struggle. A struggle is a battle. You struggle when exerting force against your thoughts. Struggles arise when you act by what Monkey Mind says, rather than out of your intentions.

Let us first look at what happens when you deliberately go against your thoughts, that is, defy Monkey Mind's warnings. As you have learned, your task as a hero is to recognize, observe and dismantle the structures that hold your thoughts in place. Was there any mention of getting rid of those thoughts? Of suppressing, or working against them in anyway? No. Remember the exercise where you tried not to think about a hot-fudge sundae. What happened? It was impossible to *not think* of it.

Your thoughts and feelings are like the waters of a river. Sometimes they flow in turbulent rapids. Sometimes they rest in quiet eddies and lie in tranquil pools. They are always there. If you try to dam them up to cross the river, they collect and spill over with ever greater force.

People who are successful do not spend energy trying to change the course of the waters in the rivers of their minds. Instead, they observe them and learn how best to navigate them.

My friend, Ellie, a white-water river raft guide, once told me that she has the most fun when she is conscious of the river's mood and flow. During those moments she steers her raft in a way that is exciting, creative and yet safe. She feels alive and awake. She uses lots of physical energy. Even in challenging moments along the way, she performs with ease if her actions are appropriate to the river's flow. She does not battle the boulders, wishing the currents would change.

"Do not push the river!" is a saying that must have derived from a similar kind of experience. It represents a great deal of wisdom about authentic action. It speaks of using the energy of the river to your own advantage. No need to fight it or deny it exists. Does it seem incongruous: working hard with ease? The following example may help to clarify this.

Paul: I learned a valuable lesson last month. Five months ago, I agreed to climb Mount Shasta with some friends. I planned to train for it, since it's a difficult climb. Well, I didn't train. I remember thinking: "I don't have the time. It's only a one-day hike. How difficult could it be?"

To my credit, I did walk a few miles each week, but it wasn't enough. Comes the day of the hike. I set out with everyone else. One hour into it, my heart is pounding in my ears. I tell myself: "Keep going. Everyone else is." I'm having a terrible time. My buddy, Mike, is hiking next to me. He looks great. Sure, he's sweating, but he's enjoying himself! He trained for this. One hour later I have to stop. I feel lousy. Talk about a struggle! I'm out of commission. I had to hike back down and wait for the others. They got in that evening. Tired, but happy. Me? I'm sore and exhausted, hitting myself over the head with thoughts like: "You jerk. Can't you do anything right?" I've had enough of doing things that way.

In this story Paul struggles in several ways: on the trail with the inner voice that prods him past his endurance; back at camp when he makes himself wrong; before the hike when he tells himself, "I don't have time for this."

To work with ease, allow spaciousness in your heart for everything that is going on in your head. Continue down your path anyway. You can do this best when you learn to observe what actually is going on in your head.

Symptoms of the Monkey Mind in Action

The following is a checklist of symptoms that show when you are under the sway of Monkey Mind. The following list includes examples of thoughts and conversations we all have. They distract us from really looking, seeing, telling the truth and taking authentic action. Identify the different ways your inner chatter distracts you. This will present you with the opportunity to catch yourself engaging with Monkey Mind. Then you can consciously redirect your attention to taking authentic action. This is especially useful when you are struggling.

Sometimes all it takes to wrest yourself from the grip of Monkey Mind is to tell the truth when you are acting or thinking foolishly. This takes courage and a big heart. As a hero, you have those qualities; all you need to do is reach inside yourself and draw them out.

Your Monkey Mind is particularly robust where your relationship with money is concerned. It stands at the edge of your structures of knowing, urging you to halt and retrace your steps. Going outside your usual structures of knowing about money creates loud mind chatter.

On the right are the symptoms of Monkey Mind. We couch them in terms of money here. They apply to all aspects of life.

The essential quality of a Monkey Mind experience is your sense of dis-ease, that is, a lack of ease. You feel locked into place, adamant, as though it were a matter of survival to maintain your position. Your body is tense and poised for an attack. Or you feel mired in a swamp.

Can you become aware of how much of your life is run by Monkey Mind? Yes. The next exercise will give a good look at the answer. As a result, you may learn to catch yourself dancing with Monkey Mind. The key here is to discern the times you are *not* acting or thinking according to who you really are in your heart. Bringing your Standards of Integrity and life's intentions with you is valuable as you do this exercise. Looking at them will bring you back to yourself.

Monkey Mind Checklist
SYMPTOM: Example

1. BEING VAGUE: I'll balance my checkbook sometime soon.

2. DEALING WITH THE PAST AND FUTURE AS IF IT IS THE PRESENT: Income tax time has always been, and will always be an ordeal for me.

3. DEFENSIVENESS: I am *not* being defensive about my credit card expenses!

4. TAKING THINGS PERSONALLY: Look, are you questioning my professional judgment here?

5. RESIGNATION: It doesn't make a bit of difference whether I plan for this vacation or not. I'll never go. I'm too busy. I don't have the money.

6. QUALIFYING STATEMENTS: Well, I'll *try* … and *if* it works out, we can *probably* take the next step to develop a budget.

7. EXCUSES: I'm late because I overslept and then I ran out of gas.

8. EITHER/OR THINKING: Either I get to keep my credit card or I'm not going to feel secure.

9. PARANOIA: Nobody listens to me. They think I don't have anything valuable to say.

10. FRAGMENTATION: Part of me likes this book and part of me doesn't like it at all.

11. MAKING COMPARISONS: Why does it seem like no one has as hard a time as I do with their taxes?"

12. RATIONALIZING: I'll accept this money under the table just this once. After all, doesn't *everybody* do it?

13. JUSTIFICATION: I deserve that expensive meal. I've been working hard all week.

14. DEFLECTION: I know I spent a lot of money. But, hey, I didn't spend it all. I still have checks left!

15. BEING A MARTYR: No one really knows how hard I work.

16. PETULANCE: Being cantankerous, cross, or grouchy, as in: If I want your advice, I'll ask for it. Until then, just leave me alone!

17. IMPULSIVENESS: I want what I want *right now.*

Exercise: Dancing with Monkey Mind

What You Will Need

Have a small spiral note pad to carry around with you and jot down the observations you will be making over the next few days. Have the Monkey Mind Checklist so you can identify the symptom.

Time For This Exercise

Record your observations for two or three days. This gives you sufficient data from which to draw conclusions.

The Exercise

Jot down at least three times you engage in Monkey Mind thinking each day. Do it the moment you notice the symptom. What was the symptom? Did you say it aloud? Did it appear instead as an internal dialogue? If you find you forget to keep records, have compassion for yourself. You are removing a mask from the face of a style of thinking you have used for years. Then, go back to it. If you remember any conversations, note them. If not, go on to the next instance. Make your notations brief. It may look like:

* **Monday, 10:15 a.m.** Comparison. Bob doesn't look worried about our presentation. I sure am. What's wrong with me? (Spoken to self)
* **Monday, 12:45 p.m.** Being vague. I'll get this budget done sometime next week. (Spoken to supervisor)
* **Monday, 4:30 p.m.** Defensive. I am not always too busy to talk with you! I've just had a hectic day, that's all! (Spoken to wife)

Discussion

Examine what you wrote during the last two or three days. If you have even a few notations, commend yourself! This is rigorous work. Now, let us look at what those notes say. Let the next questions guide your observations. It is best if you can share what you see with someone with whom you feel comfortable.

1. Were most of these thoughts internal, or did I voice them?
2. What are the themes here? Is there a medley of my favorite Monkey Mind conversations?
3. How does my body feel when I am gripped by each of these symptoms? Am I tense? Do I have a sinking feeling? Do I tighten my stomach? Do I clench my jaw?
4. Was I able to catch any of the symptoms before they became full-blown? In other words, was I able to intervene early on? What was it like to do this?
5. Are there any special Monkey Mind conversations I have about money? If so, what are they? When did they arise?

There is Dancing ... And Then There is Dancing

Monkey Mind is the reactive aspect of your mind. The Tibetan Buddhists call it *sem*. As Sogyal Rinpoche points out is his book: *The Tibetan Book of Living and Dying*, *sem* is always influenced by outward circumstances. It is like a candle flickering in an open doorway. It moves this way and that with every puff of air that passes by. Plotting, scheming, gathering evidence for its decisions, Monkey Mind is in perpetual motion. From this we may draw the following conclusion.

Monkey mind is an incessant chatterbox. It is not going to go away! This is both good news and bad.

The bad news is that Monkey Mind is with you for life. The good news is you can now relax. You don't need to waste any energy trying to change the way Monkey Mind works. Trying to alter what your mind says forces you to dance with it, keep to its rhythm. Your attention and energy can be free to focus upon possibilities that surround you. You cannot do both at once.

You can devote your energy to changing Monkey Mind, or you can take that energy and infuse your dreams. You can either dance with your Monkey Mind, or dance with your goals and dreams. Pick one.

As we will see, time and again, in this book, ease and enlightenment may be nothing more than a simple shift of attention. This is both a gentle and subtle act. No change is necessary in your ceaseless inner dialogue. In fact, you take it with you on your hero's journey. No need to wait for it to go away before you go for your dreams. You might just place Monkey Mind in a basket, held under one arm, as you go on. Your attention can remain focused outward instead of inward. Anyway, when we are worried, it is often too dark inside. We use a little joke in the course to remind us of this. Groucho Marx once said, "Outside of a dog, a book is man's best friend. Inside of a dog, it's too dark to read!" Keep your eye on the light of possibilities. The darkness is just a shadow.

Peace with Honor

The way to peacefully coexist with Monkey Mind is to leave it alone. Just let it be. Writing about the solution to the tyranny of Monkey Mind, Sogyal Rinpoche offers guidance: "Just as a pool of water becomes clear when the mud is not stirred up, so the mind settles when you just let it be without trying to mess with it." A simple exercise used in biofeedback is wonderful to practice this "hands off" approach.

Exercise: Centering in Here and Now

What You Will Need

Nothing except a quiet place to sit. You may settle on the floor or in a chair.

Time For This Exercise

Start with ten minutes. Increase to twenty when you are comfortable with this technique. Do this once a day for one week. If possible, pick the same time each day so you get a routine going.

The Exercise

This method asks you to focus upon your breath. Sit in a comfortable, yet upright, position. Rest your hands, palms down, upon your thighs. Close your eyes. Breathe in, allowing the air to fill your lungs gently. Keep your tummy soft. A soft tummy gives Monkey Mind less to hold onto. Remember to fill even your upper lungs with air. Breath out, feeling the breath as it leaves your nostrils. Pause at the end of the breath for a moment before you breathe in again. Be like a wave that waits a moment after it breaks upon the shore before returning to the sea. Do this throughout the exercise. Feel and observe your breath as it moves in and out.

Your inner chatter will become noticeable. Periodically, the babble will get louder. Thoughts having nothing to do with the present will float through your mind. Each time this happens, let them pass. Everyone reports that they find themselves following thoughts unconsciously. When this happens to you, just release that thought and create emptiness again. When the time is up, you have a sense of the constant noise that underlies daily life. Sometimes we think this noise really means something. You have had a chance to see how it changes from moment to moment, not based on anything in particular. It could be hard to be attentive to life if you thought that chatter meant something.

Discussion

Almost universally, people are amazed at how much unbidden, unrelated, even contradictory conversation goes on in their minds. What did you see? Are you beginning to grasp the nature of Monkey Mind? Share your discoveries with someone. If you do this exercise in a group, have each person contribute one observation. The goal of this exercise is not to eradicate the inner dialogue, but to observe it.

After doing this for one week, you may notice a heightened awareness of times when Monkey Mind is present. When you see and tell the truth about the symptoms you exhibit, they no longer have a hold on you. You have dismantled them. Until next time, that is! But at least you increase the amount of time in which you experience who you really are under the reactive chatter. Other people see more of your authentic self as well. Observing your mental process, and letting it pass increases your power to peacefully coexist with Monkey Mind. This power will serve you well on the hero's journey toward your goals and dreams.

If you have any final doubts about whether Monkey Mind is *you*, ask yourself this question, as we sometimes do in the *You and Money* course: If the Monkey Mind conversations are you, who is the one listening, or hearing them? Who you are is much greater than Monkey Mind, and therein lies your power.

A Word of Caution

Some people have discovered that one way of dealing with Monkey Mind is to infuse it with an intense perception of danger. After an initial burst of chatter, Monkey Mind gets quiet and focuses intently on the task of keeping alive. It has no time for anything else. Many who mountain-climb and hang-glide report this experience:

Armand: When I climb, it's just me and the rock. Very simple. No thoughts. I put my hand where it fits and lift myself up one more foot. Then it's on to the next crack or foothold.

There are two aspects of Armand's experience: an exhilarating climb and a quiet mind. Armand was a master climber. He recognized that this method for warding off the internal dialogue can be habit-forming. He had known others who tried to recapture the mind-bending experience again by increasing the fear quotient. Many had met with accidents. He was always vigilant about taking unnecessary chances while climbing but aware of the temptation:

Armand: It's part of my discipline to keep within safe limits. I remember reading an article on hang-gliding which said that most master gliders are no longer alive. They kept pushing the edge until it was just too much. I saw that could happen to me in climbing.

Take a moment and look at your own life. The above talks about the extremes of creating danger to overpower Monkey Mind. Are there times where you create emergencies, real or imaginary, to give your mind something upon which to focus?

Janette: I admit it. Crises do calm me down. It sounds crazy! When there's an emergency I feel focused. I get in a problem-solving mode. During those moments everything else in my mind goes away. It's like when the copier broke at work yesterday. We had a report to get out by 5:00 p.m. My administrative assistant and receptionist were panicked. Me? I'm calmly taking the thing apart to see what's wrong. So now I'm looking to see where I actually *create* crises in my life. One place is tax-time. I wait until the last possible moment to do them. I'm always there at the post office at 11:59 p.m. on April 15th. Tired. Exhausted. But calm.

A Fool for Enlightenment

One day I discovered something that has helped me for years. The price I paid for this was a few moments of humiliation. It was well worth every spiritual penny. This is what happened:

There I was in front of the first *You and Money* course I ever taught. The participants were to have brought in their homework on balancing their checkbooks to the penny. Most of them had not done the work.

"Until we can understand the assumptions in which we are drenched, we cannot know ourselves."

Adrienne Rich

My chest got tight, my arms heavy. It felt like I was about to sink through the floor. I started giving them a lecture about their lack of commitment and guts. I was a woman possessed. Not a pretty sight.

Stopping to take a breath, I noticed that the place was very quiet. My friend, Rita, stood at the door of the room. She motioned me to come outside. Excusing myself, I stepped out of doors with her. Our exchange went like this:

Rita: Okay, what's wrong? You sound so angry. You're being very rough on them.

Me: This is it! I'm not going on with this course. I can't lead it. It's just too much for me. If someone better led it, everyone would have done their homework. But not with me.

Rita: Sounds like you're having a fit. What's happening?

Me: I'm *not* having a fit. It's the truth! I can't lead this course.

Rita: What do you mean you can't?

Me: What do you *mean*, what do I mean? I just can't do it. I don't have what it takes to do a course on money. Or any course. I should have listened to myself when I began this. I knew I couldn't do it.

I stopped my fit long enough to look up at the window and see the group was waiting for me. Twenty noses were pressed comically against the glass. Twenty pairs of eyes peered out at me. It looked so funny I started to laugh. I felt like a fool!

Well, that laugh dismantled something. I remember saying to Rita how familiar the whole thing felt. Whenever I started something, my first reaction was that I could not possibly do it. I never felt up to the task, and it felt like I was sinking.

Making a long story short, my work with the Basic Assumption was born. Going back to the course, I apologized for my behavior. Everyone was relieved, including me. I talked about this sinking feeling and the "I can't" pattern that went along with it. It had been with me since I could remember.

Before *You and Money* I had led workshops with a friend, ValJon Ferris. We helped people uncover the early decisions that had shaped their options in life. Called *basic assumptions,* they are attempts to cope with early crises. They are decisions that inform our perceptions of how life works. We are driven to gather evidence to support them.

In my previous work with basic assumptions I had not encountered the fundamental, deep-in-the-cells experience like I did that day in the *You and Money* course. In that brief moment, I came face to face with the key Basic Assumptions in my life. We all carry these Basic Assumptions with us and they become the way we organize our views about ourselves, others, and the world. Nowhere do Basic Assumptions come up more potently than in our relationship with money.

> "Personal constructs are sets of conscious ideas about one's own abilities and character, the behavior other people expect of us in various situations, how others are likely to behave in response to us, what they mean by the things they say, and so on. They are important determinants of personality and behavior."
>
> *George Kelly*

I have assisted more than two thousand people to discover their Basic Assumption in subsequent *You and Money* courses. The process is intense and profound. We look at it now because it is useful for you to begin to uncover this fundamental limiting decision.

Getting a Bead on the Basic Assumption

We begin our inspection of the Basic Assumption by visiting a notion that has been around since the 1950's: the flight or fight response. The flight or fight response comes as a reaction to the perception of danger. As Herbert Benson, M.D., describes in his book, *The Relaxation Response,* our ability to survive was linked to the well-developed nature of our flight/fight response. The literature on stress is full of research on the harmful effects of being in situations where this response is evoked on a regular basis. Some researchers have noted a third response to emergencies, making it the flight/fight/freeze triad.

In my work with people, I have found there is one response that is strongest for each person. For some, it is the flight response. For others, fight or freeze gains ascendancy in an emergency. Do I know how a particular choice is made? No. We will probably find that genes predispose each of us to one of the three responses.

Your personal bias toward flight, fight or freeze shapes

your Basic Assumption. For example, my Basic Assumption is; I can't. It is a flight response. I do *not* like it. I would like a fight-type Basic Assumption. But here is what I have discovered:

Whatever your Basic Assumption is, it is the one you like the least.

You have a natural aversion to your own Basic Assumption. One reason for this is that it is the limit you personally have placed upon possibility. It is your private show stopper. It also reflects your inner ring, or who you are afraid you are. Recall the diagram from an earlier chapter:

Remember we said the outer ring reflects who you *pretend* to be. The inner circle is who you are *afraid* you are.

Another way to say this is that your inner ring points to what you worry the awful truth is about yourself.

Everyone with whom I have worked has a Basic Assumption. It never goes away. It usually stays the same over the years. However, when you see what it is, the Basic Assumption may lose power over you. It is like what Ram Dass said: The internal dialogue is still there. It just does not stay around as long. By seeing it, you pull the cover on your Basic Assumption.

The Source of Your Basic Assumption

How is your Basic Assumption formed? This is how it works. There you are as a toddler, minding your own business. Something happens that is a shock or a loss. Let's say, for example, you wake up in the middle of the night, scared by the dark. Your night light is off because the bulb burned out, leaving you alone and confused. On a pre-verbal level, your mind races to make sense of the circumstances. The body wants to fight, flee or freeze depending upon your bias.

A little later in life, Monkey Mind takes over and wraps some words and images around the experience. And then it forms a conclusion: "I'm not sure" (how to take care of myself, how to do anything about this) or "Life is hard" (I can never be safe, or count on anything) "I don't know" (what to do, how to save myself) "People are a _ _ holes" (Where is my mom when I need her, whose fault is this?)

This conclusion is a structure of knowing, and once set in place, it takes on a life of its own. Without being aware of it, you begin to gather evidence to prove it is correct. Or you gather evidence to prove the opposite -- that it is not true! That is where the first circle, who you pretend to be, comes in.

The opposite of my "I can't" Basic Assumption is: I can too! In my case, I say it with a defensive tone in my voice and a shrug of my left shoulder. When I am under its sway, I will do anything to prove to people that I am capable. Even super-capable! I will go to extremes to outdo myself. That was happening when I invested that $35,000 in exchange for an unsecured *promi-sorry* note. Friends cautioned me. I was out to prove they were wrong and that I could make a good financial deal without their opinions, thank you!

As you can see, the Basic Assumption creates a limited, or false, picture of who you are.

The task of the hero is to uncover this unauthentic aspect of self. You do this by questioning your conclusions about life. You also keep before you the reflec-

Example of a Basic Assumption Tree

Life is hard

People are a_ _- holes

I don't know

Something's wrong with me

I'm stupid

△ = Basic Asumption
○ = Tributary

tions of your authentic self: your Standards of Integrity and life's intentions. You compare this against your driven behavior. Who you are *not* soon becomes very clear.

It is unlikely that you will find your Basic Assumption by reading this book. Finding the Basic Assumption requires a process that is an intense and often profound experience for participants in the *You and Money* course. The process also requires the support of a specifically structured group. However, you could discover what I call the tributaries or offshoots of your Basic Assumption. By tributaries, I mean the decisions that come *after* your Basic Assumption. These are more available to your conscious thought.

Above is a structure that symbolizes how your Basic Assumption looks in relationship to its offshoots.

The Basic Assumption lies at the core of your decision tree. You are not conscious of it. This is because it is like the air you breathe. You are immersed in it. Furthermore, it does not show up as a decision, but as *the truth*. For example, when I am gripped by *I can't,* there is no way to convince me that this is simply a decision I made long ago as a child. No matter that it is not logical or coherent, it is just too real to me at the moment. It would be like telling someone who is convinced he is drowning that the water is a figment of his imagination. I can always find proof and justification for what I'm feeling.

Your Basic Assumption emerges every time you are about to do something new, different or unprecedented. An aspect of Monkey Mind, it activates and starts its over-cautious chatter. Not surprisingly, the Basic Assumption is there with you any time you approach the border between the meta-physical and physical reality.

Marlene: My Basic Assumption is: life is hard. Many years ago, before I discovered this, I remember signing up for a quilting class. Our first assignment was to get some cloth that was uniquely beautiful or meaningful in some way. We were each going to create our personal work of art. I had two weeks to gather the material. Five days before the class I got it in my head to go to a swap meet thirty miles away; I'd heard there was some old, beautifully patterned cloth for sale there. Sunday morning I woke up at 6:00 a.m. to get there on time. It's foggy. It's cold. But there I am, driving to this swap meet! The punch line was that they weren't open. It was the wrong weekend. But this was how I typically handled new situations: by making it harder on myself, and others, than was necessary.

As you leave the Basic Assumption for its tributaries, the decisions become more obvious to your conscious mind. In other words: you *hear* your tributaries in your head. By contrast, your Basic Assumption is a way of *being*. Trying to see your Basic Assumption is like taking your eyes out and turning them around to see the back of your head. For ex-ample, if you had asked Marlene if she thought life was hard as she was driving to the swap meet, she probably would have answered, "No. It's not that hard at all. Why do you ask?" She might have even turned the question around and directed it at you, perhaps implying that there was some-thing wrong with you for thinking about life that way.

The Basic Assumption expresses itself in many ways. First, your tone of voice shifts. Your posture may undergo some change. Your facial expression may alter. You may sense tense-ness in various parts of your body. Your heart may start pounding. These groups of symptoms occur time and again. They become like old familiar, if unwanted, company. Many people try to muscle their way through the Basic Assumption reaction. Others stop and wait for it to go away. Of course, they wait forever.

Your Basic Assumption and its offshoots shape the sorts of things your Monkey Mind tells you. When you recognize them, you do not have to be run by them.

Here are some examples of the decisions that form your Basic Assumption or its offshoots. I have cleaned up the language of the fight Basic Assumption. You will know what I am talking about anyway. I do not encourage the use of the fight language outside the course room. However, nothing seems to better capture the essential nature of the fight response as do those two harsh words. Many people have gotten lots of relief out of actually saying them instead of *being* them.

Flight Basic Assumptions:	Freeze Basic Assumptions:	Fight Basic Assumptions:
I'm dumb	I don't know	Leave me the f _ _ _ alone!
I can't	I'm not sure	People are a _ _ holes!
Something's wrong with me		F _ _ _ you. You can't make me!

Parents have told me they can tell when their children are making limiting decisions about life. They can do nothing to stop the process. It has a life of its own. This was made clear to me during a recent visit to a famous amusement park in Florida.

I was walking in front of a five-year-old girl and her father. She had a cartoon character hat on, was wearing an amusement park T-shirt, and was holding a balloon in her free hand. Obviously, her father had recently purchased all these items for her. She asked her dad as they walked along:

"Daddy, will you get me an ice cream?

"Not right now, honey. It's almost lunch time.

"Oh," she said. "You *never* get me anything I want!"

A spoiled child? A needy child? A budding *People are a _ _ holes*? Who knows for sure? Every child has his or her moments like this. All you do know is that your children are making a decision right then and there, no matter what you as a parent say or do! It is not going to do a bit of good for this little girl's dad to point out to her that he just got her at least three things she had asked for: a balloon, a T-shirt and a hat. She has made up her mind based on her most recent request, and that is that!

What comes next is an exercise you can repeat many times. As you do, you will flesh out the outer branches of your Basic Assumption decision tree. This alone will provide you breathing room to take bold steps toward your goals and dreams.

Exercise: Trials and Tributaries

What You Will Need
Your notebook and pen are all that you need.

Time For This Exercise
This exercise can be done in ten to fifteen-minute bites. You may want to do it a number of times over the course of the next few weeks, taking one or two questions each time. This will not interfere with any other work you do in the book. Doing this many times helps you map your responses, to see the patterns that develop. In this way, you are creating at least the outer limbs of your Basic Assumption tree.

The Exercise
Write your responses to the following questions in this format. Keep them short and to the point. Be absolutely candid.

This is no time for quasi-liberal or enlightened answers. As comedian Joan Rivers would say: "Can we talk?" In other words, tell yourself the truth; you might as well. You are the only one who is going to hear it, unless you actually choose to tell a friend. Note your body sensations and posture. If you are consistent in following the format, you will be able to see a pattern of responses emerging.

1. You have just inherited one million dollars. A relative asks for a fifty-thousand dollar, unsecured loan.
    a. What is your first thought? Be honest.
    b. What are your body sensations right now? Are you tense, tight, hot, or cold?

2. Think of a time when you failed to complete something you promised you would do. Be specific. Think of names, dates and places.
    a. What were your reasons for not keeping your promise? What happened?
    b. As you think of it now, whose fault was it that you failed to do it? Why? (Do not answer "mine" unless that is what really occurred to you to say.)
    c. Note your body sensations? What are they?

3. The past ten years has shown an upsurge in the number of personal bankruptcies filed.
    a. In your opinion, what causes someone to go bankrupt?
    b. What do you feel as you say this?
    c. Note your body sensations.

4. Think of a work or personal relationship where you know you are not operating within your Standards of Integrity.

  a. What has kept you from clearing this up?

  b. What do you feel as you say this?

  c. Note your body sensations.

5. You are about to stand up in front of a group of people you hardly know. You are going to tell them, to the penny, how much money you bring home each month.

  a. What thoughts come to your mind as you think of doing this?

  b. Do any emotions emerge?

  c. Note your body sensations.

6. You have been asked to give the year-end summary presentation to the president of your company. You have been given you two hours to prepare.

  a. What did you think as you read this? Note anything down, even if it seems unrelated.

  b. Why would you fail at this task?

  c. Note your body sensations.

7. You are being asked to compute your net worth.

  a. How hard would this be for you? Why?

  b. What feelings come up for you?

  c. Note your body sensations

8. You have just received a letter that your income taxes for the last two years will be audited.

  a. What do you think happened to cause this to occur?

  b. How will you handle the situation?

  c. Note your body sensations.

9. You are leaving a record store with some purchases. As you go through the security gate, the alarm sounds. A salesperson rushes toward you to stop you from leaving.

  a. What is your first thought? What would you do?

  b. What are your feelings as you think about this situation?

  c. Note your body sensations.

10. Name one dream you have had for some time which you have given up.

  a. What is it? Be specific.

  b. When did you give up on this dream? What were the circumstances?

  c. Note your body sensations.

Discussion

These questions are by no means easy to answer. They are designed to surface your tributaries. Were you able to arrive at some distinct phrases? List what they were. Make sure they are declarative. Statements like, "I think that few people are really trustworthy," or, "It seems to me that there are very few people in the world who are truly trustworthy" are not declarative. A declaration is precisely that: "You can't trust *anybody*!"

Did you find your answers to be fight, flight, freeze, or a combination of all three? While your Basic Assumption is one of those responses, your tributaries can be any of the three. Discuss what you have found with a friend. Are you willing to give them permission to tell you when they think you are doing a flight, fight or freeze response? This will give you great feedback. You may ask them to tell you what your facial expression looks like during those times.

Do the phrases seem familiar? Are there other times in your life when you have heard them in your head? What were you doing? What did you do next? Really take the time to explore any ways these statements have worked in your life.

Miracles Are Real

The next chapter will reeducate you about miracles. You will see how to make way for them and how to recognize them. The work you have done has set the stage for these new skills. You are clearing your path.

Summary

People who are successful do not spend energy trying to change the course of the waters in the rivers of their minds. Instead, they observe them and learn how best to navigate them.

When you work with ease, you allow spaciousness in your heart for everything that is going on in your head. You continue down your path anyway. You can do this best when you learn to observe what actually is going on in your mind.

Your Monkey Mind is particularly robust where your relationship with money is concerned. It stands at the edge of your structures of knowing, urging you to halt and retrace your steps. Going outside your usual structures of knowing about money creates loud mind chatter.

You can devote energy to changing Monkey Mind, or you can use that energy to infuse your dreams. You can either dance with your Monkey Mind or dance with your goals and dreams. Pick one.

Monkey Mind is an incessant chatterbox. It is not going to go away! This is both the bad news and the good news.

Whatever your Basic Assumption is, it is the one you like the least.

Your Basic Assumption and its offshoots shape the sorts of things your Monkey Mind tells you. When you recognize them, you do not have to be run by them.

CHAPTER NINE:
The Two "M"s: Money and Miracles

The Two "m"s: Money and Miracles

"Miracles rest not so much upon healing power coming suddenly near us from afar, but upon our perceptions being made finer, so that for the moment our eyes can see and our ears can hear, what has been there around us always."

Willa Cather

In this chapter you prepare to experience miracles in your relationship with money. With full respect to the religious definition, we are approaching this as Willa Cather did, on the secular level. We are coming to it from a particular point of view, which is:

Miracles are nothing more than ordinary events that lie outside your current structure(s) of knowing.

In a sense, miracles are commonplace. Their potential for occurring is around us always. They are only hidden from view by the way we think about the world.

Much of what you now consider to be commonplace once seemed like a miracle to you.

Your first breath was miraculous. Your first baby step was full of wonder for you and your parents. Do you remember the first time you were able to ride a bicycle? How about the day you first drove a car alone? What was it like to receive your first paycheck? Before experiencing these events you probably thought you knew what to expect. Were those expectations accurate? In retrospect, did you really have a clue how the experience would feel? Probably not, but when they did occur, these events were awesome and wonderful. They were miracles. Take a moment to note other miraculous events in your life that may now seem commonplace to you.

You can naturally use miracles to help yourself grow and develop. In Chapter 7, you saw that you can navigate through life by creating, using, and then dismantling structures of knowing. As a result of the dismantling, you become open to the miracles that lie outside. When you discern a miracle and interact with it, your structure of knowing expands to incorporate the event. (Remember the diagram on page 141?)

As you really experience the miracle, the foundation of your perceptions grows. The miracle then becomes integrated into your current structure of knowing. As a result, what once seemed miraculous loses its air of wonder and mystery. It takes on a quality of ordinariness. It becomes unremarkable or transparent and loses your attention. Then, it is on to the next miracle!

Jake: I remember first learning to drive. Finally, I got to drive a car alone. Was I excited! I turned on the ignition and saw my whole life as a traveler before me. For the first two weeks, I'd jump at any chance to drive. If Mom needed groceries or any errand done, I'd be there, eager to do it. After four weeks, the novelty started wearing off. One afternoon Mom asked me to run to the cleaners for her. I did it, but it seemed like a hassle. The thrill of driving on my own was wearing off. Now? I take driving for granted. It's just a means to an end. There's certainly no thrill as I start the car each morning for my commute to work.

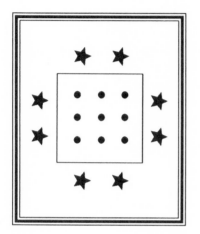

Can you remember how impossible some of your accomplishments once seemed? Having a peaceful and satisfying relationship with money is just as possible as any of those accomplishments. It is just a matter of being able to move beyond your current structures of knowing. How is this done? You clear away unfinished business that obstructs your journey. You will be learning to do so in this chapter.

The Miracles Surrounding You

Miracles begin to show up when you can fully recognize and benefit from them. As you mature, miracles may not be as evident as they were when you were very young. Your structures of knowing get denser; in the process they obscure the miraculous. The more you think you know about life, the less you are open for reality and its surprises. Having beginner's mind is, therefore, an advantage and you can enjoy its gifts at any age.

Living your life as a hero's journey molds you to be successful in attaining the miraculous. For example, in the story of the Holy Grail, Percival did not just meander up to the Grail and nab it. He prepared, making sure his own house, spiritually and otherwise, was in order. As a result of that order, he was able to recognize signs that guided his quest. Percival could withstand temptations that might have distracted him from his path. He thus succeeded where other knights of the Round Table had failed. He found the Grail and brought it to King Arthur.

Your journey to discover miracles in your relationship with money is much like Percival's search for the Grail. It is essential to put your own house in order regarding money. Thus unencumbered, you are free to easily and successfully attain your goals and dreams.

The distractions you encounter are often the products of Monkey Mind. In the last chapter, we looked at the nature of this Mind. It swings from worry to worry like a monkey leaping about from branch to branch in the jungle. It is never silent for more than a few moments.

As you venture toward the outer edges of your structure of knowing, Monkey Mind's chatter grows louder. If you are prepared, it does not distract you from your path.

Many of the world's greatest motion picture directors will say that days occur in a film's shooting when things seem to be going all wrong. Perhaps the weather is intensely hot or cold. The cast gets sick. The equipment breaks down. Permission to shoot at a specific location is suddenly denied. At these points Monkey Mind jumps into action. It yells: "If you had any sense, you would quit right now. Let's get out of here!" This is the decisive moment. Does the director stop, listen to the chatter, and stray from his or her course? The best of them move outside their structures of knowing, ignoring what Monkey Mind says it should look like. They continue to reach for their vision in spite of it all. They put themselves in the position to produce a miraculous result.

George Bernard Shaw wrote about the importance of operating outside customary reason. In *Man and Superman,* he said: "The reasonable man adapts himself to the conditions that surround him. The unreasonable man adapts the conditions to himself. All progress depends upon the unreasonable man."

By doing the work in previous chapters, you have seen how your structure of knowing about money has influenced your life. You have faced the fact that your inner chatter, composed of doubts, fears and worries may never go away. Now you are considering the idea that this chatter increases as you abandon the predictable, and pursue new horizons.

Conventional wisdom often suggests that we not move forward until Monkey Mind stops. Unfortunately, this way of thinking too often keeps us moving nowhere. By contrast, the hero knows that he or she can still succeed accompanied by the mind chatter.

Let us look again at how Monkey Mind can distract you. It can prevent you from going beyond the boundaries of your structure of knowing and into the realm of the miraculous.

Matt: We've just been asked to submit a bid for all the finished woodwork in a big new housing development. What a break! It looks like a sure thing, and means a lot of money for our shop. We'll have more work than we can handle for at least a year, maybe longer. I'll have to hire at least ten new experienced carpenters. We may need a new bookkeeping system and will need to hire another clerical person. Hmm, I don't know. It makes me nervous. It'll be a lot of work. Don't get me wrong. I want to go for the contract. I'm excited, but thinking about it makes my head spin.

Will Paul adjust his way of life to dance with this miracle? He will have to, because this miracle is outside of what he currently knows and does. This can be a little scary. It *does* feel safer doing what you know, doing what you are accustomed to thinking and feeling. Besides, Monkey Mind gets so raucous when you push outside the known and familiar! The alternative, however, is no expansion, leading to stagnation. Your dreams are so much bigger than that.

Paul may not ultimately take this big new job. He may want it but be too afraid to rock his boat. If this were to happen to you, how would you know what to do?

The answer to this question requires that we draw the distinction between what is *valid* and what is *relevant* about your inner chatter. Paul's anxiety, doubt and worry are valid. By valid, we mean that they are authentic and genuine. It is possible that, with his current organizational structure, he cannot deliver on such a big project. Since he's never done such a big job before he has no proof that he can pull it off. You can pick up Paul's anxiety about shifting how he does business. Monkey Mind may be telling him everything that could go wrong. It may urge him to turn back. His concerns are legitimate. They are reasonable given his current structure of knowing. But remember, all progress depends upon the prepared, unreasonable man.

Now comes a different question. Is his internal dialogue *relevant*? That is, does it have a direct bearing upon whether or not he should go on toward grasping this miracle? Maybe not. Look at the following questions:

1. Should Paul wait until his thoughts and feelings subside before he submits his bid? Probably not. No matter what is going on inside him, something needs to be done now if he is to go ahead.

2. Is this chatter a sure sign that something is wrong with his own intelligence or ability? No. It is a normal response to something that represents a big step. Everyone has loud internal voices during those times. Still, it

is interesting that we often think that something *is* wrong with us because we have anxiety or fear at a new opportunity.

3. Will the intensity of this chatter ever diminish? Maybe it will, but it is always ready to come back again. Chatter will resume when Paul is again poised to challenge his own structure of knowing.

So, if you do not go by the inner monologue provided by your own structure of knowing, what *do* you go by? First, look and see if what you are about to do corresponds with your life's intentions. One of Paul's intentions was: to be financially successful by having a large business. Obviously, this new job is relevant to his intention. It is germane to his dreams. Among his

Standards of Integrity was to be creative and adventurous. These had heart and meaning for him. The chatter? He did not use it as a signal that he should not proceed. He did not wait for it to go away. He saw it as valid, but irrelevant. He took the big step and applied for the contract. Paul also hired a business consultant to help him with the expansion. They awarded him the contract.

Dancing with your intentions and Standards of Integrity, instead of Monkey Mind, provides opportunities for miracles.

Look at the difference between a miracle and an opportunity. An opportunity is an auspicious opening. It combines circumstance, timing and place to produce conditions that are favorable for an event or action. Opportunity includes events that are predictable, not requiring a stretch, as in: Have you had the opportunity to read this morning's paper? Some of these events can be boring or commonplace if they are recurrent. Miracles are events that show up in the opening that opportunity creates. They are not an extension of the past. A sense of awe or wonder is attached to them.

How to Prepare for Miracles

To have miracles, you must be willing to do whatever it takes to gear up for them. Preparation helps you see if your mind chatter is relevant to your vision. You have more freedom for authentic action. You remain focused and undistracted.

One of the best ways to get ready for miracles is to clear away whatever is impeding your ability to respond quickly and with ease to new opportunities. Unfinished business, unfulfilled promises and neglected responsibilities present hurdles, sometimes conscious and sometimes not, that trip you up in your journey. When you have a clear, open road, miracles just seem to flow forth, sometimes with no effort at all on your part. For example, an architect once told me she has one sure way of getting a new contract. She does a thorough job on the ones she already has. She said:

> "There is no such thing as a minor lapse of integrity."
>
> Tom Peters

Ellen: You know that old saying about Nature abhorring a vacuum? Works for me! If I want a new project, all I have to do is make sure I'm thoroughly finished with what I'm already working on. Then, other projects seem to show up. Is it magic, or does this happen because I'm freer to look at new possibilities? I don't know. I really don't care. I'm just glad it does!

Concluding unfinished business may not seem exciting. Nevertheless, whatever is incomplete in your life draws energy to it until it is finished. It may be a natural law. You have to exert force to hold completion in suspension. You become tired, concerned, and preoccupied. You are disempowered from going full speed ahead.

A promise is your word, whether spoken or implied. It is a contract you make with the universe. Unfinished business is a broken promise. The breaking of a promise initiates a series of events that drain your power. When you keep your word, you gain strength to bring your dreams from the metaphysical to the physical.

Gay Hendricks and Kate Ludeman, in their book, *The Corporate Mystic: A guidebook for visionaries with their feet on the ground,* found that people who are successful intuitively know and operate from this principle. For example, no matter how far they traveled, every business leader they interviewed for this book showed up on time. They showed that they took themselves, and others, seriously. They also made it a point to keep promises in all areas of their lives.

Keep your word and you live within your Standards of Integrity. Not living within your Standards of Integrity is a drain that saps your energy.

In previous pages you have looked at the many different

aspects of your Standards of Integrity, that is, the internal guidelines that show you how to live a fulfilled life. When you demonstrate these standards in your actions, life is sweet. You are free to use the miracles that surround you. When you go against your standards, you turn yourself into hamburger meat, pushing and struggling against your own best efforts.

Where money is concerned, unfinished business comes in many forms. Unpaid bills, unfulfilled contracts, unbalanced checkbooks, and the lack of car insurance are a few examples.

Here is an illustration of how unfinished money business affects our ability to attain our goals and dreams. Imagine a playing field for any sport you like. Picture that field or court filled with trash and old equipment. Not a pretty sight! Aesthetic appeal is not the only problem here. What is more important is that there is not much room on the field to play a truly inspired game.

> "The first problem for all of us, men and women, is not to learn, but to unlearn, to clear out some of the assumptions."
>
> *Gloria Steinem*

Unfinished money business makes our relationship with money onerous. The incomplete items clutter the playing field. They threaten to trip us up. We become wary and worried. Unpaid loans are a prime example of unfinished money business. If you owe money to someone and have not made payment arrangements, you may be faced with a situation like this:

Tony: Uncle Alex lent me five thousand dollars around eight years ago so I could finish college. I haven't talked to him about repaying it. I just don't have the money yet. Besides, every Thanksgiving when I see him, it's hard to talk with everyone around. Last summer he invited me to his beach house for a family reunion. I've wanted to go there for years! Two days before I was to go, I got sick, and I hardly ever get sick. I missed the party!

Would Tony have gotten sick if he had harbored no ambivalence and fear about talking to his uncle? His illness may have had nothing to do with the unpaid loan. Yet, you can sense the *dis*ease he feels where his uncle is concerned. This discomfort hampers him from playing freely. He may never know for certain if there was any connection between his getting sick, and his unfinished business with his uncle. We do know that if he had cleared up his past obligations he could have gone to the family gathering and had a wonderful time.

Many people learn to endure a lot of unfinished money garbage in their playing arena. It is as though they are players in a tennis match, trying to do their best while jumping over bottles, beer cans and other assorted trash. Such an environment provides no room for excellence, grace or the joy of accomplishment.

Many of us expect that our relationship with money will always be burdensome. We see this as the natural state of affairs. Our load of unfinished money business goes with us when we go to the bank to apply for a mortgage. It is there when we plan to go on vacation, or look at future retirement or at our childrens' education. The condition is usually held in place by resignation. Monkey Mind says: "There's nothing you can do about it. Everyone has some trouble with money."

If you wish to experience the true power of money to fuel your goals and dreams, clean up the debris on your path. Do everything you can to complete unfinished business, both personal and professional. Whatever is incomplete or unfinished in your relationship with money impedes the flow of that energy in your life.

Make Ways for Miracles

Cleaning up unfinished money business can be challenging. It can seem mundane and not very spiritual. But it is the very stuff of authentic action to clean up messes in the physical domain to make way for the metaphysical. When you clear these obstacles you strengthen your ability to continue on your hero's journey.

Take the time to prepare yourself for this necessary step. Once you get past Monkey Mind chatter and clear the playing field, you create a much simpler, more constructive relationship with money.

Allow yourself to be willing to do the next exercise. To be willing is itself a choice requiring heart and courage. Your mind may find reasons to stay where you are. It will suggest that you cling to what you think you know, even when what you think you know is uncomfortable or undermining. The advice is not out of malice. On the contrary, Monkey Mind is concerned for your survival. It is convinced that safety lies in maintaining the *status quo*. It does not matter to Monkey Mind that this means doing the same thing over and over again, even as you go on expecting different results.

Exercise: Taking Care of Business, An Inventory

What You Will Need

You will need your notebook, your Standards of Integrity, your life's intentions, and Symptoms of Monkey Mind.

Time For This Exercise

Give yourself twenty to thirty minutes to answer this inventory.

The Exercise

You are about to see where you have unfinished money business. Read each item carefully and note your immediate reaction. Is Monkey Mind chattering away at you? If so, what is it saying? Write down what you have uncovered before you do anything else.

If you see that an item applies to you, look at your Standards of Integrity and life's intentions. Ask yourself this question: "What am I more interested in, my Monkey Mind conversations or my goals and dreams in life?" Use this question to mediate any internal dialogue about why you should not bother handling this item. Write down whatever is true for you about this item. Be specific. For example, if item "5" relates to you, list the credit card(s), their interest rates, and how much is owed for each.

Go through this list now, noting any areas where you might find some unfinished business:

1. Checkbook(s): balanced to the penny?

2. Car, health, fire, theft, earthquake insurance: have necessary coverage?

3. Will or revocable living trust: useful and established?

4. Durable power of attorney: necessary and complete?

5. Credit cards: high interest rates, high balances?

6. Medical, dental or eye exams: needed, due again?

7. Tires, brakes needed, the servicing of your car: up-to-date?

8. Parking or speeding tickets: any unpaid?

9. Saving for the holidays: account necessary and initiated?

10. Paying income and property taxes on time: need a consultation on completion?

11. Malpractice insurance: necessary and paid for?

12. Borrowed items: need to return? (Oh, yes, anything from jewelry to garden equipment.)

13. Financial records: accessible, in order? (Not in a mess somewhere in a shoe box.)

14. Billing for services: being done on time, any old ones pending?

15. Allowance system for your children: established, consistent?

16. Monthly budget: prepared, followed?

17. Overdue bills: mutually acceptable agreement for repayment arranged?

18. Student loans: late, on time, completed?

19. Home repairs: needed, planned, savings plan started?

20. Professional advice (legal, accounting, financial planning): needed, arranged, payment planned?

21. Retirement accounts and plans: never too early to start, what is the status?

22. Any other items not mentioned above that you know are unfinished.

You may have additional items that do not appear on this list, personal items that do not exactly match the way they are stated above. Do yourself a big favor. Write down anything else that the list suggests to you. List even those items that seem impossible to clear up or have been around for years. One reliable rule of thumb: if something comes to mind during the exercise, even if it seems illogical or not obviously related to money, include it on your list. You will see how that item relates to money as you continue.

Now, the action part of this exercise. Before you do anything else about money, balance your checkbook to the penny. Do it even if you need to have a friend or spouse help you, or you have to go to the bank or a bookkeeper for assistance. No matter what your head is telling you right now, just do it! To the penny. Go back as far as you have to in to order to get your checkbook to reconcile with your bank statement. *Do not close the account and open a new one!* This might be tempting, but it will not prepare you for miracles.

If balancing your checkbook has never been a problem for you, congratulations! For many, it is one of the hardest things to do.

When you balance your checkbook you are making a declaration of your willingness and intent to be a conscious custodian of energy. Since life is a hologram, this will affect other areas of your life.

Later you will engage in an exercise that presupposes a balanced checkbook. You will look at what your checkbook has to teach you about your spending patterns and priorities. But for right now, applaud yourself for taking this task to heart.

For the rest of the unfinished items, take at least one step toward the completion of each item on your list. Do this within the next two weeks. For example, if you owe someone money and have not begun to pay it back, call or write this person and set up a mutually agreeable timetable for payment. If you do not have a will, living trust, or durable power of attorney, make an appointment with an attorney to draw up these documents. Notice what Monkey Mind is saying to you about doing this. And then do it anyway!

Take action on incomplete items. It is one of the most powerfully direct things you can do to prepare yourself for miracles in your relationship with money.

Even if you are tempted, do not skip over this part. Put a date next to each item to indicate when it will be complete. Complete all items as soon as possible. Take care of the ones that are easiest first -- after balancing your checkbook, that is!

You may not know how to complete some of the money items you checked. For example, if you have unpaid student loans it may be possible to get twenty-four months forbearance on the loan, or negotiate lower monthly fees and payments. Options are also available to clear up credit card debt. If you are stumped for how to handle debts and unpaid loans, consult with your local Consumer Credit Counseling agency. Their staff will work with you and your creditors to consolidate and come up with a manageable monthly payment plan. Check to see if your situation is appropriate for their services.

Discussion

Wherever possible, use people who will help you go outside your usual structures of knowing about what it takes to clear up things. They may suggest easier ways to complete items than you currently imagine. Be open. Why suffer needlessly?

If you are an entrepreneur or have a professional practice, and are having difficulty collecting from others, take note. One place to look for the source of this trouble is whether you have repaid all of your educational loans. Unpaid school loans serve as a drain on money energy. You know at some level that you have not kept your end of the bargain to repay the energy that helped you get your start. Thus begins a what-comes-around-goes-around cycle when it comes to your collecting accounts receivable. Defaulting on student (or any) loans also damages your credit.

Do you know in your heart that chronic debts are a matter of concern for you? I suggest a wonderful book that has brought relief to thousands of people, no matter what their income. It is recommended reading for all *You and Money* participants. It is called: *How to Get Out of Debt, Stay Out of Debt, and Live Prosperously,* by Jerrold Mundis. This book describes specific ways to end the debt cycle while providing for what you truly want in life. Mundis says: "Clearing up your debts doesn't mean eating cat food while you're doing it."

What do you find as you clear away these impediments to your hero's journey? I suggest you keep a diary that records whenever you notice a miracle regarding money.

Paulette: I was blown away by this! I started paying off some old school loans. My Dad heard about this from Mom. He called and told me he was proud of my taking responsibility for my finances. One month later he told me that he would help me make a down payment on my first house! I felt great about accepting his offer.

Share your results with friends. Ask for their support as you take action. To provide centering and cheer you on, keep your life's intentions and Standards of Integrity before you. You are taking more action to prepare yourself for miracles than just about anything else you could do!

Waking Up About Money: It's About Time!

You are learning how to handle energy powerfully and wisely. Money is one form of energy, and so is time. In our culture, it takes time for most of us to earn money. Therefore, time and money are linked. For example, let us suppose you want to take a cruise to the Caribbean. It costs approximately $1,100 for eight days. How long does it take you to earn that amount of money? Seen in this way, what costs money also costs time. This is one of the central themes of Joe Dominquez' book: *Your Money or Your Life*. You must look not only at how you want to spend your money but at whether or not the time you invest to earn that amount of money is worth the return. Examining these matters promotes conscious stewardship of energy.

Do you want to be an investor? Do you want to use the money you have to create more? Doing the next exercise will help you save and channel money to those ends. All you have to do is wake up.

Money can allow you to help yourself, your loved ones and your community reach important goals. In fact, your ability to donate money or time to your favorite causes will increase as you become more conscious of both forms of energy. The following exercise will help you gain conscious control over your money and your time.

Exercise: Plugging the Leaks in Your Money Raft

What You Will Need:

You will need a small spiral pad like the one you used to note daily symptoms of Monkey Mind. Let it be small enough to carry in your pocket or handbag. You will also need your notebook.

Time For This Exercise

This exercise takes two weeks. It is a tracking exercise, so exact amounts of time each day will vary. One thing is for sure: it will definately take a lot less time than your Monkey Mind is telling you right now.

The Exercise

Carry the note pad with you. For two weeks, keep track of every penny that runs through your hands. Divide your daily sheets into three columns: cash, check and credit cards. Note each expense, no matter how small, under each category. Make sure you do it at the time you spend it, not later. For example, if you buy a newspaper to read while commuting to work, write that expense down immediately.

You are not keeping track of this money to create a budget. You are doing it to increase your consciousness about the ways money energy flows through you. If you have your own business and write business checks, keep track of those as well. Money leaks occur both at home and at the office. If you work for someone else and write the checks for them, do not list those.

Even if you forget to do it periodically, start up again. Do not worry about duplication, like charging something on your credit card and later paying the credit card bill with a check. All of this should be written down. Notice what Monkey Mind says about this right now. Which symptom is it exhibiting?

Joel: I remember Monkey Mind telling me: "You don't want to do this. This will take too much of your time. It's stupid, besides. Just skip this part. You've done this before. It doesn't accomplish anything." I said, "Thank you for sharing", and did it anyway. It wasn't so bad. It was an eye-opener.

As you track your expenses, ask yourself the following questions. Write your answers in your notebook for later examination.

1. Regarding the way I use money, what is the difference for me between leaking and spending?
    a. When do I go unconscious about spending money? Is it during a particular time of day? A particular mood?
    b. Upon which items do I spend most unconsciously? Are they what I really want at the time I buy them?
    c. If the items are other than food, do I put them to good use? Do I get my money's worth from them? Do they lie around unused? What do I see

about this?

   d. Where do I spend money consciously? How does this experience differ from leaking money?

   e. Do I really value everything I buy? Does what I buy bring me pleasure?

2. Is there a parallel here with how I leak or spend my time?

   a. Do I leak time with unimportant activity? If so, what is it? For example, do I waste time looking at television?

   b. Do I leak time by compulsive activity? Do I spend hours and hours exercising, organizing or fixing?

   c. When am I most likely to leak time? How does this contrast with time that I spend consciously?

   d. Do I promise to do something for myself or others, only to become distracted with meaningless activity?

   e. Do I spend as much time as I want with friends and family?

3. If I fix the way I leak money, what will happen to the time I use to earn it?

4. Is it possible for me to work less and have more of what I truly want?

Discussion

As you study your two-week spending record, do you notice any patterns? Are there any black holes that suck away your money? For example, how much do you spend on convenience food?

Rick: I spend three dollars a day for cappuccino and pastry at work. It came to $60 a month. I added $2 more each day for incidentals like soft drinks or fruit in the afternoon. I found I was spending enough money each year to fund a down payment on a small car, not counting the occasional unplanned lunches or dinners at restaurants. I found that I go for quick convenience food on my way home when I feel too bushed to prepare a meal.

Margo: How I waste time really surprised me. I buy all these good books, take them home, and never spend time reading them. I'm in front of the television set, staring at a program that barely interests me!

You are becoming aware of your patterns of spending money not to deprive yourself, but to empower you to make conscious choices. You do not want to leak out the energy over which you have custodianship. You want to bring your dreams from the metaphysical into the physical. Becoming aware of leaking versus spending will give you real choice and satisfying spending habits. Many *You and Money* participants have found creative solutions to the problem of leaking money and time.

Alex: I saw how much money I waste on stuff, so I developed a system. Every time I spend money on convenience food or entertainment, I put twice that amount away in a savings account. I use the savings to add to my investments, like buying mutual funds. It's amazing how much I've invested in the past two years! Knowing I'm going to spend three times as much on a movie also gives me the chance to choose if I really want to see it. If I do, no problem.

I've just made an investment at the same time!

Heather: I go through the TV guide every week and circle the programs I want to watch. Then I watch them, and only them. I cut down the time I watch television by twenty hours a week! I have also budgeted time for reading. I've joined a reading club. We have a blast together! Something else, I think better of myself. I had criticized myself for not doing anything worthwhile with my time. That is over now.

Building the Strength to Dance with Your Goals

Oscar Wilde once said: "There are two tragedies in life -- not getting what you want and getting what you want." Have you noticed that when you attain important goals in life you need an adjustment period? That is because goals, if they are worth playing for, lie outside the boundaries of predictability. You have to stretch outside your structures of knowing to achieve your goals, grow into them, and enjoy their benefits.

In the next chapter you get a pay-off for all your determination and courage. You will be creating great goals that have meaning and value for you. You will learn what a goal really is. Be ready for a surprise! You will also get another chance to be even clearer about your relationship with money. Ease on your journey will increase with each exercise.

Summary

Miracles are nothing more than ordinary events that lie outside your current structure(s) of knowing.

Much of what you now consider to be commonplace once seemed like a miracle to you.

As you venture toward the outer edges of your structure of knowing, Monkey Mind's chatter grows louder. If you are prepared, it does not distract you from your path.

Dancing with your intentions and Standards of Integrity, instead of Monkey Mind, provides opportunities for miracles.

A promise is your word, whether spoken or implied. It is a contract you make with the universe. Unfinished business is a broken promise. The breaking of a promise initiates a series of events that drain your power. When you keep your word, you gain strength to bring your dreams from the metaphysical to the physical.

If you wish to experience the true power of money to fuel your goals and dreams, clean up the debris on your path. Do everything you can to complete unfinished business, both personal and professional. Whatever is incomplete or unfinished in your relationship with money impedes the flow of that energy in your life.

Keep your word and you live within your Standards of Integrity. Not living within your Standards of Integrity saps your energy.

When you balance your checkbook you are making a declaration of your willingness and intent to be a conscious custodian of energy. Since life is a hologram, this will affect other areas of your life.

Take action on incomplete items. It is one of the most powerfully direct things you can do to prepare yourself for miracles in your relationship with money.

In our culture, it takes time for most of us to earn money. Therefore, time and money are linked.

CHAPTER TEN:
Intention-Based Goals

Intention-Based Goals

"To save the mind from preying inwardly upon itself, it must be encouraged to some outward pursuit. There is no other way to elude apathy, or escape discontent; none other to guard the temper from that quarrel with itself, which ultimately ends in quarreling with all mankind."

Fanny Burney

For a moment, be willing to set aside everything you think you know about goals. The purpose of this chapter is for you to go outside your current structure of knowing about them. What if you discovered that what you think you know about goals has actually kept you from creating ones that are satisfying and attainable? You would be in good company. Everyone in the *You and Money* course has a story to tell about a thwarted goal, the one that got away.

Notice if your memories of your past goals are filled with delight, or the effort it took. You have probably succeeded in attaining goals, but was it fun? The introduction of the goals section of the course is often met with an initial groan. There is an alternative to dreading goals. I have coached thousands of people to create meaningful goals and get what they really want, with ease.

The problem with most "goals" is that they are not empowered by what we really want out of life. And, much of the time, we think we are too busy to find out what we really want. If a genie were to slip out of a bottle and ask us our heart's desire, we might be stumped for an answer.

Oh, yes, most of us know what we *should* want. We may have memories of what we *used to* want. We usually have some half-formed dreams in the back of our minds. These are desires we tell ourselves we will fulfill *someday* when we get the time or the money. We also have convincing reasons for why we cannot pursue what we want right now. These reasons fill the space where our dreams used to be. Hidden in our souls, however, are still those wonderful dreams we want to have and contributions we want to make. We find them by opening our minds and hearts to the key to attaining goals.

Why is it that setting goals does not always excite us? Identifying them should contribute to a sense of power in our lives. So, what in the current process tends to produce anxiety and doubt instead?

Carl: Just thinking about making goals leaves me cold. I don't know how to do it. Besides, let's say I finally pick one. How do I know it's the best goal for me? How do I know I'm not just fooling myself?

Lynne: You could call me a goal junkie. I set goals every week. I'm in sales, so my goals include cold calls I have to make. I've heard that successful people have goals, and I certainly want to be successful. How do I feel when I make my goals every week? Relieved. For about fifteen minutes. Why don't I get a real bounce from them? I don't know.

Rhonda: I don't believe in goals. At least not formal ones. I believe in trusting the universe instead. If something I want is meant to happen, it'll just show up. Take money, for instance. I don't have much, but it shows up when I need it. So there's no need to set a goal for what I want.

Tim: Everyone else must know how to achieve their goals. For me, trying to figure out my goals is a bust. What do I really want? How hard will I have to work? Then, will I be able to enjoy the results?

Take heart. You were born with the natural ability to generate, project, and attain goals. It is your birthright. You still have what it takes. Look at when you were a child. Your intentions and goals came naturally and easily. Ask most kids around age nine or ten years old what they want to be when they grow up. You will get a long list of life's intentions:

* I want to be a nurse.
* I want to be a baseball player.
* I want to be an explorer.
* I want to be an astronaut, and a teacher, and a cowboy.

Do you know any kids under the age of thirteen who could not give you a long list of what they want for their birthday or Christmas? Okay, okay, you might not like the list, but the list represents goals. They are specific and concrete. My nephew, Ben, even arranges his lists in order of importance, with the first items being gifts "to die for."

Do you remember the first goal you worked for as a child? For me, it was working for money to buy my mom a gold-plated pin for her birthday. I was twelve. The pin was in the shape of a shaft of wheat. I was so proud because I had gotten it for her. Years later, that pin serves as a memento. I still feel good when I look at it because it represents the first time I was able to set and achieve a goal.

What happened to your ability to create goals? Who knows for sure? Maybe during your teens you decided to "grow up" or "chill out." Maybe you did not get the things you wanted. Or, found that it was not cool to get so excited about life's possibilities. Many people can remember when they decided to shelve their goals and dreams and "get with the program." So, you may have entered young adulthood with lowered expectations and heightened cynicism.

Not only do you have dreams in your heart, you have the ability to make them come true. This is one of the gifts of being human. The question for you to answer here is whether or not you are willing to reawaken this capability. Do so, and you will set the stage for an exciting future; your future.

You may ask if this is a promotion of consumerism. Far from it. Stephen L. Goldstein, in an article for the *Miami Herald*, spoke about whether or not we have the ability to finance education, health and other ailing sectors of our social system. He observed that:

"The problem in America is not that we don't have money. The problem is that we have gotten used to having so much money that we simply cannot imagine doing without what we have come to regard as necessities -- like tortilla chips, marshmallows and potato chips, on which we spent $6 billion in 1991. We finance our foibles. We wager $18.8 billion each year on lottery tickets. We spend $15 billion a year on toys, instead of reading to them [our children] for free ... we have bought 450,000 plastic pink flamingos in 1985. Objectively speaking, haven't we gone mildly mad?"

Goldstein speaks to the madness of a life driven by blind consumerism. While you may not agree with the intensity of his argument, it is difficult to deny that far too much of life seems to run according to whimsical response to marketing. It is one reason fast-food has grown to be such a large industry. The quicker the service, the more we buy. Check this out the next time you take yourself or your family for a hamburger or pizza.

There is a difference between a goal and a whim. Whims are based upon impulse and immediate gratification. This spontaneity brings spice to life. However, it can become habit-forming. Remember, one of the symptoms of Monkey Mind is the unwillingness to delay gratification. A goal exists in a definite span of time. Unlike a whim, you must sometimes delay gratification to focus your energy on a goal.

Your hero's journey is enhanced by your ability to create and sustain interest in a genuine goal that takes time to achieve. This will nurture your spirit.

Having time-based goals brings clarity and power to our lives. Goals are sure antidotes for a life led by impulse. For instance, when you rely upon impulse shopping, it saps your energy. It is especially true when you worry about how to pay for what you just bought. The worry replaces the freedom or peace of mind to create your dreams. Who wants a clutter of purchases to replace life's fulfillment? Not you.

I have talked with thousands of people who have the newest VCRs, the latest exercise equipment and the most advanced cappuccino machines. When bought on a whim, these items soon gather dust. When bought as the result of a true goal, there is pleasure in their acquisition and use. The difference is consciousness -- spending money instead of leaking it -- and setting goals makes that difference.

The purpose of your work here is to recognize and attain what you really want. It is about using your gifts to bring joy to yourself and others. Before we proceed, let us check out what you think and feel about goals. You have done a good job telling the truth in other areas. Clear the air here, as well. Use this process fully to make way for the good stuff.

Exercise: Goals or Ghouls? -- You Be the Judge

What You Will Need

You will need your notebook and a pen or pencil.

Time For This Exercise

You will need ten to fifteen minutes for this process.

The Exercise

On a new page in your notebook, write the word "goal." Take two minutes and write down every thought or feeling that occurs to you when you see that word. Be honest. Write it all down, whether or not it seems to make any sense. You can write whole phrases or single words. If you notice a body sensation, write that down as well. What do you see? The following examples may spark your examination.

Jessie: At first, my mind went blank. Then came words like "play", "inspiring" and "free." But, as I listed those words, I saw I hadn't felt like that about any goals lately.

Mark: "Productive, useful, purposeful, on target," came to mind. All that's okay, but where's the *fun*?

Roger: I didn't want to do this exercise. I thought, "This will be too hard, and besides, I can't achieve the goals that are really important to me."

Esther: I got annoyed at the thought of looking at the word "goal." Why should I have goals? It seems like a lot of trouble. Maybe I should just hang out.

Bob: As I did this exercise, I saw that I like to create goals. But once I do, they seem to go flat. Maybe I'm just an idea person.

You may have a reaction to the word "goal" unlike any of the above. That is fine. Just look at what you wrote. Would you have written the same thing when you were ten years old? Would your mood have been the same?

Next, on the same piece of paper, make a list of at least ten goals you have that would take time or money to accomplish. Can you even think of ten? Does it seem like a burden to do this?

Discussion

Read these goals to another person. How do you feel? Would you want to post this paper where you could see it every day? Would you be just as happy tearing it up and using it for hamster litter? Be honest. There may be some that are great, but some that bring up discomfort. How does this compare to the way you might have experienced the exercise when you were ten years old?

Excitement and Goals

Having done the goals exercise, let us take a moment to re-think our understanding of this word. The dictionary defines a goal as: "an area or object, toward which play is directed in order to score." How many of the goals you have listed line up with this concept? Do you see play peeking out from behind any of your words?

The definition I just gave for a goal is not the only one. But use it for your work here. If you are like most adults, play is not usually associated with goals. We most often see goals as requiring fortitude, strength, perseverance and a set jaw.

Imagine a rating scale from one to ten. A score of one means, "I do not want this." A score of ten means, "I want this very, very much." Honestly assign a number. How would you rate each of the goals you listed above? There may be some that excite you. Others may be a big yawn.

Being Dragged, Kicking and Screaming, Into Heaven

One reason you may not be excited about your goals is because they are not goals. Surprise! They are tasks that should or ought to be done. Some common tasks that people confuse with goals are:

* Getting rid of credit-card debt.
* Creating a will or revocable living trust.
* Opening a retirement account.
* Hiring a money manager.
* Fixing the roofing, plumbing or heating at home.
* Filing forms or documents on time.
* Buying health insurance.

These are not goals. So, what are they? They are tasks that will clear the way for you to play for your goals. They are not that trip to the Caribbean, the special extra items for the baby's room, that romantic dinner, that gift for your mom and dad. Not even near. Notice the difference in the feeling of those items and the ones I mention in this paragraph. In your heart, you recognize the difference. It just may not be clear to the part of your brain that has been picking so-called "goals".

They are items of unfinished money business. If they apply to you, put them in your unfinished money business list. Set dates when you will complete them. You will give yourself breathing room that engenders success and peace of mind. One key for determining whether you have a task or a goal is to ask yourself: "Will I be relieved when it is done?"

If the answer is yes, then it is a task, not a goal.

When you complete a goal, you feel joy. When you finish a task, you feel relief. People who are driven tend to strive for relief, mistaking it for joy. People who are successful allow themselves to experience the joy that comes from creative accomplishment.

We now edge closer to discovering some real goals for you. Remember, as you begin to go outside your structure of knowing, Monkey Mind will get louder and tell you to turn back. If this happens, turn your attention gently toward the present moment and proceed onward. Do not wait for Monkey Mind to become quiet. Bring the list of Monkey Mind symptoms with you as you do what is next. Remember, you can refocus your attention when you find it has strayed.

Taking the Big Step

Goals bridge the metaphysical and physical realms. When you fashion goals you engage in an act of creation. After all, goals are only projections of your mind upon physical reality. There are two types of goals:

Type One goals have no particular intention behind them. This increases their *Whim Factor*. They lack meaning. You cannot say why you picked them over others. They feel frivolous or trivial. You begin to journey toward them and then stop. Or, you go off in another direction. They dissipate your energy.

Type Two goals are attached to your life's intentions. These intentions anchor them and provide conduits for energy that will bring the goals into physical reality. These are the type of goals that allow for maximum creativity and fulfillment.

The process of developing meaningful goals includes differentiating them from tasks and anchoring them to one or more of your life's intentions.

You are now at the point of creating some authentic goals, as differentiated from whims. This is where you take your dreams and make them real. We begin with the first step: opening the door to your dreams.

Exercise: Opening the Door to Your Dreams

What You Will Need

Your notebook and pen; a small tape recorder. To help you in the process of creating some goals, record what follows on a cassette and then play it back to yourself. Or, have someone read it to you.

Time For This Exercise

This process need not take more than fifteen to twenty minutes. You may repeat the process as many times as you like.

The Exercise

Record and then listen to the following process. Pause for two seconds where you see the four dots.

Sit back and relax. Have both feet on the floor, hands resting gently in your lap. Close your eyes when you are ready. Take a deep breath. Feel for any tense spots in your body. Locate them, and breathe into these points of tension. As you breathe out, let that bit of tension go ....

Recall a time when you were eight or ten years old and you really wanted something. Was it something you wanted to do? To be? What was it? If it was an object such as a bike, what color was it? If it was to have a special job or life's work, what was it? Did you want to travel? Become a professional athlete? A musician? A painter? Let yourself remember what it was like to want what you wanted. Notice how your body feels as it remembers how it was for you to know you really wanted things ....

Take another deep breath. Exhale gently ....

Bring your awareness back to the present. You are sitting in a seat of power. It looks and feels just like a seat of power would .... however you might picture that in your mind's eye. It might be a huge throne in a royal palace or a comfortable leather executive's chair in a spectacular penthouse office ....

In this seat, anything you truly want to have, do, or be can be made real .... All you need to do is let yourself know what it is .... Let yourself pick what your heart really wants .... What brings you joy? Education, travel, creative projects, the perfect job and more are yours .... You have only to ask for what you want and you will receive it ....

Let yourself see, feel or hear what it is you really want .... What is it that makes you glad or excited? .... Find the words for what you want and say them to yourself ....

Whether you have become aware of some goals or not, something wonderful has happened. Sitting in this seat of power you have begun to energize your imagination. You have opened the door to discovering your goals. If you do not yet know what they are, you may surprise yourself by daydreaming or having a dream when you go to sleep at night that will reveal something to you about your goals. Whenever this happens, write the dream or daydream down so you will remember it. You will also see that you have always known somewhere in your heart what these dreams are.

When you are ready, open your eyes. Write down whatever goals presented themselves to you.

Make a list now of all the goals you can think of that would be worth having. Note them no matter how much you think they might cost, or how much time they might take to get. Just look inside yourself. You may hear Monkey Mind saying: "But how will I get it? This is too difficult. I don't have time or the money. I have no direction." Stand back for a moment. Ask yourself: "Which am I more interested in, dancing with my doubts, or dancing with my goals and dreams?" Choose the dreams to dance with, regardless of how Monkey Mind chatters.

Let the goals come from the top of your head and the bottom of your heart. List whatever comes up, no matter how silly or frivolous it might seem. This is no time to censor yourself. You have probably done that for too long already. Keep going until you have at least 10-15 items listed. Feel free to repeat the closed-eye activity as often as you like. Each time will open you more to this process of digging for goals.

I have included a partial list of the types of goals people in the *You and Money* course have chosen over the years.

* Replant my garden
* Sponsor a local child for educational travel
* Take my children to an amusement park
* Go white-water rafting on the Colorado River
* Write a storybook for children 6-8 years old
* Open a restaurant
* Buy a new home
* Be a benefactor for the Red Cross
* Buy a computer
* Get an airplane pilot's license
* Redecorate my home
* Go to Tahiti with my honey
* Have an investment portfolio of $2,000
* Write a screenplay
* Have my first art exhibit
* Enroll in a Ph.D. program
* Reach the Golden Circle award for real estate sales

Discussion

How did it feel to get in touch with some goals? Exciting? Scary? Vulnerable? Were you bursting with creativity, or dried up like an old desert watering hole? How many passes did it take before you came up with a list? Did Monkey Mind come up with some new objections? Did one or more tributaries of your Basic Assumption rear their heads? Now is the time to talk about issues such as these with someone you know. You have started a process that will continue long after this exercise.

Dancing with Your Dreams

You now have a list of goals. We will hone them further by discovering if what you listed are goals, tasks or ongoing processes.

First, look at all of your items. Pretend you have a *Want-O-Meter* in front of you. Every time your hand passes over one of the goals you wrote, that meter registers how much you really want it. Start with the first item on your list. On a scale of 1-10, with ten being the most you could want this and one being the least, what rating would you assign that goal? We are not setting priorities here. You may have all 10's or all 1's, or anything in between. It is all up to you.

Take a deep breath. Remove any items that do not have a score of eight or above. You are winnowing out all items that you really do not want. This may eliminate some or all of your list. You may have to return to the previous exercise to come up with another preliminary list of goals. When I ask this of the participants in the *You and Money* course, a collective groan again rises from the group. I remember one man saying with a sardonic laugh: "Great! Now she's going to *make* us have what we want!"

To master the art of creating meaningful goals, you must learn to see what you truly want. This involves the discipline of laying aside, at least for a moment, whatever is *not* what you want. Thus, you cultivate the ability to generate energy by letting go of insignificant elements that dissipate it.

Returning to your list of goals, choose one that you are willing to have by one year from today. When you choose a goal you embrace it as a possibility. This is often difficult, given the nature of Monkey Mind. For a moment, become unreasonable. Look at what you want to be, do or have within this year. Pick one. In that simple act lies more courage than almost anything else you could do.

If you have chosen a goal, congratulate yourself! You are stepping beyond your structure of knowing. You are re-invigorating an ability you have had all your life: the ability to choose what you want. We now take the next step of insuring that your goal possesses all the qualities of a true goal.

Creating Powerful Goals

A goal is a projection from your mind into physical reality. It has the same features as items in the physical, save one. It exists in the future rather than the present. Nevertheless, we must treat a goal in every respect like a physical object. To do this, we make sure it is imbued with qualities represented by the acronym SMART. Each quality must be present for an item to qualify as a goal; if *any* of these are missing from what you wrote, that item is not a goal.

S: is for "specific." Is your goal explicit and precise? For example: "I want to be happy," is not a goal. It is an intention. It is not specific, but refers to an ongoing feeling state. "I want to learn scuba diving by next summer," is specific. One pitfall at this point in creating goals is the tendency of Monkey Mind toward vagueness. Being vague about what you want will keep you in a state of suspended animation.

M: is for "measurable." How will I know that I have learned scuba diving? One way is by getting a certificate. "I want to get my scuba-diving certificate," is a measurable goal. I will either have it or not. There is no *wiggle room*.

> "Integrity is finding the way of life and of being that will be true to its own nature."
>
> *Ira Progoff*

A: is for "attainable." A goal needs to be a stretch for you. For example, to say that you are going to save $600 a year when you are already saving $50 a month is not a stretch. It is easily within the realm of predictability. A goal needs to depart from business as usual. At the same time, pie-in-the-sky goals are a set up for failure. To say that you are going to run a marathon next month when you have not yet begun to train is to give yourself an unattainable goal. Many people create unattainable goals. Quite predictably, they do not achieve them, and get discouraged or indignant about the entire process of goal-setting. Remember, make the goal worth playing for, yet not so unattainable that you obviously will not get it.

R: is for "relevant." This is where we take care of the *Whim Factor*. Take out your life's intentions. To which intentions does this goal relate? For example, one of my life's intentions is to be adventuresome. Another one is to be physically fit.

You will be amazed at how the goals you really want are attached to at least one of your life's intentions. This is what I mean by being relevant. Everything relates to everything else. Write the intention(s) satisfied by this goal next to it.

We now check for the way this goal relates to your Standards of Integrity. First, in going *for* this goal, are you going *against* any of your standards? Is the goal outside your integrity in any way? Does it ask you to lie? Are you being irresponsible in trying to attain it now? Again, you will most likely find that if this goal is related to one or more intentions, it does not violate your standards. However, checking this out is still advisable.

If you maintain your Standards of Integrity, you propel yourself forward to meet your goals. The way is clear and easy. If you violate your Standards of Integrity in any way, you may unconsciously keep yourself from getting your goals. Or, if you do attain them, you will suffer along the way.

Next, does proceeding with this goal *demonstrate* one or more of your Standards of Integrity? For example, one of my standards is to be courageous. If I learn to scuba-dive, whether or not I am afraid, I demonstrate courage.

This process may seem laborious at first. You are learning to create integrity-based goals. They will have the living spirit that sustains you on your path.

T: is for "time-based." You must anchor your goal in time. To do this, give a date by when you will accomplish it. You are making a promise to yourself.

When you set a date for the completion of a goal, you show that you are earnest about getting it. This is a powerful step to take. At the same time, it is a step that many of us avoid. We prefer to say, "Next summer sometime," or "I'll do it next year." This takes the teeth out of your goal. In sales terms, it is like doing all the work to make a sale and not closing the deal. A definite date closes the deal you make with yourself. In this way, you are taking yourself and your goals seriously.

A goal is not an open-ended process. You complete it, rejoice, and go on to the next one. As a matter of fact, when you reach a goal it disappears! It is no longer a goal. It has been actualized.

Making Your Goals Solid and Effective

People make some common mistakes when crafting their goals that can produce a lot of frustration. For example, losing or stopping something is not a goal:
*   I want to lose twelve pounds.
*   I want to quit smoking.

These are laudable ambitions. They may even save your life or at least make things easier for you. But they are not goals. They are tasks. There is no excitement in doing them. You would not wake up one morning and say: "I just love detoxifying from nicotine!" Similarly, you could lose twelve pounds in many ways. One way is by being ill and unable to eat. Besides, how do you know that what is best for your body is to lose precisely twelve pounds?

It is possible that there are goals hidden beneath those

tasks. This is how you discover them:

1. Look at what you really want for your body. What are your life's intentions? For example, you may find that one intention is *to be physically fit*.

2. Look at one goal that would demonstrate that you are physically fit. Something you want to do on a level of eight or above. You may discover that you have always wanted to hike in New Zealand, run a 10K, go white-water rafting on the Colorado River, or bike from inn to inn on a trip to Vermont. In some cases, you may have put this off until you lost that weight or stopped smoking. Yet this strategy has gotten you nowhere.

3. Are you willing to have a goal that demonstrates the intention to be physically fit? If you say yes, you are on your way outside your structure of knowing. For example, if you choose to bike from inn to

> "Mastery isn't reserved for the super talented. It's available to anyone who is willing to get on the path and stay on it -- regardless of age, sex, or previous experience."
>
> *George Leonard*

inn, you will need to exercise to prepare. Exercise will help you lose weight (maybe not as much weight as you think if you are adding muscle). The exercise will most certainly support you in stopping smoking. But it is the goal that will inspire you. You will see the new abilities and experiences that become available when you have a body that is physically fit.

Golden Keys to Success

If you have completed the process outlined above for one goal, congratulations! If you continue on this path, and follow my coaching in the next chapter as well, I promise you miracles! Great teachers have always highlighted the importance of having goals to be successful. For example, Napoleon Hill, author of *Think and Grow Rich,* talked and wrote about the one consistent difference he saw between people who are successful and people who are not. According to his findings, only those who wrote down their goals enjoyed success and prosperity in their lives.

You are successful if you can take a dream, articulate it as a goal, and know that you will keep your promise to yourself to attain or even surpass it.

Continue with the process until you have identified three goals that you are willing to have within one year from now. You will take these goals further toward completion in the next chapter.

Building the Strength to Dance with Your Goals

Look again at your preliminary list of goals. You will find that most require money and time to energize them into existence. It may be obvious by now that a powerful relationship with money is one key to having the goals you truly want.

You are about to engage in an exercise that will increase your power where money is concerned. You are going to calculate your net worth.

There are two reasons why we do this exercise now. First, in discovering your net worth, you may come up with even more goals regarding money. For instance, have you considered opening an investment portfolio? Becoming proficient in the arena of stocks and bonds? If so, you are going to need to understand and be able to calculate your financial assets.

The second reason is more to the heart of the matter. When you increase your awareness of every aspect of your relationship with money, you also increase your power. Your net worth is your scorecard. It tells you how your current money game is going. Not looking at it is like a tennis pro playing and refusing to see his or her score.

Another way to see it is that your net worth represents the amount of money energy over which you currently have custodianship.

Right now, take out your list of the Symptoms of Monkey Mind. Just do it. I know you are having conversations in your head about skipping over this part of the book.

What are they? Where do they fall in the symptom list? Take heart. You are not alone. No one *ever* jumps out of their seats with enthusiasm when we come to this part of the *You and Money* course.

It may take more courage for you to compute your net worth than it would to go on a fire-walk. This may be the first time you have seen your net worth. Or, you may have had an accountant do one for you so that you could get a loan. In either case, doing one will help you wake up and get you in shape to dance with your goals. The increased awareness will cause a shift in your power to have what you want with ease.

Exercise: Your Net Worth -- Awakening a Powerful Relationship with Money

What You Will Need

First, get a net worth form. They are easy to obtain from banks, real estate agencies, financial planners and books about personal financing. They are also available in computer programs designed to help you with financial planning.

Next, have your notebook with you, since you will be answering some questions about what you have found.

Time For This Exercise

The time to compute your net worth varies. When in doubt, ask someone who has done one to help you out. This will make the process easier.

The Exercise

First, complete the net worth statement. Do it, even if you have done one as recently as one year ago. A net worth statement includes places for you to list your assets such as:

Personal Property	Liquid Assets	Investments
* House	* Checking	* Stocks
* Car	* Savings	* Bonds
* Furnishings	* Treasury Bills	* Partnerships
* Jewelry	* Money Market	* Rentals
* etc.	* etc.	* etc.

Your net worth form will also ask you to list your liabilities such as:

* Mortgages
* Business Debt
* Credit Card Debt
* Car Loans
* Life Insurance Loans
* etc.

You compute your net worth by subtracting what you owe from what you own. It is a snapshot in time. It is only true in this moment. Besides any guidelines that might be included with the net worth statement you get, make certain you cover the following:

1. When figuring your net worth, be conservative. If you list your business as an asset, look to see if you really know you can sell it for a certain price.

2. Regarding furniture and personal items, compute how much you could get for them if you had to sell them within the next two weeks.

3. As you go over your assets, use this time to update your insurance to cover any items you have added or that have increased in value over the years.

4. If you are married, discover with your spouse the best way for each of you to compute your own financial net worth statements. Do you have pre-nuptial agreements or anything that you owned individually before your marriage? What are the community property laws in your state? This may be difficult to discuss. Anything regarding money that you are unconscious about will impede your ability to realize your goals.

Discussion

If you have discovered your net worth, you have given your hero's journey a boost. For some, this is one of the most difficult things to do. It is natural for all sorts of thoughts and feelings to emerge as you do this work. Seeing what comes up is just as valuable as knowing your score. Whatever you see has been there all along. It is time to dismantle some old structures of knowing. Get out your notebook and answer these questions. If possible, discuss them with a friend or in a group.

1. Does it feel like this net worth statement is measuring your worth as a person? Tell the truth. Remember, one Monkey Mind symptom to which we all fall prey is *taking things personally*. If this is true for you, now is the time to write and talk about it.

2. Were you pleasantly surprised at your net worth? Unpleasantly surprised? Upset? Once again, keep in mind as you do this that your net worth is just a snapshot in time. Seeing it can be a great wake-up call.

3. Are you interested in increasing your net worth? Would it be all right for you to get a higher score? Are you satisfied with the score you currently have?

It is a good idea to revisit your net worth every six months. Some *You and Money* graduates have made graphs to show the increase in their net worth over time. They set their targets for attaining a certain amount of money by a certain time and then chart their results. This can be very rewarding. You may have more control than you think over how to spend or invest your money.

Toward a Higher Score

Would you like to increase your net worth score? There are four ways to do this: earn more, spend less, invest, and clear up debt. There is a fifth way to increase net worth that is not available to everyone: inherit it. We are about to see the largest inter-generational transfer of wealth in this nation's history as baby boomers inherit money from their parents.

You may think you have to earn more to increase your net worth. However, you may not have to earn more to have more. Each time you pay an overdue bill or reduce your credit card debt you are *increasing* your net worth. Once again, Jerrold Mundis' book, *How to Get Out of Debt, Stay Out of Debt and Live Prosperously,* offers helpful guidelines for reducing debt, and by that, increasing your net worth.

Regarding spending less, recall the exercise in the last chapter on the difference between leaking money and spending it. Did you pick up some ways to stem the unconscious flow of money through your hands? This is a good time to put what you discovered into action. It is the time to simplify. As Sarah Ban Breathnach wrote in her book, *Simple Abundance: A Daybook of Comfort and Joy:*

"Many people believe that simplicity is doing without. On the contrary. The true simplicity as a conscious life choice illuminates our lives from within. True simplicity is buoyant and bountiful, able to liberate depressed spirits from the bondage and burden of extravagance and excess. True simplicity can elevate ordinary moments, dreary lives ... from the mundane to the transcendent."

As you simplify your life, the way becomes clear for you to attain what your heart truly desires. You come to have goals that are not tasks, but the outward projection of your spirit. You no longer need to plug up the leak in your life created by driven behavior. You begin to distinguish Monkey Mind from the earnest, still and quiet voice within that speaks to you of vision, purpose and contribution.

The next chapter goes even further in giving you tools to dance with your goals. You will discover a method that has been specifically designed to empower your journey; it is called "Creating a Treasure Map." Keep going. Remember Rilke's words: "step outside of your house ... enormous space is near."

Summary

✎   Your hero's journey is enhanced by your ability to create and sustain interest in a genuine goal that takes time to achieve. This will nurture your spirit.

✎   A goal is an area or object, toward which play is directed in order to score.

✎   When you complete a goal, you feel joy. When you finish a task, you feel relief. People who are driven have learned to strive for relief, mistaking it for joy. People who are successful allow themselves to experience the joy that comes from creative accomplishment.

✎   The process of developing meaningful goals includes differentiating them from tasks and anchoring them to one or more of your life's intentions.

✎   To master the art of creating meaningful goals, you must learn to see what you truly want. This involves the discipline of laying aside, at least for a moment, whatever is *not* what you want. Thus you cultivate the ability to generate energy by letting go of insignificant elements that dissipate it.

✎   A goal must contain the following five attributes. The acronym for this is SMART.
*   S is for specific.
*   M is for measurable.
*   A is for attainable.
*   R is for relevant.
*   T is for time-based.

✎   If you maintain your Standards of Integrity, you propel yourself forward to meet your goals. The way is clear and easy. If you violate your Standards of Integrity in any way, you may unconsciously keep yourself from getting your goals. Or, if you do attain them, you will suffer along the way.

✎   You are successful if you can take a dream, articulate it into a goal, and know that you will keep your promise to yourself to attain it or surpass it.

✎   Your net worth represents the amount of money energy over which you currently have custodianship.

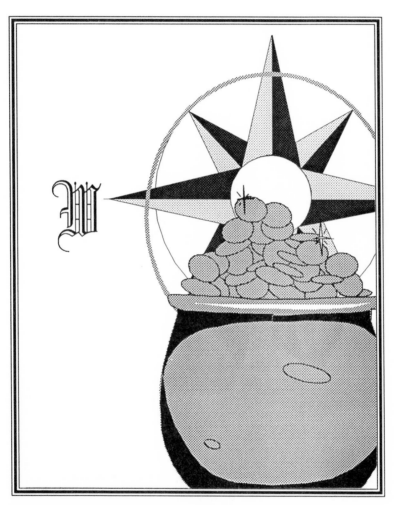

CHAPTER ELEVEN:
Growing Into Your Goals

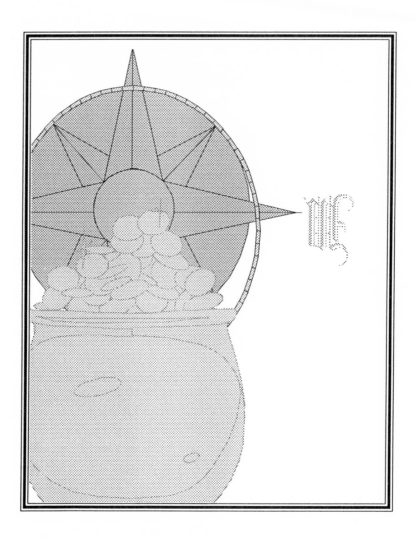

Growing Into Your Goals

"Whatever you can do or dream you can, begin it. Boldness has genius, power and magic in it. Begin it now."

Johann Wolfgang von Goethe

Goethe's quote has inspired many to dare to reach beyond their current structure of knowing to achieve their greatest potential and realize their dreams. One of those so inspired was W.H. Murray, author of *The Scottish Himalayan Expedition*. Murray wrote about commitment and its importance in all human endeavors. He said:

"Until one is committed, there is hesitancy, the chance to draw back, always ineffectiveness. Concerning all acts of initiative and creation, there is one elementary truth, the ignorance of which kills countless ideas and splendid plans: that the moment one commits oneself, then Providence moves, too. All sorts of things occur to help one that would never otherwise have occurred. A whole stream of events issues from the decision, raising in one's favor all manner of unforeseen incidents and meetings and material assistance, which no man could have dreamed would have come his way."

There is something both exciting and scary about having goals with meaning and power. They change who you are. The very act of creating such goals takes audacity and courage. At some intuitive level, you know that your journey toward them will reshape your identity. You will be taught things you never knew about yourself and your world.

Let me show you what I mean about the power of goals to mold us. Recall when you first decided to learn how to drive a car. Did you have a vision about how driving would expand your life? And did your life expand? Mine did.

I remember my first car, a high school graduation present. It was not much to look at, but it moved. I would sneak away from home in the middle of the night and drive down to the cargo loading docks at the Port of Long Beach. I would park and watch ships from all over the world emerge from the fog to pull up and disgorge their treasures. I remember the sense of freedom and independence I felt, being there while most of the city slept. I was proud of my adventurous spirit.

Here is another example of the transformative nature of goals:

Spencer: I've looked forward to this promotion for years. I'm finally projects manager at the plant. I head up a team of twelve people. I remember the days when I'd get irritated on the job. I'd say it was the manager's responsibility to keep things going right. Now I am one! My whole perspective has changed. I worry about whether I'm up to it. I do know that this is causing me to grow in ways I hadn't imagined.

Have you ever noticed that when you attain the really big goals in life, you need an adjustment period? Remember, goals worth playing for lie outside your boundaries of predictability. They draw you outside your structure of knowing. You have to grow into them to fully enjoy their benefits. All this requires change. Change means increased stress.

Some years ago, the Navy commissioned a study on the effects of change on people's health. After extensive interviews, the researchers, Holmes and Rahe, created the "Life Stress Index." This indicates a person's responses to major changes in his or her life. This ground-breaking study found that illness often results when people confront more change than they are able to comfortably integrate into their lives. This principle held true whether the changes were positive (inheriting money, getting promoted, or buying a house) or negative (loss, death in the family, or failure in business).

I remember watching the *Today Show* on television in 1980. Tom Brokaw was interviewing a couple who had just won a multimillion dollar lottery the day before. Both looked exhausted. They were in shock. They answered his questions in a monotone. If you had not known differently, you might have thought that they had just suffered a terrible loss in their lives. In a sense, this was true. They were losing their old identities with the influx of all this energy.

Now, you might say: "Please! Give me a loss like that! I could handle it!" That may very well be. Or, it may not. It is important to delve into this issue.

The Icarus Syndrome Revisited

This chapter gives you tools to help you integrate your goals with your life. This happens when you grow into them. Failure to integrate or grow into their goals is the primary reason most people never attain them -- or get into trouble and lose them once they have been attained. We all know of cases where people, unprepared for fame, fortune or power, meet with disaster. They may seem to fly high for a while. They purchase all sorts of things they believe they wanted. They find themselves in a terrible financial bind a few years later. One lottery winner told me: "It sounds crazy, but it was like

I couldn't get rid of the money fast enough. I really wasn't ready for all this power."

You may remember the Icarus Syndrome I spoke of earlier. Icarus was given wings, his fondest dream. But he flew too close to the sun, where his wings melted, and he plummeted back to earth.

All of us have our own personal version of the Icarus myth. There are times in our lives when we are unprepared for the opportunities that are offered to us. It is not a pretty sight! We are squashed against our opportunities like a flying critter meeting the windshield of a speeding car.

The next exercise allows you to get more in touch with your own variation on the theme of scorched wings.

Exercise: The Icarus Syndrome -- A Personal Recollection

What You Will Need
You will need your notebook and a pen or pencil.

Time For This Exercise
This should take no more than twenty minutes. Add another fifteen if you are sharing what you wrote with another person.

The Exercise
Note your answers to the following questions in your notebook:

1. Recall an example of the Icarus effect in your life. Have you ever been presented with an opportunity, only to botch it because you were not prepared for it? When did this occur? What happened? Be as specific as possible.

2. What decisions, if any, did you make about continuing forth on your hero's journey? Did any of your Basic Assumptions tributaries make themselves known to you?

3. In retrospect, what might you have done to better prepare for this situation?

Discussion
Share your answers with a friend or group. When I did this exercise, I recalled a time early in my business career when I decided to make an audiotape about success. Everyone who listened to it said it was good. But when I realized how little I knew about marketing and distributing, I stopped. I did not grow into the opportunity to learn. Years later, I still have this tape. It does not represent my current thoughts on the subject. However, it would have been a great introduction to my work ten years ago.

Channeling Energy: How to Fly, Instead of Flail, with Your Goals

Goals are a means of focussing the energies of money, time, love, creativity and physical well-being. Goals are benchmarks that tell us whether we are successfully demonstrating our intentions. One of the thrills of being human is to learn how to channel energy successfully -- to manifest in physical reality what has, until then, only been living in our hearts. Goals pull us forward, encouraging us to take an idea and transform it into reality. Those goals can be anything: writing a book, making a quilt, producing an invention, or painting. Maybe you want a business, a pilot's license, a home, a savings account, a diploma, to create a community assistance program, find a medical cure, or go on vacation. Successfully attaining goals is one of the fulfilling experiences of life! You are designed for that adventure.

You are made to have what you want. It is not a matter of deserving it. When you do not know what you want, you get cranky. Fail to learn the skills necessary to get what you want, and you become your own worst enemy. Then you become needy, greedy and cynical. What a mess! What a way to live! You are not here for that type of life. Shooting yourself in the foot repeatedly is exactly the opposite of your intention. To extend that metaphor, you want two good feet to walk up and claim your heart's desire.

A happy paradox is created when you know you can prepare for and have, what your heart desires. You begin to want less. Your choices reflect what will bring quality to your life and the lives of those around you.

When you get used to having what you truly want, you become less driven. You are not grasping and greedy. Greed is the result of dissatisfaction. It occurs as a response to the void created by driven behavior. The antidotes to greed are satisfaction and enjoyment. The trick is to slow down long enough to appreciate what, according to Willa Cather, "has been there around you always."

One day I met a woman who worked at a bakery. She told me that the first three weeks she tasted everything in sight. It felt like a holiday. When eating chocolate cake, she would finish the whole piece. She responded to an inner voice that told her: "Eat this up, there may not be any more chocolate cake again for a long time."

After a while, she found herself eating less. She ate only what really called to her. She said, "I was getting used to the idea that I could have cake whenever I wanted it. In a strange way, I felt more secure. I ate more slowly. I appreciated every bite. I was no longer gulping it down." By the time I met her, she was down to one dessert a week. She had begun losing the weight she had gained.

Are you really willing to get used to having what you want in life? All it takes to move forward from this point is to be willing to take a stand for what you want, and prepare for it.

Attaining your goals is an outgrowth of two factors: conscious declaration and personal preparation.

The first factor, conscious declaration, is like the commitment expressed previously in W.A. Murray's quote. Your creation of three goals for this year is a conscious declaration. You have promised yourself that this *will be*. You have taken a stand and projected your intentions into the physical plane. Circumstances will form themselves around your proclamation. You will find opportunities where there had previously seemed to be none. Is the universe aligning around you? Are your perceptions of already existing opportunities being made finer? Both may be true.

To clarify what we mean by preparation, let us take a further look at some scenarios of what happens when we are *not* prepared for achieving our goals. What happens to us when we have not taken the time to look into the impact our success might have on our daily lives?

* You start a new business, but have not researched what it will take to run it. You find yourself working too hard and investing too much money. Broke and exhausted, you cannot enjoy what you have created.

* You have finally gotten your pilot's license. To pay for the flying lessons, license, and for a timeshare in an airplane, you must work long hours. You never find the time to fly.

* You decide to run a marathon. You do not spend the time or money for the support or coaching you need. You get injured on your first run and must stop.

The hero's journey toward a goal starts with the questions: Am I willing to expand beyond the person I currently consider myself to be? Am I willing to be adventurous? Am I willing to prepare to have it?

Any goal worth pursuing lies outside your current structure of knowing. To reach it, you need to dismantle this structure. You must expand the framework of your current image of yourself. It is true whether your goal is to be an opera singer, a manager, a business owner, an artist, or an author. Here are just a few examples of how our perceptions and relationship to the world can change as we achieve our goals:

* Once you are a pilot, weather takes on a new meaning, as does the perception of physical space.
* Once you have a child, your identity as an independent person shifts. The cry of your infant gains your attention like nothing else in the world. A good night's sleep takes on a whole new meaning -- a goal you would give anything to attain!
* Once you are a home owner and the roof leaks during a storm, you can no longer call the landlord. It is your job now.

Consider the case of someone who finally suceeded in growing into a goal:

Mitch: My intention is to have a successful private practice. I set a goal of making $1,500 a week. When I first began as a therapist, the hardest thing for me to do was to collect money from clients. Sometimes I'd let clients' bills pile high because I felt awkward charging for my services.

> "One remains young as long as one can still learn, can still take on new habits, can bear contradictions."
>
> *Marie von Ebner-Eschenbach*

Occasionally, bills would get so high that the client would quit therapy, discouraged about how much he or she owed me. So, I wouldn't get paid. It was a mess. The same with insurance billing, I put it off forever. By the time I hired a business consultant, my accounts receivable was $10,000.

I'm glad I got help when I did! I collected only $6,000 of the $10,000 owed me. Now I collect payment at the end of each session. My clients are more relaxed and realistic about what they can afford. In cases of need, I have a sliding scale. I bill the insurance companies every week. I learned that accounts receivable are definitely *not* the same as money in the bank!

If you are willing to be shaped by your goals, you are in for an adventure. The journey shapes you as you progress toward your goal. It is a natural and exciting path to growth.

The Treasure Map: A Physical Picture of Your Goals

Treasure Mapping your goal is a way to begin your journey toward achieving it. Remember Napoleon Hill's discovery: people who are successful write their goals down? That being so, can you imagine how much more effective it would be to create a graphic, colorful representation of your heart's desire? A Treasure Map is just that, a colorful, detailed, and graphic representation of your goal. It represents your best effort to create a comprehensive, visualization of how your life will look when you have attained what you want.

Treasure Mapping begins the process of taking your goal from the idea stage to physical reality. It acts as an energy magnet or goal generator boosting your energy. The very act of creating a Treasure Map puts you firmly on the path to success.

The urge to create a visual representation of what we want is in our blood. Have you ever seen ancient pictographs in caves? They are paintings or carvings left by prehistoric human beings. If you have, a sense of kinship may have arisen for you. Archaeologists and anthropologists have interpreted this amazing art. They say that the ancient artist believed the picture of a bison on the wall of a cave brought "bison energy" forth. On an everyday level, we can still experience this process. Look at a picture of the car you want. Find a travel brochure with the mountains or beaches you love. Do you feel the excitement? Can you put yourself in the picture?

"It is only by following your deepest instinct that you can lead a rich life and if you let your fear of consequence prevent you from following your deepest instinct, then your life will be safe, expedient and thin."

Katherine Butler Hathaway

It is time for you to consciously energize your goals. You will awaken an ability that may have been dormant within you. We are going to call forth the spirit of that which you are pursuing. This is a simple process, although it might not immediately seem so. You may have many years of inertia to overcome. Perhaps you told yourself that it was silly to be guided by your dreams. The act of creating Treasure Maps for your goals is an act of vulnerability. It contradicts Monkey Mind's chiding:

* You're acting like a kid playing *let's pretend*.
* This will never work.
* You better make sure nobody sees what you are doing.
* Getting what you want is way too complicated!
* Are you sure you want to make such a big deal out of this?

Over the past fifteen years, I have consulted with people on approximately 8,000 Treasure Maps. During the *You and Money* course, each person comes up with three goals, and with Treasure Maps for each one. I have seen and heard about miracles associated with them. Here are some examples:

Alan: I Treasure Mapped a Victorian-looking home, white with blue trim. I cut out a magazine picture of a house and put a picture of myself in front, holding a Sold sign. It was dated eight months into the future. I had no idea how I was going to come up with a big down payment. Four months later, I was riding my bike when I saw a house with a For Sale sign. The owner had to move because of a promotion, and was willing to carry the paper with a small down payment. I bought the house. It was almost an exact copy of my Treasure Map picture.

Christie: Two months after I did a Treasure Map about wanting to make money while traveling around the world, I met a cousin at a family reunion. He was going to travel the South Pacific, teaching scuba diving. I remembered my Treasure Map. I'd already gotten my scuba diving certificate. I decided right then to get my instructor's license. Why pass up a way that might make my dream come true? I wrote my cousin in Tahiti. He'd landed a great job with a cruise line teaching resort diving courses. They needed another instructor. I flew down and got the job.

These are only two of the hundreds of stories I have heard from people in the *You and Money* course. Others traveling this path have achieved the following:
* Published books and screenplays
* Recognition for Successful Entrepreneur of the Year
* Award-winning architectural project completed in record time, with ease
* Trekking the Himalayas, with the time and money to do it enjoyably
* First art exhibit a success
* Becoming a respected and highly-paid business consultant
* A new wardrobe with a well-conditioned body to fit into it

Your Treasure Map will focus your energy toward your goal. All manner of unforeseen incidents will begin to come your way. You will become more aware of already existing windows of opportunity. Or maybe, conscious intention really does create the probability that something will happen, as quantum physicists think! Whatever the case, the Treasure Map helps you prepare for your success. With the intentional focus that a Treasure Map represents, you will likely realize your goal in full.

Exercise: How to Create Your Treasure Map

Are you willing to have what you want? Are you willing, even if it means doing something new or different? If your answers to these questions are yes, use the guidelines for creating a Treasure Map. Make sure you follow the instructions to the letter. Again, you will go outside your structure of knowing. I developed these guidelines carefully over the years. Start right now taking your dreams seriously and do exactly what successful people before you have done.

What You Will Need
* Scissors and two glue sticks.
* One piece of poster board, around 18" x 24" for each goal. White is the best color.
* Colored construction paper: about five pieces for each map.
* Magazines, brochures and catalogues with colorful pictures. Having those that depict the general subject of your goal is best. For example, get architectural or home magazines for a home, travel magazines or brochures for a vacation, and business magazines for career goals.
* Magazines or brochures with catchy or inspirational phrases that can be cut out and pasted on your map.
* Calendars with dates at least 1" high, that can be cut out.
* A recent photograph of yourself and whoever will share this goal with you. Please note: make sure you get their permission before placing anyone but yourself on your Treasure Map.
* Your notebook.

The Exercise
In the *You and Money* course, making Treasure Maps is a group process. You work together, give feedback, and share ideas. The sheer energy and synergy of the group helps overcome the inertia of your old structures of knowing. Consider making your Map with at least one or two friends. After all, everyone who has a dream or a goal can use some company as they begin their journey toward it. Everyone can benefit from having a Treasure Map of their own. As you help each other, you can find pictures and words to share. Support each other to venture outside your structures of knowing. Entertain and include novel ways the goal can look.

1. Take one of the goals you identified in the last chapter. Make sure it conforms to the SMART criteria we described earlier: Specific, Measurable, Attainable, Relevant, and Time-Based. Each goal you map must have a "want rating" of eight or higher.

2. Create a phrase that describes your goal. Put it in the present tense. For example, instead of saying: "I *will be* at the beach with my children, April 14, 19__," write: "I *am* at the beach with my children, April 14, 19__."

3. First, take your photograph(s) and glue one on each Treasure Map. Place them anywhere you like. This is the first big step in putting yourself (and anyone else you have chosen, with their permission) on the journey toward your goal.

4. Look through your magazines and form the goal phrase from words you cut out of magazines or other print media. Do not write these words or print them from your computer. As you look for words in these magazines, you are broadening your options. You may find an even better way to express your goal. Glue this goal phrase on your Treasure Map, preferably somewhere toward the top. If you wish, cut out a piece of construction paper and use it as a colorful backdrop for your goal phrase words.

5. Find colorful pictures that represent your goal. Use the magazines, brochures and catalogues you have collected. Do not draw anything on your Treasure Map. Your drawings are influenced by the very structures of knowing you are moving beyond. Whether it is a car, a home, a new job, a trip around the world or an academic degree, find pictures that make your goal crystal clear.

6. As you place the pictures and glue them down, make sure you fill your Treasure Map. You want it to explode with color as it embodies your goal. Do you want a car? Get a picture of the exact car of your dreams from a magazine. You can even place another picture of yourself inside it. How about opening a business? You may want a picture of you, perhaps sitting at a desk or standing in front of your store, equipment, ranch, etc. Let your imagination flow. One woman wanted to begin a career as a motion picture photographer. She found the type of camera she would be using and had her picture taken with it. A man who wanted to open a homeless shelter got a sign, printed it with the shelter's logo, and got his picture taken standing in front of it.

7. As you work on your Treasure Map, take time out to breathe. You are doing what you have been born to do. You are bringing a dream into reality. You are showing that you respect yourself and take your goals seriously. **Respect your goals. They come from your heart.**

    When you notice thoughts or feelings becoming strong, take out your notebook and write about them. What are you saying to yourself? What emotions are coming up? Have these stopped you in the past? If so, when? You are re-creating your ability to picture and claim your goals. You will encounter your old obstacles along the way. This is a natural process.

8. Clip words and phrases that reflect how you will feel when you attain your goal. Make sure what you choose are *feeling* words. They must be words that represent emotions. Words like *important*, and *successful*, and phrases such as "the best just gets better," are motivational, not emotional. They may be placed on the Treasure Map. But they are not *feeling* words. Here are some examples of feeling words:

admiring	certain	enchanted	fascinated	joyous	strong	warm
adoring	cheerful	encouraged	free	joyful	satisfied	wonderful
amused	comfortable	energetic	glad	loving	secure	zany
appreciative	confident	energized	grateful	moved	sensitive	zealous
blissful	courageous	enthusiastic	gratified	optimistic	thankful	zestful
boisterous	daring	enthralled	great	passionate	tender	
bold	determined	exhilarated	happy	patient	thrilled	
brave	eager	exhuberant	hopeful	playful	valiant	
calm	ecstatic	excited	intrigued	relaxed	vibrant	

You might use colorful construction paper as a backing for the words. This helps them stand out on the Map.

As you go through magazines and brochures, it may surprise you to discover how few feeling words we use. We rely upon concepts: "Go for the gold!" "Be a winner." "You deserve the best." These expressions are not reflections of the heart-centered emotion for which we are looking. Hunting for feelings and placing them on your map puts you into the immediate experience of the goal. The immediacy of feeling words will draw you down your path. If you glance at an ancient pictograph, you can sense the feelings of its creator. The experience is vivid, even after thousands of years.

9. Include, in clearly visible type cut from a printed page, brochure or calendar, the exact month, day and year that you will attain your goal. The date is where the *rubber meets the road*. This anchors the goal in physical reality. Make it bigger than you think you should. Then it will be just right.

10. Add the intentions that support your goal to the map. It, too, should be a phrase composed of words clipped from magazines. Have intentions, as much as possible, begin with the words "to be." Examples are: To be financially successful; To be an artist; To be physically fit. Again, you might use some colorful construction paper as a backdrop. This sets the words off from the rest of the map.

Discussion

You have just completed an important project. It is time to share your experience with others. What were your thoughts and feelings during the process?

1. Did any Monkey Mind conversations emerge? Did you write them down?
    Be sure to note them. What was it like to work through these conversa-
    tions, without waiting for them to go away?

2. What was it like to hunt for feeling words? Has this process broadened the
    types of words you use to express your emotional states?

3. Is your Treasure Map colorful and graphic? What do you perceive as you
    look at it? Now is the time to add any parts that are missing.

Show your Treasure Map to at least two people who have not helped you
with it. See if they can tell what the goal is without you explaining it. If they
are confused, look for what is missing from the map. People should be able to
tell at a glance what it is about. You want to come away from your Treasure
Map feeling that the total image you have created is imprinted in your mind.

Place the map where you can easily see it. Look at the map once a day for
thirty days. Read the goal, intention and feeling words. The process has begun.
Good for you!

Continuing to Clear the Way

Next, you will further prepare for your goals.

**When you engage in bringing the metaphysical into
the physical, your life has spark and focus.**

If you recall, we had you compute your net worth in the
last chapter. If you have done this, you are waking yourself
up. You are empowering yourself to become conscious. I
know that this is not a particularly *exciting* activity. It may
seem mundane. That is because it *is* mundane. The root of
the word mundane is "earthly." You are dealing in the physical realm in a focused way. In doing this, you are giving
yourself an antidote to driven behavior. Driven behavior
clouds your awareness.

The following exercise asks you to examine your credit
report from two independent credit agencies. If your net
worth is like a score, your credit rating is like your handi-
cap. That is, it indicates the ease with which you will be able
to negotiate money matters. This is useful to know as you
begin your path toward your goals. According to bank of-
ficers, one frequent source of heartache is a credit rating that
shows you are a poor investment risk. People are denied loans
based upon this. The rating is independent of how much
money you make. It is based upon how promptly you pay
your debts. It also reflects whether you owe more than you
can comfortable pay back. I have known millionaires who
have had difficulty negotiating financial matters because of

a poor credit rating.

Do this exercise. Allow yourself to know what is there. I promise, you will have more power to go for your goals just out of your willingness to do this! You are displaying the hero's courage. This is not an exaggeration.

Your credit record is subject to inaccuracies and errors. For example, one woman found that, according to a credit agency, she was married to her adult son! Every time he wrote a bad check, it showed on her credit report. By writing a letter to the credit agency she was able to get this error corrected, instantly improving her credit rating 100 percent! One man found he was being confused with someone with the same name. The other person lived 3,000 miles across the country and had recently filed for bankruptcy.

You may have some items to address on your credit reports. There are many different credit reporting agencies. Lenders subscribe to one or more and use them to check your credit rating when you apply for a loan. You can correct errors in one report only to have them turn up in another. However, if you can show a lender at least two corrected reports from respected credit reporting agencies, you will have no problems.

Exercise: Now That You Know Your Score, What is Your Handicap?

What You Will Need

Obtain at least two credit reports from independent credit reporting agencies. Each report may cost between $8-15. It is money well spent. You will learn in advance if any factors preclude achieving your goal. These reports must be current. If you have one from more than three months ago, you are not necessarily getting the accurate information you need. Make sure they are *bona fide* credit reports. You do not want computer printouts like the kinds available at car dealerships and real estate agencies. Check the codes that are used, and the methods each agency uses to clear credit items.

Have your notebook with you as well.

Time For This Exercise

Time requirements will vary, depending on the contents and format of your credit report. Expect to spend at least ten minutes studying each document.

The Exercise

1. Look for any items that point to a question about your credit. You may have a poor credit rating because of your own mistakes or oversights. What are they? Can they be corrected? One mistake people often make is failing to close out accounts that are not currently in use. If, for example, you have ten credit card accounts that together give you the potential for charging $20,000 worth of goods, it may count against you. Cancel out those accounts and your credit rating may go up. Look at the back of your credit reports for remedies suggested by the credit agency itself, and then follow through on those suggestions.

2. If you are in doubt about any item(s) you may want professional consultation. Is this a legal issue? A mistake in accounting?

3. Write the items you need to clarify or rectify in your notebook under Incomplete Money Business. Put a date next to each, noting by when you will have taken the appropriate action. *Take care of the items as soon as possible!*

Discussion

Share with a friend what you have found from doing this exercise. If you know precisely what is on your report, you can respond realistically when negotiating money matters. Often, a truthful, up-front account of the mistakes shown on your report will allow people to work with you in finding solutions. In addition, you can have the items removed through working with the agency that reported them.

What internal conversations did you notice while looking at your credit report? Were you relieved? Worried? Are you allowing your discomfort to be present, while handling what needs to be fixed?

Discomfort is a natural part of growth. Every time you grow, you will encounter it. Instead of being relieved when you avoid discomfort, you actually extend it! Facing it with compassion produces wisdom, because you will see how irrelevant it usually is to attaining your goals and dreams. This is cultivating the heart of the hero.

The Journey Continues

The next chapter prepares you to embrace the possibilities in your life. It is about gratitude and contribution. We also revisit your Standards of Integrity.

Summary

✐   A happy paradox is created when you know you can prepare for, and have, what your heart desires. You begin to want less. Your choices reflect what will bring quality to your life and the lives of those around you.

✐   Attaining your goals is an outgrowth of two factors: conscious declaration and personal preparation.

✐   The hero's journey toward a goal starts with the questions: "Am I willing to go beyond who I currently consider myself to be? Am I up for the adventure? Am I willing to prepare to have it?"

✐   Respect your goals. They come from your heart.

✐   When you engage in bringing the metaphysical into the physical, your life has spark and focus.

✐   Treasure Mapping begins the process of taking your goal from the idea stage into physical reality. It acts as an energy magnet or generator, boosting your energy. The very act of creating a Treasure Map puts you firmly on the path to success.

✐   Discomfort is a natural part of growth. Every time you grow, you will encounter it. Instead of being relieved when you avoid discomfort, you actually extend it! Facing it with compassion produces wisdom, because you will see how irrelevant it usually is to attaining your goals and dreams. This is cultivating the heart of the hero.

CHAPTER TWELVE:
The Nature of Abundance

The Nature of Abundance

"Gratitude unlocks the fullness of life. It turns what we have into enough, and more. It turns denial into acceptance, chaos to order, confusion to clarity. It can turn a meal into a feast, a house into a home, a stranger into a friend. Gratitude makes sense of our past, brings peace for today, and creates vision for tomorrow."

Melody Beattie

We come now to the heart of the matter; the nature of abundance. This subject invariably emerges as we proceed upon the hero's journey. It is so important because it frames our perceptions.

The gateway to abundance is gratitude. The key to gratitude is to be willing to affirm what is present. Integrity and contribution amplify the power of affirmation.

Are you willing to experience abundance in your life? We begin by looking at what abundance is, and then each factor that promotes it: gratitude, affirmation, contribution and integrity. Having done what has been suggested thus far, you are now engaged in the process of clearing your hero's path. Now you have identified your goals, intentions and Standards of Integrity. You have looked at the symptoms of Monkey Mind, and the tributaries of your Basic Assumption. You recognize how driven behavior and your fears of scarcity affect your daily life. These are heroic accomplishments.

This is the perfect time to discover the true nature of abundance. To do this, let us return to the diagram about who you are on page twenty-eight. If you recall, the outer layer indicates who you pretend you are. The next layer reflects who you are afraid you are. The star in the middle indicates who you really are. Monkey Mind inhabits the two outer layers. It jumps back and forth, chattering at us about past mistakes and future disasters.

To the extent that we fall prey to this voice, life will be hard. We worry about not having enough time, love, money, physical energy or creativity. In this frame of mind, we are convinced that more will be better. Just give us more of everything, especially money, and our problems will be solved.

The experience of abundance occurs at the level of the person you really are, your true self. Your true self, or who you really are in your heart, is the foundation of your being.

It is not affected by what goes on in physical reality. Who you really are exists as potential. You give form to this potential through your intentions. Your true self is mirrored in your Standards of Integrity.

Your true self is timeless. That is, it occurs outside the realm of physical time. Who you are in your heart lives in the present moment. It is through appreciation of the present moment that you can experience abundance.

To appreciate the present moment is to acknowledge, cherish and savor it. This is a tall order. We sometimes have to pass through many layers of discomfort before we get to the appreciation part. And the trick, as we will see, is to appreciate and cherish even the discomfort.

Abundance and The Hero's Journey

Let us go outside our usual structure of knowing about abundance. As we have seen from the words of gifted thinkers and teachers, the well-lived life is a conscious life. When we are conscious, we are aware of everything. We are living fully. To live fully is to be present to all of life's ups and downs. This gives us a clue to the nature of abundance.

Abundance is everything. It is the good and bad moments, happiness and sadness.

This recalls that saying from the Bible, *Ecclesiastes* 3:1-8: "To everything there is a season, and a time to every purpose under heaven. A time to be born, and a time to die; a time to plant, and a time to pluck up that which is planted ...." Truly, if life teaches us nothing else it teaches that there is a time for comfort and a time for discomfort, a time for joy, and a time for sadness. This is abundance.

We all hope that abundance means more. More of the good, sweet-smelling stuff of life. But abundance is all of it, even the bitter moments that serve as lessons and wake-up calls.

Scarcity is not the opposite of abundance. It is an inseparable aspect of abundance. Scarcity is the perception of limits. Limits are necessary in order for us to operate in the physical domain. It is therefore a condition of life. It is part of abundance. We do not have to fear scarcity or try to get away from it. We learn and grow from it if we are willing.

If you were really to take this all in, you would find that there is no need to run from your discomfort. Discomfort is a sign of an imbalance. Bringing balance to areas in your life that have an imbalance provides for some of your best lessons. Therefore, even the imbalance is necessary.

If abundance is everything in existence, then what is prosperity? Prosperity is the outgrowth of being willing to say yes, *emphatically* yes, to all of it. Prosperity occurs when you are willing to be present to everything put before you, the bitter and the sweet. Prosperity is a state of growth. It is the continued expression of who you are in your heart, and you contact it the moment you say "I am willing."

This may be a lot to swallow all at once. Look inside to see the truth of the matter. People who thrive are people who are willing to say yes to their lives. They have not blocked themselves from the difficult moments. They are open to everything: pain, despair, joy, love; everything. You know that if you try to cut out feeling pain, you dull yourself from feeling joy as well. If you are like me, you have tried to do this at some point in your life. Does it work? **The hero inside you arises when you are willing to say yes to everything on your life's path.**

> "What brings fulfillment is gratefulness, the simple response of our heart to this given life in all its fullness."
>
> *Brother David Steindl-Rast*

Are you willing to say yes? Are you willing to experience the sweet, happy, delightful moments in your life? No matter what Monkey Mind says? Are you willing to experience the discomfort and imbalance in your life? Are you willing to use it all to grow and thrive?

The Fine Art of Gratitude

Spiritual thinkers tell us that it is important to develop an approach to life called gratefulness. Brother David Steindl-Rast, theologian, has given this a lot of thought. He says we have gotten what makes for a full life all backwards. We wait for good circumstances to happen to us before we are grateful. However, the experience of a life well-lived is based on bringing gratefulness to our everyday circumstances, no matter what they may be.

The principle of gratitude is a key ingredient to growing into your goals. It more easily brings goals into being when gratefulness prepares the space for them. To have a goal to try to get away from an uncomfortable or painful circumstance only prolongs the very circumstance you seek to escape. There is no breathing room for creativity. Gratitude shifts your energy. You are no longer in the fight, flight or freeze mode. Your belly is soft and receptive. You breathe deeply. You are open to possibility.

Gratitude is present when you see that everything that occurs in your life can be used to show you how to live fully as a human being.

Living life fully means living every aspect of life. This includes the experience of joy, sadness, love, hate, scarcity, and inspiration. As Pema Chodron puts it in her book, *The Wisdom of No Escape and the Path of Loving-Kindness:*

"Being satisfied with what we already have is a magical golden key to being fully alive in a full, unrestricted, and inspired way ... It doesn't do any good to get rid of our so-called negative aspects, because in that process we also get rid of our basic wonderfulness. We can lead a life so as to become more awake to who we are and what we're doing rather than trying to improve or change or get rid of who we are or what we're doing. They key is to wake up, to become more alert, more inquisitive and curious about ourselves."

How do you become grateful for everything? It starts by being willing. You may not *want* to be grateful for whatever is in your life. You may think it is a bad idea to be grateful for a difficult circumstance, because it will "empower" that circumstance. For example, you may find you owe $1,000 more on your income tax than you had anticipated. Or, you are downsized out of a job. How do you wrap gratitude around that? Would it be foolish to do so?

You may feel worried about making too much of the good circumstances in your life. After all, things might change for the worse. Maybe the Fates will get jealous. This is not logical. It is, however, a superstition that shows up in many cultures. For example, my older Jewish relatives, upon seeing a healthy and beautiful baby, would cry out: "It's too bad she is so ugly and sickly." This would hopefully keep the evil spirits from working their mischief upon the child.

I remember one woman in the *You and Money* course was having difficulty coming up with goals. She finally told us she was recovering from breast cancer and was afraid to make goals lest she not live to meet them. At the same time, she was terrified of expressing gratitude for the lessons that the illness taught her. She thought this could bring the cancer back.

Gratitude does not mean that you jump for joy at whatever occurs in your life. It does mean, however, that you note, bear witness to, and are willing to learn and grow from whatever is put before you. You are willing to have it be there. You are doing nothing to run from the situation.

For most of us, the moment of acceptance and gratitude is usually preceded by doubt, fear and worry. Even Jesus, in the Garden of Gesthemane the night before He was crucified, asked God to remove the cup of suffering from His lips. This is the essence of the Passion. In those moments, He demonstrated what it was to be both human and Divine. At the culmination of this suffering, He declared: "Thy will be done!" This is the quintessential example of: "I am willing!" The way is open for Him to continue on.

> "Bless a thing and it will bless you. Curse it and it will curse you ... If you bless a situation, it has no power to hurt you, and even if it is troublesome for a time, it will gradually fade out, if you sincerely bless it."
>
> *Emmet Fox*

Awakening the Grateful Heart

One way to kindle gratitude is to practice noting that which occurs to us in everyday physical reality. So much of our time is spent with Monkey Mind in the past or future. We do not linger long enough to see what is here in the present.

Observation gives power to the present moment. The moment can then be used to awaken the grateful heart. This is the foundation of affirmation.

When we affirm, we are literally *making firm*. We are giving substance. We observe, note our relationship with what we are observing, and are willing to have it be there just as it is. This takes guts. We do not always feel up to it. However, we can be willing even when we fear we cannot meet the challenge.

There are three ways to engage in creative affirmation. The first is to note and give substance to your daily lessons. This is difficult. Most good lessons do not appear beneficial when we first encounter them. To discover that you have lost a job seems more like a closing than an opening. It feels terrible. At the moment you first experience this loss, it would be useless for anyone to tell you: "Oh, but you will learn so much from this! Be grateful!" No, first you need to grieve, complain or get angry. Then, and only then, do you have the opportunity to say: "Yes. I am willing to experience this. I am willing for this to be a lesson for me." It might look like this:

Mark: I lost out on an organizational development consulting job.

Me: What happened?

Mark: I guess I didn't come across well. This really burns me. I thought I did a great job.

Me: Tell us about being "burned up". (I am not trying to "logic" him out of how he feels).

Mark: I really wanted the job. Could have used the money, too. I feel like such a jerk. Maybe I came off really badly at the interview.

Me: Anything else burn you up about this?

Mark: Maybe I'm not as great as I think I am. I've been in this business for eighteen years. Maybe I've just been fooling myself all along.

Me: What else burns you about this?

Mark: (Goes on for another two minutes emptying the Monkey Mind conversations out of his head. Then he pauses.)

Me: Take a deep breath. (Mark does.) Are you *willing* to have this be here? Are you willing to have this be a message or a lesson for you?

Mark: I don't think so. I feel so stupid.

Me: I don't mean do you *want* this lesson. Or even that you *believe* it can teach you anything. I'm asking if you're willing. This is above and beyond what Monkey Mind is telling you right now.

Mark: Okay. Then I'm willing. Something happened that I hate, but I'm willing to have it be here. (He pauses.) I'm even willing to be grateful for the wake-up call this mess created. I'm not grateful now, but I'm willing to be.

Mark looked at the possibility of calling the man who had interviewed him. He was willing to ask for feedback. Was there anything he could tell Mark that might help him at other interviews? The man was impressed. He told Mark the only thing disqualifying him was that he had not given enough details when he talked about what he would do. This had nothing to do with his skill or ability as a consultant. Mark revamped his consultant brochure and presentation material. He landed a large contract within two months. But for Mark, the true miracle was seeing the possibility of being grateful despite the discomfort.

> "Accepting and blessing our circumstances is a powerful tool for transformation."
>
> *Emmet Fox*

As I said earlier, the key to gratitude is to be willing to affirm what is present. Or, as a friend of mine often says: "Play it as it lays!"

The second form that affirmation takes is being grateful for the pleasures we receive: a beautiful sunset, a letter from a dear friend, an unexpected promotion or raise at work. You might think that affirming these would be natural. After all, how much simpler can you get than being grateful for what brings you joy or happiness? In the normal course of events, we spend only a short time with everyday pleasures before Monkey Mind again directs our attention to the past or future.

The next exercise will develop your ability to engage in the two types of affirmation described above. I suggest you work with this. It will develop your *gratitude muscle*.

"No pessimist ever discovered the secrets of the stars, or sailed to an uncharted land, or opened a new heaven to the human spirit."

Helen Keller

Exercise: Basic Affirmation Training

In this affirmation training, you are going to consciously shift how you observe the events in your life. You are going to imbue them with gratitude.

What You Will Need
Have your notebook with you and any inspirational writings by your favorite authors or poets.

Time For This Exercise
You will need five minutes of quiet time at the end of each day. You may do this for one week. For the best results, engage with this exercise for thirty days. Please note that for some of us, engineering just five minutes of quiet time at the close of the day is a miracle. Try it!

The Exercise

1. Each night before you go to sleep, list three instances from your day that evoke a sense of gratitude for you. It does not matter how big or small they may seem. Keep your notebook by your bed and make your list before you turn out the light. You may find situations for which gratefulness is an easy and ready response. Examples might include a job well done, the smile of a child, or a good meal.

2. You may notice that you are unable to come up with three instances of gratefulness. This may be especially true during the first days of this practice. Ask yourself the question: "What doubts, worries or other thoughts am I listening to instead?" Write your answers on a sheet of paper that is not part of the notebook. Then, throw that paper away and go back and list instances for which you are grateful.

3. You will probably have times in which gratitude seems a highly unlikely response, given a particular difficult or distressing event in your present life. This is where the exercise becomes more challenging. Here is what you might do. It has worked for me. Ask yourself: "Am I *willing* to discover a way to respond with gratefulness to even this situation? Am I willing to see the important learning here?"

4. If the answer is no, do not push yourself into saying yes. It is sufficient that you were willing to ask the above questions and answer in all truthfulness. Find a piece of writing that inspires you and read it. It may be a sonnet, a verse from your favorite motivational author, the Bible, Upanishads, or poetry. Anything. Just allow yourself to read for ten minutes. That is usu-

ally sufficient to raise the gratefulness quotient. Then, return to the situation and ask yourself, "What is there about the situation that could evoke gratefulness? What might I learn from this?" If you find something about which to be grateful, write it down. If not, give it and yourself a rest until the next day.

Discussion

Review what you have written after the first week. Are there any patterns? How do you feel just reading what you have written?

Ron: It felt good to read what I'd written. One night I came home after a particularly lousy day at work. On my way to change clothes, I passed by the notebook. I opened it and began to read my notations on gratefulness. I felt better immediately and had a great evening with my family.

Suz: I was just about to lead a difficult staff meeting. We had found we were $10,000 over budget on a $50,000 project. Ordinarily, I'd be agitated. Everyone would be on eggshells around me. I happened to have my notebook with me that morning and spent three minutes reading over some of my entries. By the time I entered the meeting room, I was calmer. We solved the problem in record time. I got to use it as one of my instances for gratitude.

Share your results with a friend. Are you finding it possible to expand your heart around uncomfortable incidents without pushing them away? Are you willing to carry this exercise forward for a total of thirty days?

The Third Form of Affirmation

You have probably noticed by now that we are not using affirmations to deny or escape difficult circumstances. We are developing the ability to grant substance to what is already there. The third form of affirmation takes this process one step further.

You have qualities that describe who you really are in your heart. These qualities are found in your Standards of Integrity.

Affirm the attributes that are inherent in your Standards of Integrity and you empower that which already exists inside you.

Affirming who you really are is simple. It does not require a stretch of your imagination. You start by the declaration that you are willing. You then follow this with the attribute you are willing to be. This attribute is taken from your Standards of Integrity. You say: "I am willing to be courageous," or "I am willing to be loyal," or whatever is true for you.

Will you try this right now? I am not putting this in a formal exercise format. Just take out your Standards of Integrity, say: "I am willing to be ... and then follow this with one of your Standards. Then go on to the next one, and the next. Say the words aloud. See how they feel on your tongue, in your heart, in other parts of your body. Repeat them to yourself each night, preferably after doing the prior exercise. Do this for at least one week. What do you perceive? Is there a spark of gratitude present?

Alan: This was much easier for me than I expected. My mind didn't go nuts. In fact, it seemed natural. At first I knew I wasn't saying that I *was* these qualities. Only that I was *willing* to be. After a while, something happened. One night when I was saying them, I got this flash! Of course I was courageous, truthful, loyal and intelligent! That was not the question. The real question was: "Am I going to demonstrate that this is who I am?" It does no good to have these attributes if I'm not doing something with them. I'm glad to be me. It's an adventure.

Exercise: Contemplating Gratitude

The next exercise will increase your ability to bring gratitude into the present moment. It is very simple to do. Although I recommend you begin with ten minutes, you may find you can increase this to twenty minutes over time. Remember, these processes are designed to open your heart to experiencing the true nature of abundance. What you are about to do will teach you to notice how to invoke gratitude in everyday events.

What You Will Need

A small spiral pad, similar to the one you used to keep track of every penny you spent. Find a place at home or outside where you feel comfortable. If you do this in a group, make sure you are somewhere where you have enough room to walk around without bumping into one another.

Time For This Exercise

Give yourself ten to twenty minutes.

The Exercise

1. Stand in a place where you feel comfortable. Begin a slow walk. Make sure you are breathing easily and deeply.

2. Begin to consciously search for objects or scenes that bring you a sense of joy, peace, or happy surprise. As you do this, note your experience in your small spiral pad. Make sure to describe both what is going on outside and what is going on inside you. Look closely at ordinary items. Do you notice the dew on the leaves? Have you noticed the texture on the covering of your favorite pillow? For example, you might write:

* I see the shell of an acorn, with two leaves attached.
* It looks like the leavings of a squirrel. I love squirrels.
* I smell a rose. It's outer petals are red, but the inner ones are pink. It's so soft. I'm glad I found it.
* I am looking at the photo of my great-aunt Anna. She is smiling at me.
* My heart feels warm.

3. Continue this exercise for ten minutes. It requires attention. Every time your inner conversations take you away, pause. Take one or two deep breaths. Keep your stomach loose. Bring yourself back to the present moment. Search for what brings you joy, peace or happy surprise.

4. You may find nothing evokes these reactions in you. Take another deep breath. The very fact that you are willing to engage in this exercise means

you are opening the way for the experience of gratefulness. It will come, most probably when you least expect it. Deepak Chopra, in his book, *Creating Affluence*, talks about what happens when we relinquish our attachment to outcomes. For instance, you may recall when you were trying unsuccessfully to remember a name. The more you struggled with it, the more elusive it became. When you let go of the struggle, the name appeared later in your consciousness, as if by magic. That is what will happen here for you. Just being willing to engage in this exercise may be a special opportunity for gratefulness.

5. If discovering the joy in ordinary items continues to elude you, try this: Take an apple, orange, or banana. Sit down and hold it in your hands. Smell it. Take the skin off. Look at the fine lines or marks on the skin. Take a section of the fruit. Hold it to up to light. Taste it. What do you notice? Is gratitude beginning to peek out from between your taste buds?

6. Look at what you have written. In your own words, write what gratitude is for you. You have a wellspring of wisdom in your heart. Now is the time to let it come to the surface. How do you describe this phenomenon in a way that is meaningful for you?

7. How would it affect you and those around you if you were to recognize the gifts each day brings? How would this simplify how you live?

Discussion

How does your heart feel at the end of this practice? Would it be all right with you to feel this way most of the time? Or would Monkey Mind tell you: "Life is passing you by when you feel this good. This isn't real life. We're supposed to be struggling here!" Given that the chatter may never go away, you have an important choice to make:

*   Am I more interested in engaging with Monkey Mind or my heart?
*   Which brings me a sense of peace?
*   Am I willing to experience gratitude every day?

Share your results with a friend. Hearing yourself talking about your discoveries regarding gratitude is valuable. Franz Kafka wrote:

"You need not do anything. Remain sitting at your table and listen, and you need not even listen, just wait, and you need not even wait, just become quiet, still, and solitary, and the world will offer itself to you to be unmasked; it has no choice. It will roll in ecstasy at your feet."

What do you see in this quotation? Does it relate in any way to gratitude as you are coming to know it?

Contribution: The Consequence of Gratitude

Gratitude allows you to experience the gift of life. When you receive gifts, there is a natural urge to give back. This maintains a flow of energy, a balance between giving and receiving. Contribution is a natural consequence of your desire to maintain balance. It is a fundamental and prag- matic process. Biologically, receiving and contributing are as natural as breathing in and breathing out. When contri- bution is blocked, energy gets backed up, like the waters behind a dam. There is stagnation. You get cranky, tired and uninspired. Miracles are lost on you.

I have discovered the following: It puts to rest most of my own Monkey Mind conversations about donating money:

You and I are compensated immediately when we direct energy toward others. On a subtle level, you have likely seen this as you bestowed energy on objects or events by affirm- ing their existence. The result is a sense of gratitude. On a more apparent level, the act of giving is itself an affirmation of your ability to make a difference in the world. **The reward for contribution is the expanded capacity to contribute.**

Several years ago, I was privileged to hear Lynn Twist talk about money and contribution. At that time, she was raising funds for The Hunger Project. The Hunger Project is a nonprofit organization whose mission is to end world hunger. Her main premise was that we *want* to contribute to causes we consider important. The act of giving empow- ers us. I think this is because we are demonstrating our abil- ity to bring energy from the metaphysical into the physical. This is one reason we get so uncomfortable when we think that giving money is not possible for us.

Contribution can take many forms. We look at money here for obvious reasons. The energy it represents is tan- gible. The lessons you learn here about contribution can be applied to all areas of your life.

Tithing Troubles

It is a commonly accepted principle that tithing brings pros- perity. Tithing is giving one-tenth of your money to that which you consider to be your spiritual source. Charles Fillmore, in his book, *Prosperity,* wrote eloquently on the subject:

"Tithing establishes method in giving and brings into con- sciousness a sense of order and fitness that will be manifested in one's outer life and affairs as increased efficiency and greater prosperity."

The act of giving establishes balance. Energy flows

freely, coming in and going out.

When you are balanced, you naturally open up to the miracles that are there, all around you, at every moment of your life. You use opportunity. Your energy is free to create. You are open and present in the moment, open to possibilities. You perceive your life as blessed. You transmit this blessing to those around you while being prosperous.

Now, a potential pitfall applies to all of us: When we give with the thought that we will "get a return on our investment in the future," we do not create a balance. We are forming an imbalance. In fact, the conditions we then place on our giving are nothing but extensions of our own sense of scarcity. There is no sense of empowerment. On the contrary! We are waiting for the return of what we have given out. Here lies the heart of our difficulties with contribution to spiritual causes. Giving with an expectation of return for our money, spiritually or otherwise, is a setup for anger and pessimism. Monkey Mind tells us we should reap reward, and tries to invalidate or diminish all of our spiritual benefits.

Tithing, or any contribution of money, is a demonstration of our power. If we were to pray for anything, it might be for the ability to keep on contributing. This is the blessing we truly seek.

There are other examples of the potential pitfalls of contribution. This is one of them:

Wallace: I remember when I was a kid. My father gave a lot of money to our church. There were six of us in the family. We hardly had enough money to get by. One winter, I wore a coat two sizes too small. I resented my dad's giving money to the church when he couldn't even buy me a proper coat. He told us he was doing this to make sure we all went to Heaven. It was like he was afraid or something, and this was his way of escaping his fear; sort of an insurance policy. I don't give much to my church at all. I don't want the feeling I'm buying my way to salvation. I also don't want my kids to ever suffer the way we did.

We can easily point to the flaws in Wallace's logic. He went to the opposite extreme from his father because his brothers and sisters had to endure the consequences of his father's driven behavior. If you recall, one aspect of driven behavior is that you can never do it well enough. In this case, his father gave more than was necessary to create a balance. His giving created an *imbalance* of energy. He took away from his family in his misguided effort to bargain his way into Heaven. His contribution carried a "condition" that was based on fear, not on the joys of freely giving. Is it any surprise that the imbalance his family experienced was the result?

Contribution that is driven is not really contribution. It is an attempt to fill a void created by the absence of joy and gratitude. This type of giving is an attempt to escape fear. It perpetuates the driven behavior.

Integrity and Balance

This chapter concludes with an exercise designed to aid you in consciously bringing integrity into your money affairs. Integrity is a sense of completeness, the experience of balance. If you are not already doing so, you may decide to achieve balance by regular contributions to the source of your own spiritual nourishment. This could be your church, synagogue, or temple. Perhaps you will choose to invest money regularly in areas that make a difference in people's lives. A growing trend is to give to environmental, world health or educational causes in the name of loved ones at birthdays or religious holidays. One of these might appeal to you and will be in total harmony with your Standards of Integrity.

You may have discovered that you have been giving money in a driven manner. If so, I invite you to use the next integrity exercise to remedy that situation. It will help you to rebalance.

One way to thrive and prosper is to correct the imbalances in your life. That is why we spent the time we did earlier in this book on driven behavior and busyholism. You can correct imbalances by aligning your life with your Standards of Integrity. Accordingly, we now come to an exercise that will do this. It will give you guidelines for bringing these Standards from the metaphysical to the physical. Remember, your Standards are worth nothing if you are not manifesting them.

We use your relationship with money as the focus here. Imbalances in this area are usually very easy to see, sometimes too easy! So, I invite you to do the following integrity exercise to remedy that situation.

Exercise: Integrity Aerobics

This exercise is called Integrity Aerobics. It is designed to pump up your power and bring balance to your life. You do so through exercising of your Standards of Integrity. As you do this work, you may notice increased freedom in your interactions with people and money. Above all, have compassion for yourself as you do this. The work is important and sometimes difficult. You are demonstrating your willingness to dance with abundance, to be open to everything in your life. Because this will definitely make your perceptions finer, be prepared for miracles!

What You Will Need

You will need your notebook, a personal calendar, and your Standards of Integrity.

Time For This Exercise

This is an ongoing process. You will be clearing up specific items. Give yourself no more than twenty minutes for the first step. You can always come back later and add items. This is not a complete list, but merely a way to get you started. After that, each individual item you choose to examine can take from five to fifteen minutes. I recommend you take at least one hour with this exercise the first time you do it.

The Exercise

1. Locate items in your life that represent an imbalance in integrity. Use the following questions to spur your memory.
* Regarding money: Where have I lied, cheated or stolen anything?
* Regarding my relationships with people and money: Where have I hurt or manipulated others?
* Where have I been greedy, uncharitable or ignorant in my personal and business dealings?

Be very specific about your behavior. Clearly describe what you did that lacked integrity. Note the promises you did not keep. Use the following examples, taken from people in the *You and Money* course, to get you going:

Lois: I filed a false claim on my insurance. When thieves burglarized my home, I reported that they had stolen my mother's diamond ring when they hadn't. It's there in the back of my mind, every time I wear the ring.

Don: I didn't report $4,500 I made under the table at my mail order business last year to the IRS. I tell my wife I'm not worried and that everyone else does it. But whenever we get a letter from the IRS, I'm sure it's going to be a notice that they found out and I'm going to be audited.

Art: I make personal long-distance calls at work and charge it to the company. I've never told anyone, least of all my boss.

Alice: I take pencils, pens and paper from the stationery store where I work. I tell myself I deserve it because the owner pays me such a small salary. But it weighs on me. Lately I haven't wanted to go into work. When she looks at me sometimes I'm just sure she knows.

Sidney: I haven't paid child support for the past two years. I know I'm ordered to by the court, but I'm really angry at my ex. She's been living with this other guy. I'm sure she has been trying to turn my kids against me.

Make sure you list even the smallest items, even if Monkey Mind tells you that they do not make a difference. If they came up, they make a difference. What about the newspaper(s) you took without paying? The time a table server gave you back too much change and you did not tell her? The items(s) you have shoplifted? The time you bought a dress or shirt, wore it to a party, and then returned it to the department store for a refund? Raiding your child's piggy-bank without permission? Slipping into additional movies at multiple-screen theaters without paying? We all have items like this. What are yours? Cough it all up. Also, no dawdling or wallowing allowed. If you hear Monkey Mind's chatter, give it a wave and keep on going.

2. If you have done the above, even if you have listed just one item, bravo! You are getting in shape to have a powerfully free and creative relationship with money, your goals, and your dreams. Take one of the items you listed. You might want to start with a small item at first. Let us pretend you wrote: "The time I stole a tube of toothpaste from the supermarket." On a clean piece of paper from your notebook, draw a large box. Write this item on the top of the box. Write all your reasons, justifications, rationalizations, thoughts, theories and feelings that went along with this behavior. Be real about this. This is not the time to censor what you write. Write until you have emptied your entire structure of knowing onto the piece of paper. Get it all out of your head. Take a moment and look at all this stuff. How do you feel as you read it?

3. Draw another box and put: "What it has cost me to have done this and not cleaned it up." The cost will show up in terms of money, time, physical energy and emotional comfort. This is the imbalance. Be thorough with yourself. Did you return to that supermarket? If so, did you feel tense? Did you use that toothpaste? How was your next dental checkup? If you are willing, you will encounter related costs that you might never have noticed. They have always been there.

4. Look at the two boxes. Do you see the energy that has gone into maintaining this imbalance? Now ask yourself two of the questions we all face in the *You and Money* course:

*   Have I had enough of doing my life this way?
*   Am I willing to move on to more freedom?

5. If the answer is no, remember we are talking about *willing,* not *wanting.* You may be afraid to clear this up. You may not want to do it. Monkey Mind may be going a mile a minute. Are you willing? The truth is, you know you are willing or else you would not have begun this exercise. So, take a deep breath and just say yes.

6. Take out your Standards of Integrity. Look to see what specific Standards are missing from physical reality while these items go uncorrected. For example, the person who listed the above item noted the following Standards were missing when she stole the toothpaste: *honest, trustworthy, prosperous and intelligent.*

   After you have assessed what is missing, ask yourself the following: Since these are my Standards of Integrity, how would someone who is _____ (fill in the word for the missing Standards -- honest, trustworthy, etc.) clean up this situation?

   The woman above filled the sentence out this way: "Since these are my Standards of Integrity, how would someone who is honest, trustworthy, prosperous and intelligent clean up this situation?"

7. Now we correct the imbalance. We clean up the mess. For the woman above, the authentic action was simple. She went to the supermarket where she had stolen the toothpaste and told the cashier that they did not charge her for a tube of toothpaste on her last trip. She had the cost added to her present charges. She paid for it. Balance was restored.

When you begin to correct items to restore integrity, follow these guidelines:

* **Do not leave anything out.** Taking authentic action means cleaning up every mess. This goes for income tax evasion, returning stolen goods or making good on an old debt.

* **Be persistent.** One person had to work closely with his insurance company to get them to accept a check for an item he had misreported. They simply did not have a category in their computer for client reimbursements to them!

Another person filed for bankruptcy and then later retracted voluntarily before the final hearing. Her bank had already written off her credit card debt! She spent a few weeks and finally convinced them to accept her payments on the defunct account. The result, however, was that they reinstated her credit. The bank had never before done this with customers who had filed for bankruptcy.

Someone else returned $1,100 in disability overpayment from a county agency for whom he had worked. They were shocked! A reporter wanted to interview him as one of a so-called "dying breed of honest people."

One person reported that the IRS agent with whom he and his accountant were working became visibly relieved when they admitted to her that he had not paid his full taxes. He told her he was not going to make any excuses for it, and took full responsibility for what he had done. The IRS agent's response was to help him figure out a way to pay what he owed in the easiest, most painless way possible.

If you notice some cynicism creeping in here, with Monkey Mind thoughts about foolhardy do-gooders, take a deep breath. Ask yourself the question: What interests me more, holding onto my cynicism, or having my goals and dreams become reality? Pick one. You cannot have both.

*   **Clean up items in a way that works for you and will not get you in any trouble. If you are going to clean up an item with legal implications, get advice from an attorney first.** If you create more of a mess through your actions, you will have a perfect rationale for not correcting imbalances in the future. It may be necessary to get legal, personnel, or human resource consultation before you tell your boss about the phone bill. You may want to consult a tax attorney or CPA before going to the IRS. There are ways to clean up these situations without putting yourself or others in jeopardy.

*   **If cleaning up the mess has to do with another person, get support. Use a friend, counselor, or loved one so that you do it in a way that demonstrates your Standards of Integrity.** It does no good to lay your guilt at someone else's feet. Get proper coaching before handling the situation. This is bringing balance about with integrity and compassion.

*   **Take specific authentic action.** In almost every instance, you know what to do. You have a wellspring of wisdom in your heart. It is time to show this. Set a date by when you will take action, and do it! For example, one man remembered a time twenty-five years before when he stole $16 from a summer camp's store. He recalls being too sick the following year to attend that camp. Coincidence? The camp itself no longer exists. To create balance, he took the $16 and added interest over the years. He then donated that $250 to a local charity. Balance and integrity were restored.

If no specific action comes to mind, sit with it for a while. Get counsel from someone you know who will support you in handling this matter. It does no good, for example, to talk with someone who might collude with you about not having to do anything.

*   **Take a few minutes and acknowledge yourself every time you complete an item. Do not just rush on to the next one. Every hero needs a moment of replenishment. Let someone know what a good job you are doing; reward yourself with a little fun.**

Discussion

Do your Integrity Aerobics with increasingly difficult items. The more you resolve, the more balance and energy you will experience. Knowing that Integrity Aerobics gets easier with time is important for you. As you experience more relief, you will see integrity missing before it shows up in your behavior. You can then cut it off at the pass. For right now, acknowledge yourself for being willing to see who you really are and taking action on it.

What do you experience as you work through the items in this exercise? You may want to make a point of acknowledging instances for gratitude every night before you go to sleep. Do more instances seem to arise? Are there openings and opportunities where there seemed to be none? Were they always there, just waiting for you to be clear enough to perceive them?

One of my favorite stories comes from a woman who wanted to travel the world for her company. At the same time, she owed $6,000 in taxes she had not reported from consulting she did on the side. One month after she sent her check for this amount to the IRS, her company offered her a job traveling the world. Her new salary more than made up for any money she had paid in taxes. One happy person!

The rewards for this work are best summed up by one man who said: "I sleep better at night. I'm not afraid to read my mail. I don't have to keep track of any lies I've told. My business has been expanding as never before. It's simple. And yes, it is just fine with me that things have gotten easier."

The Journey Continues
The next chapter shows you how to handle the inevitable obstacles that will occur as you start for your goal. This will give you more ways to handle them so that you keep on track and proceed with ease.

Summary

✐   The gateway to abundance is gratitude. The key to gratitude is to be willing to affirm what is present. Integrity and contribution amplify the power of affirmation.

✐   Abundance is everything. It is the good and bad moments, happiness and sadness.

✐   Scarcity is not the opposite of abundance. It is an inseparable aspect of it.

✐   The hero inside you arises when you are willing to say yes to everything on your life's path.

✐   Gratitude is present when you see that everything that occurs in your life can be used to show you how to live fully as a human being.

✐   Observation gives power to the present moment. The moment can then be used to awaken the grateful heart. This is the foundation of affirmation.

✐   Affirm the attributes that are inherent in your Standards of Integrity and you empower what already exists inside you.

✐   The reward for contribution is the expanded capacity to contribute.

✐   The act of giving establishes balance. Energy flows freely, coming in and going out.

✐   Tithing, or any contribution of money, is the demonstration of our power. If we were to pray for anything, it might well be for the ability to keep on contributing. This is the blessing we truly seek.

✐   Contribution that is driven is not really contribution. It is an attempt to fill a void created by the absence of joy and gratitude. This type of contribution is an attempt to escape fear. It perpetuates driven behavior.

✐   When you begin to correct items to restore integrity, follow these guidelines:
* Do not leave anything out.
* Be persistent.
* Clean items up in a way that works for you and will not get you in any trouble. If you are going to clean up an item with legal implications, get advice from an attorney first.

* If cleaning up the mess has to do with another person, get support. Use a friend, counselor or loved one so that you do it in a way that demonstrates your Standards of Integrity.
* Take specific authentic action.
* Take a few minutes and acknowledge yourself every time you complete an item. Do not just rush on to the next one. Every hero needs a moment of replenishment. Let someone know what a good job you're doing; Reward yourself with a little fun.

CHAPTER THIRTEEN:
Turning Iron to Gold:
Obstacles into Miracles

Turning Iron to Gold: Obstacles into Miracles

"As a man's real power grows and his knowledge widens, ever the way he can follow grows narrower, until at last he chooses nothing, but does only and wholly what he must do."

Ursula LeGuin

This chapter is about the nature of obstacles and breakdowns. You will be looking at ways to identify and successfully deal with these inevitable companions on the hero's journey. First, let us look at what an obstacle is:

An obstacle blocks, or threatens to block, progress toward your goal. In advanced stages, unworkability is present. The desired outcome is not being attained.

Do you ski? The process that occurs when you learn to ski is a metaphor for obstacles on a hero's journey. If you do not ski, find a situation in your life that evokes obstacles. They are everywhere.

When you first learn to ski, *everything* is an obstacle. How to use your poles, put on your skis, stand up and move; everything takes energy and deliberation. You probably started out with the short, wide skis that are very forgiving. Such skis take you over the patches of dried grass or dirt you might accidentally hit. You ski slowly.

As your skill advances, you get narrower skis. You begin to carve graceful turns around moguls, but these skis will not carry you over grassy patches. They are made for grace and mastery and are less forgiving than wide skis. When you ski more swiftly down the slopes, the smaller patches of ice now become obstacles. At high speeds, small imperfections on the trail can send you face-forward into the nearest snowdrift. You may have seen this happen even with Olympic skiers in competition.

The more powerful and knowledgeable you become, the more aware you are of the obstacles on your path. It will become obvious that you must clear these obstacles away. You have no other choice. In this sense, ever the way you can travel grows narrower.

Obstacles happen. They are often painful, unhappy events. You never hear people say: "Oh, boy! Something else in the way! Whoopee!" Still, obstacles are necessary to the hero's journey. They define your lessons in life. No obstacles, no growth. No growth, no journey.

Why We Have Obstacles in Our Lives

Goals, intentions, and obstacles go hand in hand. There is no way to have one without the others.

I forget this truth every time my face is pushed up against the snowdrifts in my life. Like me, you may have wished it were not so. Let us examine this truth further.

An obstacle is an event that gets in your way or delays progress toward your goal. It occurs because you select a path toward a goal. Without a goal and a path, an event would not be an obstacle. For example, if you were interested in buying a house, you would experience not qualifying for a mortgage as an obstacle. Otherwise, you might not care. Another example: inability to obtain an ISDN line for Internet service would not be an obstacle if you were not interested in speedier downloading.

"Difficulties make you a jewel."

Japanese Folk Saying

While we experience discomfort with them, obstacles keep us interested. They keep life's games from being boring. Life's luster fades without some degree of personal challenge. We seek challenges to achieve mastery and growth. It is a hero's way to test his or her mettle. Having no obstacles could actually drive us crazy.

I heard the story of a ruthless gambler who dies and goes to hell. He is ushered into a fully-equipped casino with a bucket of chips. Here he is to remain forever, to play to his heart's content. He will never lose, no matter what. The man smiles, convinced he is in heaven, and steps up to the black-jack table. He wins every hand. Bored, he steps up to the craps table. Once again, he wins every time. No fun. He plays roulette, slots and poker. No losses, no threat of failure. No excitement. Everything is predictable. Locked in this room for eternity, the man goes crazy.

There is another way to view obstacles that will take you outside your customary structures of knowing:

Obstacles surface as you take your goal from metaphysical to physical reality. Such impediments are created by this movement, like ice that builds up on an ice-breaking boat.

Every time you put action into the physical domain, you will meet with a reaction. If not, there would be no limit to your action. Your energy would go forth unimpeded. It would disperse just as light projected out into the heavens finally disperses. This is the basic premise behind Newton's First Law: for every action, there is an equal and opposite reaction. Obstacles are the sign that physical reality is pushing back. Believe it or not, it is a confirmation that you are progressing along your chosen path.

The Nature of Obstacles and Breakdowns

How often do we think of obstacles as being a validation and natural consequence of setting goals? We usually take them as a signal that something is wrong with our intention, our goal, or ourselves for having that goal. When faced with an obstacle, we experience a host of physical, emotional, mental, and even spiritual symptoms. Sometimes we are stopped dead in our tracks.

Of course, we actually seek some obstacles out because they are inherently fun. Examples of this are found in athletic activities. We run a marathon, play tennis with a well-matched opponent, or look for the best way to ski around the moguls while making our snowy, pine-scented way downhill on a particularly difficult run.

We may often feel joyful, but for now, we will deal with less joyful or exciting experiences. We will look at the kinds of situations that are uncomfortable and discouraging to face. We will look at the times Monkey Mind is saying: "I told you to turn back. Now, look at this fine mess you've gotten us into."

> "For a long time it had seemed to me that life was about to begin -- real life. But there was always something to be got through first, some unfinished business, time still to be served, a debt to be paid. Then life would begin. At last it dawned on me that these obstacles were my life."
>
> *Alfred D'Souza*

You do not have to get mad at Monkey Mind when this happens. After all, it is only interested in your survival. It relies on habit and sticks to whatever is predictable. It likes some novelty, but when confronted with situations that are confusing, paradoxical, or that run counter to well-established routines, it tries to attract your attention. If you listen to it, you may stop what you are doing and retreat back into your more comfortable structures of knowing.

In this chapter, you will see how to identify and handle both obstacles and breakdowns on your path. We will use this definition of a breakdown:

A breakdown is the psychological, emotional, physical or spiritual discomfort that accompanies your *perception* of an event as an obstacle.

A breakdown is your inner reaction to an event. That is how it becomes an obstacle. You can learn to deal with obstacles effectively. The key is knowing how to identify the precise areas of discomfort you experience. Then you can begin to dismantle your perception of the event as an obstacle. Once you do so, you can take authentic action appropriate to the event and your goal. If you think about it, this is the good news! To go back to what Tallulah Bankhead said, "There may be less to this than meets the eye."

You can be like people who are successful. They are willing to experience the discomfort of breakdowns while handling their obstacles and proceeding toward their goals. They are willing to learn from these events/obstacles about how to better travel their path.

To travel with ease, learn how to recognize when Monkey Mind has captured your attention. When an event appears as an obstacle, Monkey Mind can distract you from seeing the nature of the event and the specifics of your personal breakdown. You may even fail to identify the obstacle until it has become more pronounced. Or, you might try to drive over and/or around it. This evasion can create some real hardships, primarily because it puts off the inevitable. When you discern Monkey Mind in operation, you can acknowledge its chatter while focussing on finding a constructive way to handle the obstacle. It is your first step toward making your way through the obstacle with efficiency, speed and ease.

How to Tell When Monkey Mind is Operating

Imagine you invested some money with a friend. He owns an antique furniture store. Your intention is to be financially successful. Your goal is to earn at least 10 percent on your investment after one year. You will also gain equity in the antiques. For various reasons, the store does not do well and finally has to close its doors. The failure is an obstacle in the path of achieving your goal. It leads to a breakdown. Soon you hear Monkey Mind, chattering away.

That is what happened to Roger. The following is a dialogue I had with him in the *You and Money* course. Get out your Monkey Mind Symptoms Checklist. Can you spot any symptoms in his words? If so, what are they?

Me: So, how much money did you lose?

Roger: I'm not certain. It was over a period of time. Fifteen, maybe twenty thousand dollars.

Me: Is there a way for you to find out exactly how much you lost?

Roger: My accountant knows. I don't need to know to the penny. That's not what's important here.

Me: What if I told you it *is* important for you to know exactly how much you lost?

Roger: Then I'd tell you you're wrong. What's done is

done. There's nothing I can do about it.

Me: You're really frustrated with the whole thing, aren't you?

Roger: That's not the half of it. If my brothers find out about this, they'll laugh at me. They'd never do anything this stupid. At least I didn't mortgage my house to do this, like Burt did. Now, *that* was risky!

Me: How did you get into the deal in the first place?

Roger: Well, that Burt's a smooth talker. I trusted his business sense. Maybe I'm too trusting.

Me: What are you going to do about this?

Roger: There's nothing I *can* do. I know one thing for sure, though. I'm going to stay out of the investment game. I don't have the stomach for it.

What is missing from the above conversation? Movement. He has not yet identified the obstacle and breakdown. It is as if Roger were sitting on a tree stump at the side of his path. His head is in his hands. His eyes are closed while he talks himself out of looking at what could be corrected. This posture alone is a good indication that he is caught up in Monkey Mind. There is no room for growth. He could stay with that same conversation for years.

Eventually, Roger let himself be coached. He became willing to look, see, and tell the truth about what happened. Opportunities opened. As a result, he and Burt found a group of bed and breakfast owners who bought the antiques. In the end, the sale made Roger and Burt a handsome profit, and the buyer hired them as decorating consultants. This opened brand new horizons for them. Later in this chapter, you will have the chance to practice the process that gave them breathing room.

How to Transform Obstacles into Miracles

Let us begin to experiment with a new way to handle obstacles and breakdowns. We pick a goal that is common for many people; buying a home. For a moment, pretend that you want to buy a home for the first time. If this is actually true for you, so much the better.

Your intentions for this goal are twofold: to be financially successful and to be creative with your surroundings. Research reveals that because you are a first-time home buyer, you can purchase a home in the price range you want for $12,000 down.

Deciding to go for it, you determine that you will have to save $1,000 a month for twelve months. You get an extra job, tighten your belt, and begin the journey. In your mind, you think it is supposed to look like the figure on the left in the illustration below.

But then, real life steps in with some surprises. Four months into this plan, at point A, you are driving to your second job. By this time you have saved $4,000. You are as happy as a clam. Suddenly, your engine blows up and, guess what, your warranty expired three weeks ago. You have to shell out $3,850 for repairs. In light of your goals and dreams, this appears to be a real obstacle that threatens to stop you. What do you say to yourself as you look, for the first time, at the repair estimate for the car? Probably something profound, like, "Oh, sh_ _!" It is a universal expression of distress. That is why we call Point A an OSP, meaning the "Oh, sh_ _ point." Other exclamations Monkey Mind comes up with include:

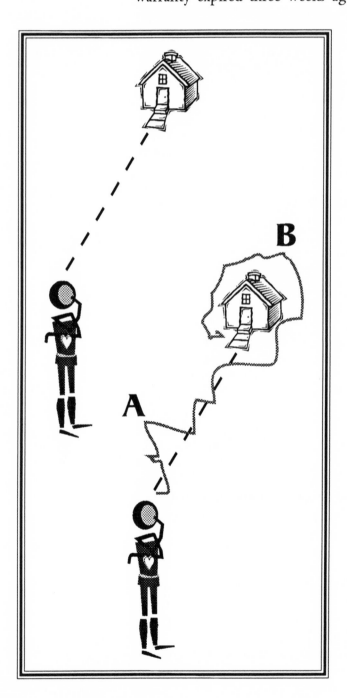

* There goes the house!
* Why does stuff like this always happen to me?
* I just knew I'd never get that house.
* My universe is telling me something.
* This obviously wasn't meant to be.
* Back to square one! I'll have to start all over again.
* This stop was definitely not on my travel brochure!

Absolutely everyone has OSPs. Unless you keep yourself in a padded cell, there is no way not to encounter

OSPs in life. Here is something to remember: **When you are facing an obstacle, and are right in the middle of an OSP, it is a sign that you are fully engaged with your goal. It is a validation.**

You may not feel that you are on the right path. You may have all kinds of thoughts about the situation, yourself and the rest of the world. Obstacles, and their resultant breakdowns, are not pleasant to experience. They cannot be denied or glossed over in any way. Given how awful it sometimes feels to encounter them, knowing what to do when you hit one is especially useful.

Returning to our last diagram, three factors constitute your journey. First, you have intentions; in this case, to be financially successful and creative. Next, you have a goal, which is your intention projected into physical reality. The goal here is to have a house. Finally, you have your plan, which is to save $1,000 a month. One, and only one, of these factors needs change at this point. Which one?

Your first reaction might be to change your goal, or at least put it off for a while. After all, you do not have the money you said you would at this point in time. It is four months down the road and after the cost of auto repairs you have managed to save only $150.

For the sake of illustration, let us make matters even worse. You have managed to get back on track. It is eleven months into the project to get your home. You have worked extra hard and saved $11,150. You found a beautiful house and have opened escrow. It closes in two weeks. One week before the close, your apartment is burglarized. This is Point B. More than $6,000 worth of computer equipment and software is stolen. You need this to finish a job due in two weeks. That job gave you much of the $11,150.

Return to the question: What needs to be changed here? The intention need not change. External circumstance does not make intentions invalid. It may not even be your goal that needs to change. The structure of knowing that needs examination is your *plan*. This may not seem like a revelation. But, in all the years I have coached people, I have noticed the first factor that is usually sacrificed is the goal, not the plan. Most people get hooked on their plans. They act as though *how it was supposed to look* to achieve the goal is more important than the actual fulfillment of the goal itself.

People who are successful consistently choose their goals and intentions over their plans.

Our plans are created out of our structures of knowing about what it will take for us to arrive at our goals. But a goal, if it is worth playing for, is a stretch. It lies outside predictability. There is no way to create a plan that will never need to be adjusted or dismantled. Especially when we are attempting something new, our plans may be incorrect from the beginning.

Consider the possibility that your plans or strategies for your life are holding you back from getting what you want. You have a picture in your mind of how your journey has to look. That picture may be insufficient to attain the goals of your dreams. In the example of the house, the plan is to save $1,000 per month. Is this really the easiest, fastest way to attain the goal? Does the plan create more problems than it solves? Has it become inflexible?

The following scenario happened to a woman in the *You and Money* course. This is how she handled the obstacle:

Brenda: When my car broke down, it felt like someone punched me in the gut. I thought there was no way I was going to get my house. Then, I remembered our work on obstacles. First, I went through the *Lead into Gold* process. I saw that I was trying to get this goal on my own, without help. I called together a group of my friends. They knew my goal and intentions. I told them I was willing to be coached to go beyond my structure of knowing. Getting others to support me was a way to manifest my intention to be creative.

We started brain-storming. We came up with four alternatives: the owner carrying paper, getting a loan from my uncle, a friend going in with me on an equity-sharing basis, and getting a $1,000 loan from each of six friends. I went to my real estate agent. Guess what! The owners were willing to carry a second mortgage if I paid $5,000 of the $12,000 I owed. It worked!

People who are successful are willing to be flexible in their strategies. For them, attaining the goal itself is far more important than being right about what it takes to get there. They are willing to be incorrect about their original plans. Brenda told me later that a thought occured to her about one month after buying this house. What if she had asked for people's support in devising a plan as she started for her goal? She might have gotten into a home a lot sooner. As it was, her strategy to save $1,000 a month was on the verge of wearing her out.

Exercise: Turning Lead Into Gold

The process for turning lead into gold is an alchemical metaphor for turning obstacles into miracles. Alchemists were philosophers and sages. They saw life as a laboratory for the distillation of the human spirit from its unenlightened state (lead) to enlightenment (gold). If one could purify his or her own spirit, the reasoning went, he or she could then learn to transmute real lead into actual gold. Some may have learned to do this. Many attained an even greater treasure. They learned to use the stuff of everyday life, both the joys and sorrows, to awaken themselves to their own essence. They discovered that lead *is* gold.

You are going to learn to use your obstacles and breakdowns to expand your awareness of the miracles that surround you. The following exercise will help. However, it will only be effective if followed by *authentic action*.

Use this exercise any time you encounter what you perceive to be an obstacle. With practice, it will take less time to complete. At first, I suggest you do the exercise together with someone else. Then you can support each other in carrying out what you get out of this work. Ideally, it can be a friend or spouse. You can compare notes, discuss ideas, and keep each other going in the process. Share what you find at each step.

What You Will Need
You will need your notebook and your life's intentions and Standards of Integrity.

Time For This Exercise
Initially, it may take fifteen to twenty minutes to examine each obstacle. If you engage in the exercise repeatedly, the process will take less time.

The Exercise
Step One: Identify an Obstacle You Currently Face.
An obstacle is something you believe blocks you from reaching a goal. Write at least three sentences about the obstacle. This is your preliminary assessment.

Step Two: Narrow Down Your Description of the Obstacle.
Look at what you just wrote. Is the statement vague or general? For example, "I am tired a lot" is a general statement. Be more specific and locate an incident that is blocking you from proceeding on your path. Let these statements help you:

Joel: I just got a notice from the bank that I didn't qualify for the loan to refinance my house. I was counting on it to help get out of debt.

Meg: I failed my counselor's license exam. It's the third time I've taken it.

Walt: We have a deadline on this construction project. I've worked with my supervisors, but they're still late on getting the specs to me. We may not execute the contract on time as I planned.

Alex: This is the fifth time this month that I've been overdrawn on my checking account. My doctor's office just charged me double on a returned check.

Michelle: My rental property is a financial black hole. Every month there's something else that needs to be fixed. This time they found dry rot under the kitchen sink.

Step Three: Examine Your Breakdown Regarding the Event.

Having located a specific incident, examine and observe your experience of the breakdown. Do it fully and you will create breathing room for yourself. There are four areas in which you can experience a breakdown: your thoughts, your feelings, your body sensations, and your spirit.

These factors are interwoven. They form your structure of knowing about the event/obstacle. You will sort out each area and look at your specific reactions. This is part of the dismantling process.

Take a page from your notebook and label it THOUGHTS. Write out all of your thoughts about the obstacle. Include all of the explanations, reasons, and theories your Monkey Mind comes up with about why this situation happened.

Joel: The bank didn't give me the loan because they don't trust me. Economic times are tough. Banks are not lending money right now. This is going to set me back. This is my own fault. I have too many questionable items on my credit report. My ex-wife charged too much on credit cards before we divorced.

Meg: I did my best. I can't pass the exam. I'm too old for this. I should have done this when I was younger. I waited too long after graduation to go back and study. The study course I took this time didn't prepare me.

Walt: You can't count on construction supervisors. Everyone knows it. All they want is their paycheck. I have to do the spec work myself. It comes with the territory. If you want something done right, always do it yourself.

Roger: I thought I had overdraft protection. This happens to me all the time. I don't know why. I don't have a head for figures. I deposit lots of money at that bank. They should extend me the courtesy of calling me before they bounce my checks.

Michelle: This is all my brother's fault. He got me into this deal. Why do I always do what he tells me? I just haven't gotten over being his little sister. I'm not good at business. Other people make money in their investments, but not me.

When you write your thoughts, include any judgments you have about yourself, the situation, or other people. If you have tried to fix an obstacle and it has not worked, write that down as well. Include any methods you used. Keep listing your thoughts until nothing more comes to mind.

Now do the same thing on another piece of paper with your FEELINGS. Are you sad, frustrated, bored, anxious, furious, panicked, dumbfounded, or worried? Do you feel betrayed, abandoned or hurt? Be as articulate as possible about your feelings. Getting them all out in writing is important for you. It might look like this:

Michelle: I feel disgusted with the whole situation. I'm angry with my brother. I'm panicked that I'll run out of money.

This process asks you to establish a clear difference between your thoughts and your feelings. You are taking the cover off and looking at the component parts of your structure of knowing about the obstacle at hand. This act makes the structure more permeable and flexible. You will thus find it easier to expand this structure to include the miracles that currently wait outside.

Your BODY SENSATIONS come next. What do you notice as you write about this obstacle? Are you tired? Does your head, stomach, neck or back ache? Is your heart racing or your chest tight? Do you have a sinking feeling in the pit of your stomach? Write down all your physical sensations.

SPIRIT is the fourth area to look at. You usually experience symptoms of your breakdown at this level as a sense that something is missing. You may experience a lack of inspiration, enthusiasm, hope, gratitude, and enjoyment. On occasion, people have the feeling that the future does not hold much for them.

Walt: I am hopeless about this situation. No one is playing on my team. I know I am alone here. Despair. No joy. My future in this business looks dark. I used to be able to inspire people who work for me; not now.

At the completion of this step, take a moment to rest and quietly reflect. Do not be put off by the negativity. It is a common response. Most of us do not take the time to thoroughly acknowledge our breakdowns in life. We know that something is wrong or that we are angry and frustrated. Or, we think that all the circumstances are against us. But we remain vague in pinpointing the exact nature of the obstacle and breakdown facing us. As a result, we remain where we are. We think we should just think or act more positively. As a result, we do the same things over and over again. Using this exercise will break that pattern.

Step Four: Getting a Distance on the Obstacle/Breakdown/Event
Take what you have written, put it face up on a table or the floor and walk about five feet away. Turn and look at it. Do this even if it seems silly. Looking at it from where you stand, do you notice anything about what you wrote? Even if the writing is not distinct, you can get a sense of how much energy you have put into it. These are your perceptions and interpretations of what happened. Use the following questions to get a distance on them:

1. Do I see clearly that I am experiencing breakdown in this situation?

2. Do I see the insanity of doing the same things, over and over again?

3. Do I see my best strategies are not working, or that they may be part of the problem?

4. Have I been trying to solve this alone, without consultation or support from those who could help me?

5. Am I willing to go on, even if it means doing things differently than I have done them before?

6. Am I willing to give up plans that may no longer work?

Step Five: Restate the Obstacle/Event

What really happened? State it in terms of the absolute, bottom line, bare facts. This is where you tell the truth. The truth is distinct from your thoughts, feelings, body sensations and spiritual symptoms. It is a statement about what happened in physical reality.

Joel: I didn't qualify for a loan. My credit report contains questionable items.

Meg: I have not yet passed my counseling license exam.

Walt: I am not meeting the deadline on this contract.

Roger: I bounced five checks this month.

Michelle: I am spending more money than I thought I would on this rental.

You may have seen that this was the truth about their obstacles when you first read each person's story. But they did not. They were in the middle of it, with Monkey Mind cheering them on. This is why the above steps are so important. You are clearing the bugs off your windshield so you can see what is really before you.

So, what is the truth about this obstacle? What really happened? What did you do or *not* do? Take a deep breath at this point and wave at Monkey Mind.

Step Six: Look at Broken Promises

A closer look at the above obstacles reveals that in each case the person has failed to follow through on a promise to themselves or others. They have not yet done something to correct or balance the situation. This leaves them feeling very uncomfortable. It is at least partly the reason for their upset.

How do you get to the underlying promise? One way is to look at your Standards of Integrity. Does your behavior in this situation go counter to any of your Standards? Which ones? Write them down. Are there any broken promises here?

Joel: One of my Standards of Integrity is "intelligent." Having credit reports with questionable items that I have not personally cleared is definitely not intelligent of me. Another one is "conscious." When I applied for the loan, I was not conscious that my credit reports would reflect what they did. Not keeping these Standards has gotten in the way of my ability to refinance the house. I have not yet kept that promise.

Do you see the wisdom operating here? Joel is showing the heart of a hero. You can sense his trustworthiness and intelligence. He has gotten off the side of the road and is back on his path. Be compassionate with yourself as you do this work. Many of us never get to the point of looking at our promises, broken or not.

When you tell the truth about obstacles and broken promises, guilt often melts away. You stop blaming yourself or others. Blame is a Monkey Mind response. Instead, you simply point to what is so. This is possible to do even if the obstacle was totally out of your control. A fire or flood, for example, can generate a host of unkept promises. The hero's path through this is clear: learn from the mess, clean it up, and keep going. To paraphrase Ursula LeGuin, this is what we mean by doing only and wholly what you know you must do.

Step Seven: Look at Your Underlying Intentions

Having completed six of these steps, you are ready to look at the intentions that are being thwarted. Though it might look like it, intentions are not erased or annihilated by obstacles and breakdowns. To the contrary! The fact that you consider a situation an obstacle means that you have an intention that is currently thwarted. It is a validation of the intention, not an invalidation. If you had *not* had in intention, this incident or circumstance would mean nothing to you.

Joel: My intention is to be financially successful.

Meg: My intention is to be a competent professional counselor.

Walt: I have the intentions to be a successful entrepreneur and supervisor.

Roger: I want to be a good provider for my children, and to be financially successful.

Michelle: My intention is to be a successful real estate investor.

What intentions are being thwarted in your present situation? Write them down. If you have difficulty, enlist the support of someone who can be objective.

Step Eight: Identifying Goals You Have Been Striving to Attain

One way to help you with the obstacle you are facing is to get reacquainted with your goal. Having gotten this far, you may discover you did not clearly define your goal, or that it was not a goal. Operating without a goal, or without a clearly defined one, is a little like being an archer shooting with crooked arrows. If you know anything at all about archery, you know that crooked arrows follow very unpredictable trajectories, having little if anything, to do with the archer's intent.

Joel: My goal? A vacation in Hawaii when I am debt-free.

Meg: I want to open my private practice nine months from today!

Walt: My goal is to have five new projects completed in record time, and to give my supervisors bonuses because they did so well.

Michelle: I'm going to fix this property up and trade it for a duplex within this year.

Take time with this part of the exercise. You reward yourself with a real gift when you see your goals clearly. The goals are the benchmarks you choose so you can manifest your intentions. They are, as the archer would say, your "straight arrows."

Step Nine: How a Person With Your Life's Intentions, Standards of Integrity and Goals Would Handle the Current Situation

What is the first authentic action for you to take? By when? Be specific about this and write it down. Where have you been *doing it alone?* From whom are you willing to get support? If people offer their support, are you willing to take it?

Discussion

Practice this exercise until it becomes easier to face your obstacles and break-downs than to let them stop you. You will soon find yourself moving both mindfully and quickly through the steps. The first couple of times may be slow. But keep at it. Do them fully. You are developing your ability to be on the path of knowledge and power.

Did you allow someone to accompany you at each step? How did it feel to let another person support you? Could you get used to it? Have you made your promises clear and definite? Make sure you are specific. Good work!

The Four Guidelines

We conclude this leg of your journey with four guidelines that summarize what we have looked at regarding obstacles. Use them to wake you up to the possibilities that lie before you.

Guideline One: Obstacles and Breakdowns are Acknowledgments of Your Intentions, Not Invalidations of Them. You experience breakdowns when your intentions are thwarted. This is especially true when achieving a goal that means a lot to you begins to look impossible. Logically, you must have an intention in order to perceive that it is blocked. Your intentions are reflections of who you are in your heart, or as the ancient alchemists would say, your essence. Therefore, if you face your darkest hours truthfully, you create an opening to see your genuine intentions, ones that reflect your heart.

Guideline Two: If No Obstacles Appear On The Path Toward Your Goals, You May Not Be Challenging Yourself. This has nothing to do with ease. Obstacles arise only when you face events outside your structure of knowing. If you are operating within your current structure of knowing, no real learning is taking place. There is very little risk. Still, your energy seeks to encounter and experience miracles. That is why you keep going.

Guideline Three: If You *Only* Experience Obstacles On the Path Toward Your Goals, You May Be Doing Things The Hard Way. A consistent flow of obstacles and breakdowns is a signal that you have chosen a goal that is out of your reach at this time. If you continue on this path without modifying your goal, you could wind up with evidence about the futility of going for what you want in life. This is pure Monkey Mind. Another sign that you may be caught up with reaching your goals the hard way is if you do not ask for support. You try to achieve your goals alone. The last chapter covers this more fully. *Doing it alone* is one of the most insidious structures of knowing to dismantle.

Guideline Four: People Who Are Successful Consistently Choose Their Goals and Intentions Over Their Plans. Your plans arise from the structure of knowing you had when you set the goal. Real goals lie outside your structures of knowing. Your initial plans or strategies may hold you back. You have big dreams and they are important to you, more important than any plan. Your plans will always need to be modified, not your dreams. This is a key some people never grasp.

The Journey Continues

What you learn in the next chapter creates even more breathing room for you to expand into your goals and dreams. You will learn about forgiveness. Get ready for even more knowledge and power on your hero's path.

Summary

✐   An obstacle blocks or threatens to block, progress toward your goal. In advanced stages, unworkability is present. The desired outcome is not being attained.

✐   The more powerful and knowledgeable you become, the more aware you are of the obstacles on your path. To continue to be powerful you must clear these obstacles away.

✐   Obstacles surface as you move your goal from metaphysical to physical reality. Such impediments are created by your movement into physical reality, just as ice builds up on an ice-breaking boat.

✐   A breakdown is the psychological, emotional, physical or spiritual discomfort that accompanies your perception of an obstacle.

✐   When you are facing an obstacle, and are right in the middle of an OSP, it is a sign that you are fully engaged with your goal. It is a validation.

✐   Obstacles and breakdowns are acknowledgments of your intentions, not invalidations of them.

✐   If there are no obstacles on the path toward your goals, you may not be playing big enough.

✐   If you *only* experience obstacles on the path toward your goals, you may be addicted to doing things the hard way.

✐   People who are successful consistently choose their goals and intentions over their plans. They are willing to be flexible in their strategies. For them, attaining the goal itself is far more important than being right about what it took to get there. They are willing to be incorrect about their original plan.

CHAPTER FOURTEEN:
The Physics of Forgiveness --
The Power of Letting Go

The Physics of Forgiveness -- The Power of Letting Go

"Only the brave know how to forgive."

Laurence Sterne

Forgiveness is a source of great power on the hero's journey. It requires strength and vulnerability. When you forgive someone, you dismantle your structures of knowing about them. You lay down your weapons and armor and proceed onward. If ever there were an act of courage, this is it.

When you are on the path of knowledge and power, you travel light. You bring only the bare essentials. Enlightenment entails lightening up, letting go of structures of knowing that no longer serve you. They are like tools that have lost their usefulness. Your vitality requires you to examine and dismantle those structures regularly. If you keep your models of reality flexible, you remain open to miracles and fresh views that lie outside. This is what having a childlike mind is all about.

Forgiveness begins and ends with our own structures of knowing. Most of us are confident that what we know about others is accurate. This is especially true when we are angry or displeased with them. Attributing negative intentions to the behavior of other people is instinctual for us. This is Monkey Mind at its purest. We have names, dates, and places to prove that our conclusions are correct.

I learned about forgiveness from Father Gerry O'Rourke. At the time, he was the Ecumenical Officer for the Archdiocese of San Francisco, and priest at St. Philip the Apostle Catholic Church in San Francisco. Father O'Rourke has made it his business to teach people how to forgive others. I learned from him that forgiving from your heart is possible, even when your mind insists that there are reasons not to forgive. With immense gratitude, I have taken his teachings and adapted them for use here.

Before we go on, let us be clear about one aspect of forgiveness. When you forgive another person, you do not necessarily forget what they have done. Have you noticed how hard it is to forget a thought purposely? Think of that exercise earlier when you tried not to think about a hot fudge sundae with whipped cream, chopped nuts, and a cherry on top. Not easy, is it? Forgetting difficult situations is not necessary or even advisable. People can do hurtful things. Therapists' offices are filled with those who have tried to blank out painful portions of their life. No, distressing incidents and times are sometimes important to remember for our continued growth and healing.

If forgiving is not forgetting, then what is it? Forgiveness occurs when you are willing to lay aside *what you have said* about another because of what they did. Forgiveness means taking two big steps. First, you look directly at your evaluations, judgments, and catalogued scenarios about the person. You take stock of the thoughts and feelings going on inside you. You examine what you have said to yourself and others, about them.

> "We tend to attribute others' misbehavior to malice, while we see our own misdeeds as the results of passing circumstances."
>
> *Mike McCullough*

Second, you become willing to relinquish the permission you give yourself to entertain all of the above, ever again. Every time you hear Monkey Mind whisper in your ear: "But, he/she really *is* a jerk!" you say: "Thank you for sharing, Monkey Mind, but I have already forgiven this person."

Three components to forgiveness make this courageous act accessible to everyone, no matter how they feel they have failed at previous efforts. These are the three components to keep in mind as you go through this process:

1. **Forgiveness is letting go of structures of knowing that you have created about another human being's nature.**
2. **Forgiveness comes from who you are in your heart. It is a product of *being willing*.**
3. **Your mind takes longer than your heart to catch on. Just because Monkey Mind chatters at you about *how awful the other person is* does not mean you have not forgiven them.**

Take these elements one at a time, taking into account all that you have already learned about structures of knowing. For instance, they have a *limited* shelf-life. Though they may be useful for a time, they must ultimately be put aside. Forgiveness occurs when you are willing to consciously and systematically dismantle your structure of knowing about another person. I am not talking about *forgetting* their behavior. I am talking about dismantling the negative conclusions you have formed about them as human beings. These conclusions, along with the data you continue to gather to substantiate your opinions, take up a lot of your energy.

Forgiveness releases the energy you have used to keep your structures of knowing bound together. Just as energy is

released when an atom is split, many elements remain. Others are converted into different forms of energy. The net effect is movement and power.

Begin your act of forgiveness by answering the following question: **Who would you need to forgive to have a powerful and constructive relationship with money?** Who do you secretly, or not so secretly, blame for your misfortunes in life? Who do you hold responsible for your money problems? Do not answer "me!" Resist the temptation to blame yourself or to fall into the trap that you have consciously chosen everything that has happened to you. This is not the time to be noble, self-effacing or co-dependent. Tell the truth. Who do you feel did you harm? What has he or she done?

James: If my Dad wasn't such a bad businessperson, I would have learned how to run this export business. With him as a role model, no wonder I've made such terrible mistakes! He has really cramped my style.

Marianne: My mother was never very independent. She stayed home and took care of us kids. She wasn't enthusiastic about my going to law school. I think she was jealous. If she had encouraged me, law school might have been a lot easier to get through.

Sharon: How can you expect me to trust anyone? I've just gotten divorced from my husband. He's a playboy, sees other women on the side. He got us into debt. I'll never let my guard down again. It just hurts too much. My dreams are shattered, maybe forever!

Mitch: My business partner hasn't kept his part of the bargain over the past three years. Now I'm ruined. If it wasn't for him, this construction company would be solvent today. Now I might have to let go of the whole operation, and it's all because of him. He has ruined my hopes of being a successful businessperson.

These people have plenty of evidence for their assumptions. As you hear their stories, you might be tempted to agree with them about the character of the "transgressor." You could add insights of your own about the nature and motivations of those who hurt them. We all do this, whether it is at the dinner table or the coffee room at work. Let us get underneath this mechanism and see what is going on.

Ruined my hopes ... shattered my dreams ... cramped my style ... jealous and dependent ... these are all structures of knowing. They are metaphors. The metaphors are impregnated with thoughts, feelings, attitudes, states of mind, points of view, and memories from the past. You can almost sense their weight. Energy is invested in their development and maintenance.

They are also being used as reasons, justifications or excuses for the speaker's failures or broken promises. From what you have already learned about structures of knowing, you know it is time for you to dismantle them. Until you do, you will be sitting by the wayside. That is not for you. You are here to advance down your path to greater ease, happiness, and a truly satisfying relationship with money.

In each case, the structures of knowing are negative. They point to another person's shortcomings. There is a sense of finality and, sometimes, resignation. We call these structures of knowing *characterizations*.

When you form a characterization of another person, you see them through the grid of your assessments and judgments. This produces a two-dimensional experience of them. You are not seeing them as human beings like yourself. They appear to you as cartoon characterizations of what *you perceive* as their shortcomings.

Arguing for the Limitations of Ourselves and Others

Characterizations do not change the other person. On the contrary, the only person they deeply affect is you because they contribute to driven behavior in your life. When you attribute your behavior to what others have said or done, as in "I would be more successful if my parents had only ... ," the same behavior you fear, despise, or otherwise want to deny, is kept in place. This applies whether the behavior that keeps you down is in making bad business decisions, choosing poor investments, letting a great opportunity slip by, or getting into relationships that do not work.

Cheryl: It'll be a long time before I let anyone get close to me again. After the way George treated me, I'll keep my freedom, thank you. He left without even telling me. He abandoned me ... just walked out in the middle of the night. He had about as much heart as a lump of coal! I'm not going to let anyone get that close to me again. He taught me a lesson, believe me!

Don: Of *course* I don't know how to manage money. After all, my dad was a gambler. No, he wasn't a gambler. He was a loser. He spent everything we ever had. The biggest lesson we ever got from him was how to lose money. That was his gift!

Your characterizations limit the way you can interact with others or your memory of them. It keeps the two of you tied together in a way that stunts the growth of both of you. It will even affect your growth if the person is no longer in your life.

How do we develop these limiting and rigid characterizations about others? In any relationship, there will come a time when the other person does something you do not like or which you feel injures you or another person. Your mind notes what they did, but it does not stop there. Monkey Mind chimes in with labels about them: "This proves he's selfish, abusive and lazy. No way is he trustworthy!"

These labels and reproaches are decisions that you have made. Such decisions are powerful mental constructs. It is a choice to see the world in a particular way. To keep the decision in place, we gather other decisions to prop it up. A grid is formed. This is what I mean when I say structures of knowing begin to take on a life of their own. Undetected by their creators, they gather momentum and volume. Next, the mind collects data to flesh out the structure and prove itself correct. Monkey Mind gathers names, dates, and places to hang on the frame. You start to see a host of other, seemingly related behaviors or incidents that irritate, hurt or frustrate you. As in, "Yeah, and come to think of it, he did the same thing before. He always forgets my birthday. He's even selfish with the children. I'm the one who gets his mother presents on her birthday. He's so inconsiderate!"

Over time, your characterization of the other person becomes more and more detailed. Like a villain in your favorite novel or movie, your characterization comes alive, haunting your waking hours, popping up unexpectedly in your dreams. When you describe this characterization to other people who know that person in real life, they may start to agree with you. They have their own stories to tell, of course, because characterizations are contagious. They call out to everyone to join in. During the *You and Money* course, when a participant talks about someone with whom he or she has a grievance, everyone gets angry for them. If the object of this joint characterization entered the seminar room at that moment, almost everyone would shun him or her, though they had never met the person before!

Finally, and this happens to all of us, we get to the point of relating only to our characterization, rather than to the person. It is a lonely prospect. We do not want to be around that person because we cannot tolerate being present with our own negative thoughts and feelings. It is too uncomfortable, mostly because it is not within our Standards of Integrity to keep such characterizations alive. Our negativ-

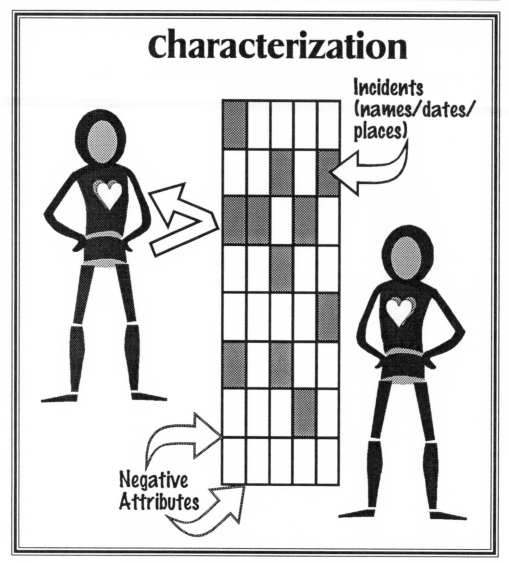

characterization

Incidents (names/dates/places)

Negative Attributes

ity becomes our burden.

How do characterizations form so quickly? The process is almost reflexive. Can you stop yourself from doing it? No. Everyone forms these structures of knowing about other people. While you cannot control the thoughts from arising, you can observe and tell the truth about them: you can be willing, if only for a moment, to see your characterizations as irrelevant. Sound familiar?

How does all this relate to your relationship with money, your goals and your dreams? As an experiment, try the next exercise. We will be looking under the proverbial rocks to find some ugly, squiggling creatures hiding there. Get out your microscope. It will be interesting and educational, even if you feel a bit squeamish.

Exercise: Looking Under the Rocks

What You Will Need
You will need your notebook.

Time For This Exercise
You will need about ten to fifteen minutes of quiet time.

The Exercise
Choose a dream or goal in your life that has yet to be attained, one you have held onto and dreamed about for a long time. Or, it could be a dream you have discarded because you were just certain it could never come true.

1. Use the mind-mapping technique you used earlier in the book to explore your relationship with money. Take a piece of paper and write down in the center one or two words that describe your dream. Now, allow your mind to start filling the mind map with all the reasons the dream or goal has not yet come true for you.

2. Look at all the reasons. Can you think of one or more people who have contributed to your difficulties? You might pick one particular reason, such as: "I didn't get the right education." Or, "My dad was a put-down artist who really undermined my self-confidence." Look for the person you blame. Was it your mom, dad, your uncle Joe who would not give you a loan for your education? Your sixth grade teacher who was uncharitable with you? Your brother for being the family star? Be honest. This is no time to look good. List the person or persons you feel stood in your way or caused you to get derailed. Say what they did, or failed to do, for you.

3. What do you feel as you write? Is there a heaviness in your chest or gut? A lack of breathing room? Anger or frustration? No matter how you manage to disguise your true feelings, when you are in the same room with this person, the feelings you now have are always present. The feelings are right out front or buried just under the surface. They are present when you hear their name or see their photograph. This is definitely not traveling light.

4. Ask yourself the following questions: "If this person had never been in my life, and there was nobody to take his place, what would then happen to my goals and dreams? After all, I would be free of all the reasons I had for not being a success. What would I be doing with my life that I am not doing now?"

Discussion
Were you able to identify people whom you believe have impaired your ability

to have what you want in life? It takes courage to do this. Whether the answer is yes or no, how did you feel during this exercise? Share what you found with a friend or fellow group member. Again, having someone with whom to process your results is important.

When you forgive another person, you cease to use what they did as *the reason* for why your goals and dreams failed to come true. Through forgiveness, you are waiving the right to use what they did against them or yourself.

As forgiveness takes over, your stories or scenarios about how difficult it is for you to deal with that person fade away. No more do you spend time talking with others about that person's character flaws and how much they hurt you. This may not be easy. I remember one woman who said: "If I can't talk about how rigid and selfish my mother is, I won't have anything to talk about with my brothers and sisters when we're together at Thanksgiving."

When you give up your characterizations, you are no longer shaped by them.

One consequence of holding onto your limiting mental decisions about another person is that you may turn out exactly like them. You know this is true. You have seen it in yourself and others. You wake up one morning to find you have become like the person you blame for your misfortune. You can hear it in your voice, or in the words you use. You exhibit the traits you most disliked about them. When you forgive, this process stops. You liberate yourself from the hold they had on you. You become your own person.

Forgiveness: Authentic Action for the Courageous Heart

Through forgiveness you get in touch with who you are in your heart. Your movement toward forgiveness is first expressed as a *willingness* to forgive. Remember, *being willing* is the most powerful authentic action you can take. The moment you are willing, you are able to draw a distinction between your Monkey Mind and your heart. You may not *want* to forgive. You may be afraid to forgive. Maybe thousands of thoughts and feelings course through your body and mind as you contemplate laying aside your characterizations. But even with all these potential discomforts, being willing transcends the mental and emotional stuff of our minds, taking on power and excitement completely outside our structures of knowing. For example, the discomfort about the prospect of forgiving someone who stole money from you could bring up many fears of the unknown. What would happen if you forgave them? Would this leave you open to terrible things like that happening again? Would it make you more vulnerable to getting hurt again? This is scary. As one participant in the *You and Money* course put it:

Sydney: If I forgive my business partner for what he

did, does that mean I give him license to do it all over again?

Remember, we are talking about forgiving, not forgetting. If someone steps on your foot, forgiveness does not mean forgetting it happened. It certainly does not mean that when you are around that person again you would stick your foot out again to see if they would repeat the offense. You are simply relinquishing the permission you give your self to use this grievance to prove what an unthinking, unconscious jerk that person is. You may still tell them: "That hurt me! I didn't like what you just did one bit!" But you are forgoing the right to use the action to dehumanize or demonize them, or to prove what a rotten person they are, or how their actions have ruined your life.

Forgiveness happens at the moment you are willing to forgive.

Forgiveness starts in the metaphysical domain and moves into the physical one very quickly. One feature of the metaphysical domain is that it is timeless. The moment you declare you are willing to forgive someone, *they are forgiven.* That is it! No lag time. It is done; there are no magical formulas to recite over and over again in the hopes that you will finally forgive that person or situation. Nothing to work on. To answer the question, "Are you willing to forgive this person?" there are only two possible answers: yes or no. Answers such as: I'll try; Maybe; I think so; or, Yeah, I guess so, are really nothing more than *no* in a not very convincing disguise.

> "We judge others. This gives us a sense of self-identity. As our awareness expands, we judge ourselves and others less, we soften, and the sense of unity grows. The hallmarks of a mystic are oceanic consciousness, universal perspective, and open mindedness. Judging, criticizing, and comparing falls away, except where it is appropriate for the ongoing enlightenment process."
>
> *David Cooper*

Monkey Mind Needs Time to Catch On

Forgiveness takes patience, no doubt about it. Monkey Mind will want to continue talking about that "awful person who offended you." Father O'Rourke taught me that it takes a while for your mind to catch up with your heart when you engage in forgiveness. Your heart forgives. Then your Monkey Mind begins once again with a litany all its own, listing all the terrible things that person said or did.

What do you do when your Monkey Mind will not stop? You answer it in the same way you always do: "Thanks for sharing, but I have already forgiven this person." And by the way, don't fall into the trap of making Monkey Mind the cause of all your grievances. For some of us, Monkey Mind may be the first *person* we should forgive.

Whatever you do, do not fight with Monkey Mind. Act with compassion. This aspect of your brain has been programmed over the years, maybe even before you drew your first breath. Remind it that these particular thoughts are no longer relevant. After a while, you will notice your mind beginning to loosen its grasp on those thoughts. They become quieter.

It was a relief to me when Father O'Rourke taught me the role the mind plays in the act of forgiveness. I had forgiven people in the past. Then I heard my mind listing all their faults again. I thought I had failed at forgiving them. This was simply not true.

You have the ability to forgive. You know how to look, see and tell the truth about your structure of knowing and then let it all go. The only question is: Are you willing?

Learning to forgive fosters your ability to distinguish between you and Monkey Mind. For this reason alone, forgiveness is important for the heroic journey.

Cultivating forgiveness affects how your mind works. You will develop characterizations about people for the rest of your life. It is part of human nature. You can recognize this with a heaping spoonful of compassion for yourself. Recall what Ram Dass said, that the same sorts of feelings and thoughts came up for him. They just did not stick around as long.

Most of us notice loud Monkey Mind conversations about ourselves. People have asked me whether they had to forgive themselves before they could forgive anyone else. My answer is no, for two reasons. First, if you look at your characterizations of yourself, you will find that ultimately you hold others responsible for why you have these "faults." It is true for most of us, even when we think we have already taken responsibility for our own shortcomings.

Second, even if the above is not true for you, forgiving another person is much more powerful and far-reaching. When you do this, you let go of the ties that have bound that other person to you in a negative way. You are setting them free. You are taking a stand that your judgments about others will no longer weigh you down. One of the oldest spiritual teachings in the world is that as you forgive, you will be forgiven. Forgiveness is at the heart of the 12-Steps, a spiritual program for the recovery from all sorts of addictions. Since forgiveness is an act of generosity, the result is often far-reaching and occasionally, surprising.

> "Surely it is much more generous to forgive and remember, than to forgive and forget."
>
> *Maria Edgeworth*

One woman in the *You and Money* course had a well-developed characterization of her sister:

Marilyn: I just knew my sister was childish and irresponsible. She owed me $800 for at least five years. She didn't give any indication that she might pay it back. I didn't *want* to, but I saw that I was *willing* to forgive her. I was willing to let go of all the things I've said about her in the past, to myself and others. One week after forgiving her, the strangest thing happened. She called me to talk. About ten minutes into the conversation she said: "You know that $800 I owe you? I'd like to begin paying you back now. I can see I've been irresponsible in letting it go for so long." Even stranger was my own reaction. I was thankful to get the money. Still, it wouldn't really have mattered if she'd paid me back or not. I felt like we were getting close again, like in the old days.

Did something magical occur the moment Marilyn forgave her sister? Or, did her sister just call Marilyn and sense that something had shifted in their relationship? Did that shift of relationship make it obvious to her sister that it was time to take care of the incompletion? To Marilyn it was a miracle, outside of her structure of knowing. Whether or not it affected paying the debt, forgiving her sister caused healing in their relationship.

It is empowering to know that you have the ability to forgive. In our heart of hearts, we want to be complete with everyone. It is a much easier road to travel. Being complete means knowing that all is well. They did and said what they did. You did and said what you did. To forgive is to release the regrets of what is in the past. It is to know what it is to be who you really are, no longer using past hurts or misfortunes as an excuse.

Begin now to look at whether you are willing to do a forgiveness exercise. There are two paradoxes here. The first is that you must forgive someone primarily for their sake and only secondarily for yours. You must be willing to see that you have held them in your mind, roasting on a spiritual spit for what they did. You must be tired of the dynamic created by your grievance.

The second paradox is that you must be in touch with your characterization of the other person. You will need to see your judgments, evaluations, anger, disgust, resentment, fear, and all other components of this structure of knowing. Why? You cannot let go of anything unless you are aware of it.

Finally, you must be ready to forgive a particular person. There may be someone from your childhood who was unkind to you. If the incident is serious and unexplored, I suggest counseling with a therapist, minister or other trained professional. Pick someone who may be easier to forgive at this time. You might start out with someone you listed on the mind-map as responsible for a specific thwarted goal or dream. You could begin with a person who has irritated you lately at the office, at home, during a sports activity, or during a financial transaction.

If you wish to go on, follow the exercise on the next page. Get ready to receive some breathing room.

Exercise: Forgive Us Our Debts -- The Forgiveness Process

What You Will Need

You will need your notebook and a quiet room. Part of this is an eyes-closed process. Ask a friend to read the process to you or you might tape-record it. The three dots in the text below always indicate pauses of about three seconds.

Time For This Exercise

Take about forty minutes for this the first time you do it. You will find that there is a practice effect: future experiences with this exercise may take as little as ten minutes. Father O'Rourke says he does this process with himself in one minute. He can see a characterization in its early stages and nip it in the bud.

The Exercise

1. Identify someone you are ready to forgive and get them clearly in mind.

2. Take a clean piece of paper and draw an oval-shaped circle that fills the entire sheet. Next, put that person's name on top of the oval. This figure now represents your characterization of that person.

3. Take a pen or pencil and fill the circle with all of the thoughts, feelings, judgments and attitudes you have about them. Write small if you must, but put everything in that circle. For example, were they unconscious, dishonest, hypocritical? Where did they drive you or other people crazy with their behavior? What are their character flaws, as you see them? Take your time and leave nothing out. Be as picky, unmerciful and derisive as you like.

    Someone once asked me, "Why dredge up all this old stuff? It's painful and I'd rather forget it." The answer is simple: If you are remembering it right now, it is still there inside you, festering away, and maybe has been there for a long time. It needs to be put on that paper where the light of your awareness can shine on it. If you see it and acknowledge it, you can consciously let it go. Trying not to look at it will only keep it around longer. Grievances denied have a much more profound effect on us than we can possibly imagine. And the more we try to push them down, the more powerful they become.

    If you have chosen a person to forgive, please take a moment to realize that you have taken a big step in healing your relationship with him or her. You and I do not usually take the time to look at all the disagreeable things we have to say about certain people. This exercise will not demean or discount you. On the contrary, it will release light into an area of your consciousness that has been in the shadows. Remember that the act of observing is the first step toward enlightenment.

    As you look over what you have written, see if you have left anything out. Add whatever is necessary before continuing. When you have finished, write: "And everything else." It signifies you are including anything your Monkey Mind may create in the future.

4.   The following are three questions that you are going to ask yourself. Again, there are two ways to do this. One is by prerecording your voice as you read these questions. Another is to have a friend read the questions to you. This is so you are not constantly referring to these pages as you do the forgiveness exercise.

     As you record it, be sure to pause after each question, speaking softly and slowly, with a calm, regular cadence. When you play it back, allow yourself to grasp the questions, then take a moment to get in touch with your true feelings.

     You may encounter a variety of emotions as you go through this exercise. This is natural, for the emotions coming up have probably been there for quite awhile. Just let them be there. You do not have to do anything with them except give yourself room to experience them.

     The answers to these questions are either yes or no. Remember, a Maybe, I think so, I'll try, or any other vague or qualifying answer counts as a *no*. This is because qualifications do not come from your heart. If they occur, it is a sign that you are not yet ready to forgive that person. Be aware that you may need to have room to say: "No, I'm not willing to forgive this person," before you can have the space to give an authentic yes.

The Process of Forgiveness
The following is to be recorded or read to you by another person:

Close your eyes, and place on your lap that piece of paper on which you have written all your notes about the person you are going to forgive ... Let your hands rest on the paper ... As you do, you might be able to feel the energy from that characterization sheet.

In your mind's eye, place an empty chair in front of you, facing you ... Allow yourself to see this person coming toward you from the horizon to your right ... Let them sit in a chair in front of you ... How do they look as they see you? Does they appear worried or wary? Now, answer the following questions to yourself as you hear me ask them:

1.   Are you willing to forgive this person *totally*? By this, we mean, are you willing to let go of everything you have written on that sheet of paper, and even things you have not written? You may not want to, may not even think you know how, but are you nevertheless willing, from your heart, to let this person off the hook? Again, are you willing to forgive this person totally? Answer yes or no to yourself.

2.   Are you willing to forgive this person *absolutely*? By this we mean, are you willing to let go of your favorite stories and scenarios about them? Are you willing to give up permission to use these stories, either with your-

self or with others, as the reason you have not achieved your goals and dreams in life? This means that every time you are tempted to use one of these stories, you will say to yourself, "Thank you for sharing, Monkey Mind, but I have already forgiven this person." So, once again, are you willing to forgive this person absolutely? Answer yes or no to yourself .

3. Are you willing to forgive this person *unconditionally*? Now and forever? This means that when you see them again, or think of them in any way, and notice you are starting to voice your old stories and evaluations, you will say, "Thank you for sharing, Monkey Mind, but I have already forgiven this person." This person may do what they usually do, which has upset you in the past. But you are hereby giving up permission to use what he/she does or says to form characterizations of them. In answering this question yes, you are willing to see that forgiveness has nothing to do with this person. It has everything to do with *what you say* about him or her. So, once again, are you willing to forgive this person unconditionally? Answer yes or no to yourself.

Whether you have answered yes or no to any of the questions, the fact that you have brought this person to sit in front of you says that you are willing for some healing to take place between the two of you ... We sometimes need room to say no before we can say yes ... There may be something you want to tell them from your heart right now ... Let them know what it is (pause for fifteen seconds). There may be something they want to tell you ... Listen to them now (pause for fifteen seconds).

If there are any questions to which you answered no, but are now willing to answer yes, allow yourself to do that now. If not, just let it be.

In your mind's eye, you can hug that person or shake their hand. They did what they did. And so did you. That is the way it is with human beings. It is possible that all is well. Are you willing to see that possibility? Now, watch them as they walk away. If you still have any feelings about them, just let those feelings be. Know that healing is now taking place in your relationship with them.

Now, open your eyes. Take that piece of paper, tear it up, and throw it away. To complete this exercise, you might also wish to wash your hands. This symbolizes that you are complete in this process, no matter how you answered the questions. Literally and figuratively, you are washing your hands of it. *(End of recorded text.)*

Discussion

If you have been working on this exercise with a friend, or if you are with a group of people, take some time to talk about what you have gotten from this exercise. If you have done this alone, write down what you have seen.

You may have answered no to one or more of the above questions. If this is so, ask yourself when you would be willing to do the exercise again. If you continue to answer no to any of the questions, it might indicate that some specific counseling on the matter is needed. Above all, this is a time for compassion for yourself.

If you have answered yes, what do you see? Is there a possibility of having a conversation with that person that was not a possibility in the past? (Note that this conversation does not need to take place for you to reap the benefits of forgiveness.) Do you notice a shift in your energy level? If so, what is it?

Learning to forgive is an ability that, with practice, becomes easier and easier. Be forewarned that you will also become more aware of people whom you have not forgiven. This awareness will stick with you until you act upon it and heal the relationship.

Forgiveness is *Your* Business

People often ask, "Should I tell someone that I've forgiven them?" Think about it for a moment. If I walked up to you and announced, "I have forgiven you," what would your probable response be? Right. Something like: "What for?" You might feel defensive. That is because the answer to the question involves my pulling up all the elements of my forsworn characterization of you! Seen in this way, announcing "I have forgiven you", may very well betray a hidden agenda on your part. The unspoken message to them might just be, "You are a terrible person, you did horrible things. You needed to be forgiven because of the jerk you were to me! I am just proving what a good person I am by forgiving you in spite of it all." That is why we get this feeling in the pit of our stomachs when someone tells us they have forgiven us. We may feel a moment of guilt for some unknown transgression that we are going to hear about. Resentment follows. Too often, the feeling is something like this: "You are forgiving me?! Oh, that's really big of you. It is I who should be forgiving you!" It is all pure Monkey Mind, over and over again.

The bottom line is that telling someone that you have forgiven them is irrelevant, and a mistake. After all, forgiveness is you being willing to let go of what you have said about them. It does not require even a single word from them to complete this process and bring you a sense of closure.

Meg: I remember after forgiving my brother, I had an occasion to have dinner with him. After a few moments of embarrassed silence, I found myself asking for *his* forgiveness for all the times I had been mean to him! He was so surprised. He started to cry!

Occasionally someone will ask about forgiving a person who has been physically or emotionally violent with them or with a loved one. It can feel threatening or dangerous to let such a person off the hook. Remember that forgiveness does not mean forgetting or rationalizing away what they have done. It involves your letting go of a characterization of them that you have created. You can become a victim of your own characterization, since it holds you perpetually in a treadmill of grievances. When you forgive someone you do not put yourself in a position of danger. Often, the process of forgiveness helps you understand how certain people can be hurtful to you. You also become compassionately aware of how you can be hurtful to others. This increased awareness allows you to be clearer in your interactions with the person you have forgiven. You need not stay in close relationship with them and you need not run.

"Once an old woman at my church said the secret is that God loves us exactly the way we are and that he loves us too much to let us stay like this, and I'm just trying to trust that."

Marilyn Ferguson

If you want to get more than your money's worth from this book, practice forgiveness daily. Notice how this affects your personal and business relationships. Are you more energized as you go for your goals? You may work up to forgiving those with whom you have had the most difficulty in life. Do this with the support of friends or professional counseling.

Going Further

Throughout this book, you have read about the value of support on the hero's journey. The intention of the next chapter is to give you guidelines for locating, receiving and giving support. This is more than a simple academic discussion. Most great works in life come from those who know that they are interdependent with the rest of the world.

Summary

Forgiveness is letting go of structures of knowing that you have created about another human being's nature.

Forgiveness comes from who you are in your heart. It is a product of being willing.

Your mind takes longer than your heart to catch on. Just because Monkey Mind chatters about *how awful the other person is,* it does not mean you have not forgiven them.

Forgiveness releases the energy you have used to keep your structures of knowing bound together. Just as the energy is released when an atom is split, many elements remain. Others are converted into different forms of energy. The net effect is movement and power.

When you form a characterization of another person, you see them through the grid of your assessments and judgments. This produces a two-dimensional experience of them. You are not seeing them as a human being like yourself.

When you forgive another person, you cease to use what they did as *the reason* for why your goals and dreams failed to come true. Through forgiveness, you are waiving the right to use what they did against them or yourself.

When you give up your characterizations, you are no longer shaped by them.

Forgiveness happens at the moment you are willing to forgive.

You have the ability to forgive. You know how to look, see and tell the truth about your structure of knowing and then let it all go. The only question is: "Am I willing?"

CHAPTER FIFTEEN:
I Did it Myself But I Wasn't Alone

I Did it Myself But I Wasn't Alone

"Somewhere a circle of hands will open to receive us, eyes will light up as we enter, voices will celebrate with us whenever we come into our own power."

Starhawk

There is a story, almost legendary by now, which is worth retelling here. It is humorous and it also conveys a message about the hazards and benefits of getting good help when you need it. As the tale is told, the following report was submitted as part of a workers' compensation claim in the 1920's:

"I am writing in response to your request concerning Block #11 on the insurance form which asks for the cause of injuries, wherein I put, 'Trying to do the job alone.' You said you needed more information so I trust the following will be sufficient.

I am a bricklayer by trade and on the date of injuries I was working alone laying brick around the top of a four-story building when I realized that I had about 500 pounds of brick left over. Rather than carry them down by hand, I decided to put them into a barrel and lower them by a pulley which was fastened to the top of the building. I secured the end of the rope at ground level and went up to the top of the building and loaded the bricks into the barrel and flung the barrel out with the bricks in it. I then went down and untied the rope, holding it securely to insure the slow descent of the barrel.

As you will note on Block #6 of the insurance form, I weigh 145 pounds. Due to my shock at being jerked off the ground so swiftly I lost my presence of mind and forgot to let go of the rope. Between the second and third floors, I met the barrel coming down. This accounts for the bruises and lacerations on my upper body.

Regaining my presence of mind, again I held tightly to the rope and proceeded rapidly up the side of the building, not stopping until my right hand was jammed in the pulley. This accounts for my broken thumb.

Despite the pain, I retained my presence of mind and held tightly to the rope. At approximately the same time, however, the barrel of bricks hit the ground and the bottom fell out of the barrel. Devoid of the weight of the bricks, the barrel now weighed about 50 pounds. I again refer you to

Block #6 of the insurance form and my weight.

As you would guess, I began a rapid descent. In the vicinity of the second floor, I met the barrel coming up. This explains the injuries to my legs and lower back. Slowed only slightly, I continued my descent, landing on the pile of bricks. Fortunately, my back was only sprained and the internal injuries were only minimal. I am sorry to report, however, that at this point I again lost my presence of mind and let go of the rope. As you can imagine, the empty barrel crashed down on me.

I trust that this answers your concern. Please know that I am finished trying to do it alone."

People who achieve their goals with ease employ a basic strategy. It is a strategy many of us overlook as we trudge wearily along the path of our own heroic journeys:

People who are successful have learned how to accomplish their goals and dreams with the support of others.

One myth we all share is that true success means going it alone. According to this myth, if we accept the support of other people along the way, we have somehow diminished our own achievement. We therefore do not deserve any praise for what we have done. If we stick to this line of reasoning, we become old before our time. It takes a lot of energy to pursue our dreams in isolation.

> "The first problem for all of us, men and women, is not to learn, but to unlearn, to clear out some of the assumptions."
>
> *Gloria Steinem*

What is Support, Really?

The definition of "support" found in most dictionaries includes actively promoting the interests of, and giving assistance and sustenance to, another person. The ongoing giving and receiving of support between people implies the knowledge that we are all interdependent. Given our interdependence, it quickly becomes clear that our greatest success comes when all of us succeed together. We are, after all, like the cells of a giant organism. The greatest health is achieved when each of its many separate parts reaches optimal functioning.

We all exist in an interdependent system. No matter how we may feel about it, we are linked socially, economically and biologically. David, a course participant, and I explored this during one of the *You and Money* courses. This conversation came at the end of a long discussion we had about interdependence and driven behavior:

David: I *hate* the idea of being interdependent. I'm going on my own for a while. One of my goals is to get a 4X4, load it with food, and go up to the mountains to be by myself for a few months.

Me: Okay, how are you going to get up there?

David: Like I said, in my 4X4.

Me: But, David, you're dependent on the manufacturer to make a good truck. And, what about the roads? Who made them? And who produced the food you're carrying? And your shoes and clothes? How about the fuel you're using?

David: Don't start *meta-fizzling* me. You know what I mean. I want to be my own person.

Me: But that's just it. We think that being our own person means isolating ourselves from the supportive energy of others. Look carefully at this because it's the source of a lot of our suffering.

David: (Becomes thoughtful.) I do spend a lot of time trying to prove I don't need anyone for anything. And I've got to admit, I'm always complaining that nobody is ever there to help me out when I need it. But I was taught to be a rugged individualist. I believe in that.

Me: Be a rugged individualist where it counts, by making your own unique contribution. Then get others to support you in realizing your dreams.

David: (Becoming reflective.) I'd like that. Then I'd get away in my 4X4 because I *want to,* not because I'm trying to escape from being interdependent. I'd be pursuing a good time, rather than trying to flee from people. I wouldn't be so driven all the time, trying to do it all alone!

We are all connected. The easiest road to success is to acknowledge this interdependence and stop pretending that we have to be the Lone Ranger (or Rangerette), on a solo hero's journey.

Think for a moment about the most significant accomplishments in sports. Athletes, whether they are members of teams or not, are aided by coaches, sponsors, family, and friends. They openly acknowledge the important role these people play in their lives. Somehow, the idea of getting and giving support seems more acceptable in this arena.

You may be able to recall a time in your own life when you accomplished something great with the support or collaboration of others. Maybe you and a friend worked together on a science project in high school. Or a friend of the family helped you finance your college education. Or an art teacher encouraged you to paint, and you produced a beautiful work of art. Or you had a coach who helped you develop your athletic abilities. Or a friend taught you to drive a car. Now, look back on the times when you did it alone, without anyone's aid. Compare the quality of these two experiences and note any differences you recognize. Was there a contrast in how you felt emotionally? How about the amount of energy it required to be successful alone? Did support carry you more easily toward your goal? How did it feel to share that success, or not have someone to share it with?

Here is a valuable lesson about getting support. It has had great impact on the successful achievement of our goals and dreams.

When you ask another person for their support, you are initiating an act of generosity from both of you. By working together, you make a difference in each other's lives.

The biggest gift you can give someone is to let them make a significant contribution in your life. The gift is complete when you consciously let them know the difference they have made.

Robert Lewis, columnist for InfoWorld magazine talks about getting and giving support at work:

"Next time you have some strange assignment or other, call five people in your organization you've never met before, tell them what you're working on, and say, "I was told you may have some good insights on how to approach this problem. Can you spare an hour to help me get my thoughts together?"

I guarantee you, at least six of the five will offer more help than you have any right to expect. And when you're done, they'll thank you. People want to create value for other people -- that's where self-esteem comes from."

Recall times in which you *knew* you made a positive impact on someone else's life. Maybe it was the time you helped a friend through an emotional crisis. Maybe it was the time you responded to a relative's request to sit down with them and talk through a business project. Maybe it was the time you became a mentor for a young person who just needed someone to listen to them.

Have you experienced yourself as being helpful to another person? Have you felt their relief or watched their sense of hope, self-esteem and strength improve? You know it boosts your own energy. In fact, when asked to look back on their most significant achievements in life, most people name those times when they helped others and saw that their efforts made a positive difference.

I remember visiting my great aunt Anna at the retirement home her first week or two there. Now, there was a woman! Ninety-five years old, sharp as a tack, used to taking care of herself. She hated being at the home but it was the only thing we could do. She had just become too frail to be alone. She looked dismal.

I was sitting down beside her and listening to her complain. This was not her old, dyed-in-the-wool gutsy Socialist self. All of a sudden, I remember saying to her: "Stop this, Aunt Anna. You're beginning to sound like an old woman!"

There was a pause. Then we both started laughing. She began to perk up immediately. The gleam came back to her one good eye. Then she became serious for a moment.

"Honey," she said: "I believe you've just saved my life."

That moment will be with me forever.

Aunt Anna gave me a gift. By responding to me in that way, she showed me I had made a difference. From this I learned that letting others know their value means more than any gift you could buy for them. It is returning the favor a thousand-fold!

> "We create our own reality because our emotional — our subconscious -- reality draws us into those situations from which we learn. We experience it as strange things happening to us ... (and) we meet the people in our lives that we need to learn from."
>
> *Edgar Mitchell*

Perhaps the best kind of support is when we give the other person room to exercise their own natural courage, faith, and confidence. When someone supports your efforts, they do not act *for* you or *instead of* you. On the contrary, the best support comes from someone who knows who you are in your heart. They recognize that you are bigger than all your doubts and fears. Armed with that knowledge such a person will not collude with you about reasons why you did not keep your promises or why you cannot fully realize your greatest talents and strengths. Instead of supporting Monkey Mind, they will remind you of your greatest skills, talents, goals and dreams.

Watch the face of a small child who is shown how to tie her own shoelaces, for example, when she finally gets the knack of it. Suddenly her face lights up with pride so bright it would light an auditorium. If you are the one teaching her, your heart sprouts wings and you soar!

When you ask someone else to support you, you are asking them to help you keep your word to yourself. You give them permission to remind you of your promises. This is most useful when Monkey Mind tries the strategy: "After all, you didn't *promise* to do it, you only said you'd *try*."

Being Supportive is not Being Co-Dependent

In recent years there has been much research on co-dependent relationships. Many books have been written on this subject. There are twelve-step programs throughout the country that deal with co-dependence. We have become sensitized to the potential problems associated with helping and being helped. People sometimes wonder if supportive relationships are somehow in danger of getting mired down in unhealthy co-dependence. Because this subject comes up so often in the *You and Money* course, I felt it should be addressed here.

There is a vital difference between supporting someone and being co-dependent with them. The difference has to do with the state of mind of the person doing the supporting.

When you are being co-dependent with another person you view them as needing to be *fixed* in some way. You take care of them because you believe they would be lost without you. You believe they would get into trouble on their own. The "co-" of co-dependence comes from the fact that *you as a "helper" are dependent on them being dependent on you*. You get a sense of false security from the belief that they could never abandon or reject you because they cannot get along on their own. In this way, co-dependence keeps you and them locked into the dynamics of limitation. You block them from developing their own capacities by always stepping in to do things for them.

As a "helper" in a co-dependent relationship you quickly get exhausted. You feel drained of energy. You feel as though you are carrying the other person on your shoulders. As often as not this leads to resentment and frustration on both sides. But true co-dependents are also very good at denying their feelings.

There is no room for creativity and initiative for the person being "helped" in this type of relationship. They may get rescued over and over again. But they are "protected" from the opportunity to learn from their genuine failures.

When you are being co-dependent, you also do not allow other people to support you. Typical co-dependent slogans in this respect are:

* If I want to get something done right, I have to do it myself.
* If anyone tries to support me, they are just meddling.
* If anyone offers support, they think I'm not good enough to do it for myself.

* I'm too busy taking care of others to ask for anyone's help right now.
* No one understands how much I have to do, how hard I work.

As you may see, co-dependence has a driven quality. Whether you view relationships from the vantage point of the helper or the "helpee," you are caught in a vicious circle of doing the same things over and over again, with little or no satisfaction for either person. You feel isolated from others. You usually end up working far harder than necessary.

When you are truly supporting someone, however, the dynamic is different. You recognize that both of you are whole and complete. You are aware of their courage, even when they doubt it themselves. You are conscious of the hero standing before you. You see that they are much bigger than Monkey Mind's chatter. You know that they have goals and dreams worth playing for. You also see that they possess a wellspring of wisdom inside and can find their own answers.

> "The only service a friend can really render is to keep up your courage by holding up to you a mirror in which you can see the noble image of yourself."
>
> *George Bernard Shaw*

Supporting another person is sometimes uncomfortable. It may not seem polite or nice to remind them of promises they have made or goals they created. And it is not necessarily easy to be in a relationship where your partner expects the best from you. Monkey Mind chatter can become loud for both of you. You may worry that you are being pushy. You may think it is best just to let the promise slide. Or you may feel constantly challenged to reach within for the very best in yourself as you support them.

In an *inter*dependent relationship you are companions, heroes traveling together but traveling your own paths. At times the other person's vision may be clouded, just as yours may be. This says nothing about your ultimate abilities, however. You treat each other with mutual respect, giving and receiving in equal measure. There is no energy drain here. There is gratitude in both giving and receiving, because the victories and accomplishments you celebrate together come from a place of generosity and strength, not from a place of fear and weakness.

Here is one clue to see when you are being co-dependent or authentically supportive: When you are co-dependent, you will feel exhausted at the conclusion of an interaction. When you are authentically supportive, you will be inspired and energized, even when you are tired.

Getting Support for Your Goals and Dreams

Okay, let us say you are convinced that getting support for yourself is important. How do you go about doing that? First, take a moment to look at your current structure of knowing about getting support from others. If you were to map that structure right now, you might come up with phrases like:

* Only ninnies and wimps need support.
* If I ask for it, people will think I'm weak and don't know how to take care of myself.
* People can let you down. Why set myself up to be disappointed?
* I'm embarrassed to ask. I don't know how.

If you are willing to go beyond your structure of knowing about support, here is the second step. Find someone you like and trust. Look for someone who will not be seduced by your mind chatter. Generally, a co-dependent support relationship is one where two Monkey Minds play into each other's doubts and fears, drowning out everything else. So, to be supportive of you the other person must not collude with you about how you do not have the time, energy, or inclination to do what you said you would do. What you need at this point is someone who demonstrates *ruthless compassion* in reminding you of your promises. You need a person who will not put up with the mischief Monkey Mind can create.

The person who supports you should not have a vested interest in the outcome. While you want to make sure that they are excited about your accomplishments, this person's own well being and comfort should not be tied to them. Such a relationship only complicates matters for both of you.

Exercise: Locating the Support that Surrounds You

Let us get you started on this aspect of your hero's journey. It is one thing to know that you need support, and another to actually go out and get it. This is a big step for most of us. Let your work in this exercise serve as the initial push into a life of success with ease.

What You Will Need
You will need your notebook, a pen and your calendar.

Time For This Exercise
You will need about ten minutes for this exercise.

The Exercise

1. Make a list of any people in your life who fit the above description of a supportive person. Look at friends, co-workers and family members. List your minister, coach, or therapist.

2. If your list is very short, or non-existent, take heart. The act of looking at how to get and give quality support for yourself will open up exciting possibilities. Give yourself a day or more to locate a person who would be a good support for you.

3. Pick a project in which you are willing to be supported. For example, you may have been planning to make a dentist or medical appointment for weeks, but have not yet done so. You might have promised yourself to walk one hour, three times a week. You may have pledged yourself to balancing your checkbook to the penny. You may have chosen to take the promotional exam at work, but have not yet begun to study for it. Any or all of these and thousands of other examples qualify for support.

4. Choose someone from your support list. Ask yourself the question: "Am I willing to give this person a success experience in supporting me?"

Do you recall times in the past when you did not allow your coach or support person to be successful? Did you spend time and energy fending them off? What methods did you use?

Denise: I stopped smoking four times last year. Each time, I'd swear it was my last cigarette. The fourth time I asked my friend Jane to support me. I promised her I'd get some nicotine gum. I didn't. I promised I'd call her every morning and let her know how I was doing. That lasted for two days. On the third day I smoked two cigarettes. The next morning I didn't call her. That evening she called me. I could hear her voice on the machine. I didn't pick up the phone. I've had enough of doing it this way. Luckily, Jane is generous and forgave me.

What strategies did Denise use to avoid support? What do you use? One of the easiest ways to disable your strategies is to tell the truth about them up front. Do you:

* Make promises you know you will not keep?
* Avoid talking to the person supporting you when you see them?
* Pretend you are too busy to talk to them when they call?
* Try to do things *your* way, even when it has not worked?
* *Nice* your coach to death? Example: "Thank you *so* much for caring. I appreciate what you're doing. Let's talk more later. Now is not a good time for me."
* Quickly turn the tables by asking them how they are doing, when you know that *you* need support?
* Threaten to get irritated, annoyed, or downright angry when you are reminded of your promises?
* Lie about what you did or did not accomplish?
* Sound terribly convincing and sincere about how you are too tired or overwhelmed to do what you promised?

We all have our favorite strategies, using them when we are in danger of not doing what we said we would do. These tactics keep us in the same rut. They are embarassing and uncomfortable to talk about. However, this momentary discomfort of self-disclosure is a small price to pay for having our goals and dreams become a reality.

5. Within forty-eight hours, invite the person you have chosen to support you on your project. Be frank with them. Tell them all of the ways you have used in the past to avoid or thwart support. When we do this in the *You and Money* course, I often ask participants to exaggerate or dramatize their most prized methods. It is usually very funny. We all can relate.

6. Tell this person the nature of your project. Make a promise for an authentic action to be taken within the next forty-eight hours. Have this action be a stretch for you, yet not beyond your reach. We want to build in the conditions for success here. Give your support person permission to call you at a set time, either to support you prior to the action, or to congratulate you after you have taken it.

7. If you really want to stack the cards in your favor, give this person a copy of your Standards of Integrity. This will give them a special knowledge of the attributes you intend to demonstrate in life. Give them permission to call you on it when it appears to them that you are operating outside of these Standards. Tell them you also want to know when it appears that you are displaying these Standards.

8. **Keep your word!** If you have not, tell the truth. Re-make your promise. Keep going.

9. Acknowledge each other for this work. You are both demonstrating the attributes of successful people.

10. If you wish, make another promise for authentic action.

Discussion

This experience of receiving support may have brought up a number of feelings and thoughts for you. What are they? Write about them in your notebook. Was this exercise difficult or easy? Did you pick an authentic action that was achievable, yet a stretch?

I usually recommend against supporting each other at the same time. You risk going into collusion with each other. If one of you withdraws, the other will be left without support. You need to have someone whose own authentic actions are not in any way tied to supporting you. For this reason, if you decide to form a success group, make sure this does not happen.

How to Form a Success Group

As you consider the possibility of being supported by others, it may occur to you to form a group of people with similar intentions. A success group is a form of self-help group, but with distinct characteristics:

*   The focus is upon success and pursuing your hero's journey. This means each person is there to be supported in keeping their promises.
*   You do not get extra points for struggling. That is because struggling usually means that you are trying to do things alone. You get to work hard, but not to the point of exhaustion. You are there to release the pattern of being driven.
*   You are willing to be supported by others, not just to be a supporter. It is often much easier for us to be a supporter than to allow others to support us. Remember that the supporters in co-dependent relationships get their sense of false power by feeling that they are in control because the other person needs them.
*   The group is not a substitute for therapy or any twelve-step program. Those programs play a different and important role. Here the specific focus is on discovering how to take authentic action. Insight is considered to be the *boobie prize* if it is unaccompanied by a demonstration in physical reality. You come away from each session with promises that will be fulfilled before the next session. This could include seeking therapy or joining a twelve-step program, if that is appropriate.
*   The group is committed to holding each member ac-

countable for who they really are in their heart. For this reason, everyone's Standards of Integrity and life's intentions are a matter of group record.

Success Group Format

The format for creating a success group is simple. Each chapter in this book is designed so that it can be easily used as the focal point for one or more sessions. Have group members read the appropriate chapter beforehand. Then open the floor for discussion of the material. The assignments throughout this book can be done before or during the group session. Make sure everyone gets a chance to speak on the topic. End with everyone declaring to the group what they will accomplish by the next session. Choose who will coach whom between now and the next session.

The Coaching Context: Blueprint for Success

Groups become powerful when they occur within a "context." A context is an intentional space where certain activities and roles occur. We live in social contexts, professional contexts, spiritual contexts, occupational contexts, and so on. This is most vividly apparent when one context clashes with another. For example, have you ever gone to a friend's party, only to be surprised by the presence of your boss or psychotherapist? Have you noticed the embarrassing or awkward moments, as you strive to find a way of relating that is appropriate for yourself in this context?

The context of a success group is that of coaching. It is a very powerful space. Each member is there because they are willing to be supported in going beyond their current structures of knowing. They are willing to support others in doing the same. The sessions should have a definite beginning and ending time. You may want to allow time for socializing after the meeting.

The context of coaching is created only when everyone in the group answers the following questions out loud. These are important centering questions.

1. **What specific qualities am I willing to contribute to the group session today, so that all of us will be successful?**

   For example, if you are tired, are you willing to be alert? If you are feeling defensive, are you willing to be open and receptive? If judgmental, are you willing to be compassionate? Each attribute or quality should be a bit of a stretch. This automatically takes you outside your structure of knowing. Make a list of these qualities. Declare what they are to the group. Do not use non-words, such as "non-judgmental." Say what you are going to contribute: "I will be open and compassionate."

Here are some more examples of attributes you can use to answer this question. You will notice that conceptual and emotional words are missing here. That is because those words do not reflect who you really are in your heart. You are pointing to more enduring qualities that can exist no matter what you think or feel.

Open	Kind	Flexible	Acknowledging
Truthful	Courageous	Attentive	Alert
Receptive	Grateful	Clear	Joyous
Loving	Focussed	Creative	Supportive
Gentle	Empowering	Generous	Appreciative

You may notice that the word "honest" is missing. This is because honesty is a way-station on the road to being truthful. For more clarity on this, refer to earlier discussions of honesty and truth in this book.

How does it feel to read those words? Do you notice a sense of opening? When you invoke these qualities, you are pointing to your intention to go beyond Monkey Mind. When a number of people declare their willingness to manifest these qualities, they are intentionally hooking themselves together at the level of being. This is essentially the same result you can achieve in a Master Mind group, such as those created by Napoleon Hill.

2. **Am I willing to dismantle my structures of knowing?**

    This question asks if you are willing to go beyond your thoughts, opinions, judgments, and evaluations about what you think you know. Remember, proceeding toward miracles can only be accomplished when you go outside your customary mental structures. Your best efforts at solving problems without support may have gotten you far. But you and everyone else need the support of others to go beyond your limitations. If you answer this question yes you are saying you are willing to go beyond what is familiar and safe. This may be uncomfortable. You may be apprehensive. Monkey Mind may be having a field day in your head. You are nevertheless willing.

3. **Am I willing to use everything that goes on in the group session as a personal lesson for myself?**

    If you answer yes to this, you are promising to create

value and meaning for yourself out of whatever happens in the group. You are willing to get all the support you need today, even if it is from watching someone else get supported in the group. You are promising yourself that you will leave the session thoroughly satisfied that you received what you needed. This question puts you in charge of learning your own lessons. If you look, you will probably find that you can learn from any situation, as long as you are willing.

4. **Am I willing to listen to the support of everyone in the group? Even if I do not agree with what they are saying ...** *especially if I do not agree with them?*

If you are willing to suspend your structures of knowing and listen to the support of others, I promise you miracles. The moment in which you do not agree with what others are saying may reveal where you have gotten stuck in a structure of knowing. You do not need to agree with the viewpoint of those who support you. It is useful to use your disagreement with them to observe yourself. Are you being defensive? Is Monkey Mind flexing it's muscles? Have these symptoms stopped you in the past from going further down your hero's path? Are you willing to experience the discomfort associated with suspending your judgment? Is it all right to get support you do not like from someone who you think has *gotten it all wrong?*

If you cannot answer yes to each of these statements, it is usually because you are not ready to interact with the group during that session. The above questions set the stage for very powerful support to take place. You are invoking the synergistic effect of the group. It is like linking a set of batteries or generators together. Alignment is a necessary prerequisite. You might allow yourself to observe the group without interacting until you can authentically answer yes to the above questions. If you remain unable to do so, use the following suggestions to identify possible causes:

* It could be a sign that you are exhausted because you have been struggling.
* It could be that you have been operating outside your Standards of Integrity in some area of your life. If it is a matter of not having done what you said you would between sessions, use the current session to tell the truth and remake your promise.
* You may be facing an issue that needs some external support, such as therapy, a twelve-step group or even a medical consultation.

In any case, allow yourself to get the help you need so that you can use the success group in a powerful way.

A Suggested Time and Format for the Group

1. Opening. Have everyone answer the questions outlined above. (15 minutes.)
2. Have everyone take two minutes to share a breakthrough since last session. (10-20 minutes, depending on group size.)
3. Read from a selected chapter of this book, doing exercises or sharing work on that chapter. (1 hour.)
4. Form support pairs until the next session. This can be done by putting names in a box and randomly drawing who you are going to support until the next session. Or, you may have someone work out a schedule so that everyone gets the opportunity to be supported by each group member at some point. Just make sure you do not end up support

ing someone who is supporting you. Once again, you both can go into collusion with each other, and then nothing gets done.
5. Write down your promises for authentic action to be completed by the next session. Keep these in your notebook. They need to be specific. Examples of vague promises are:
*   I'll be happier and more rested.
*   I'll take care of myself.
*   I'll be more careful about being on time.
*   I'll be more trusting.

These promises are not measurable as they are stated. You do not know how to tell when you have accomplished them. Specific promises have more energy. There is a sense of being on the line for something:
*   I'll have one appointment with a certified financial planner by next session.
*   I'll create three goals and come to the next session ready to Treasure Map at least one of them.
*   I'll take care of three items on my incomplete money business list.

*   I'll go to one Debtors Anonymous group meeting.

Now, these promises have workability! They may be a stretch for you. Above all, they are specific actions that someone can support you in taking.

6. Pick four times between sessions in which your support person will call and/or meet with you to remind you of your promises. They might ask if you need any further assistance.

This is what is most important about a success group:

You are in the group to learn about being supported, not to frustrate your coaches. You are in the group to learn to support others, not to be co-dependent with them. If such an arrangement is not producing results, you may need another type of group.

If you are ready, then be prepared for miracles in your life. You literally will not recognize yourself after going through this book with a support group. There is a motto coined by my friend, Dr. Patricia Elliott, after an especially productive session. Take it with you on your journey: **I did it myself but I wasn't alone!**

Summary

People who are successful have learned how to accomplish their goals and dreams with the support of others.

When you ask another person for their support, you are initiating an act of generosity from both of you. By working together, you make a difference in each other's lives.

There is a vital difference between supporting someone and being co-dependent with them. The difference has to do with the state of mind of the person doing the supporting.

Here is one clue to see when you are being co-dependent or authentically supportive: when you are co-dependent, you will feel exhausted at the conclusion of an interaction. When you are authentically supportive, you will be inspired and energized, even when you are tired.

On With Your Journey

By reading this book, you have learned how to attain success with ease. The lessons you learn here, though many are focused on money, will impact other forms of energy in your life. Always remember, you are a hero. Your path may wind in ways you could not anticipate. There is always someone in your life who is willing to support you, if you let them. Always let your dreams and goals guide your actions. And, above all, know that who you are in your heart is bigger than Monkey Mind and your circumstances. You have my love and support in this brave journey. I hope my words and those of the people mentioned in this book will serve you and those you love.

INDEX

Index

Do you want more information?

For a list of *You and Money* and other course locations

To order additional copies of this book

To order tapes

To be included on our mailing list

Call 1-800-835-9782

or visit us at

www.youandmoney.com